PERSPECTIVES IN LITERARY SYMBOLISM

YEARBOOK OF
COMPARATIVE CRITICISM

VOLUME I

Perspectives
in Literary
Symbolism

Edited by

Joseph Strelka

THE PENNSYLVANIA STATE
UNIVERSITY PRESS

University Park & London   1968

Library of Congress Catalogue Card Number 67-27116
    Printed in the United States of America
    by Wm. J. Keller Inc.

Designed by Marilyn Shobaken

FOREWORD

"PERSPECTIVES IN LITERARY SYMBOLISM" IS THE FIRST VOLUME OF A series entitled "Yearbook of Comparative Criticism" which is devoted to the study of literature based on two assumptions: that literature is an expression of the culture in which it is written, and that the study of literature involves value-judgments. Implicit therefore in comparative criticism is the evaluation of cultural phenomena; the discipline becomes in fact a search for values, which means it must also establish its standards of evaluation which are to be sought in the canons of quality of many cultures and many ages. Thus the comparative aspect is both supranational and historical; the criticism, however, is a search for universal, timeless characteristics of excellence.

This endeavor is a far cry from the positivism of an earlier day and indeed from the new criticism of our own, since the comparative critic does not limit himself to the accumulation of historical facts about the background and origin of a literary work, nor does he concentrate on textual explication alone. Rather, he sees the literary work as a gestalt that is both an aesthetic and a cultural phenomenon. As a work of art, literature not only addresses man's reason; it engages as well the imagination, the feelings, even the unconscious, and is thus capable of making a profound and lasting effect on the reader. As an expression of the writer's personality and a record of his experience in his environment, literature is a form of communication, a medium for reporting on the human condition. Indeed, more than this, it helps shape the culture of its time.

The other arts do this also, of course, and the relation between them and literature in the cultural context is an important concern of comparative criticism. Poetry and painting, music and epic, drama and dance are often imbued with a common feeling, a tone characteristic of an epoch. It is the business of the comparative critic to ascertain the quality of this tone and to note its expression in other areas of concurrent culture—for example, in social structure, the interpretation of psychological data, religious attitudes, and philosophy. Since literature deals with all phases of life and concerns every man, since it touches upon all aspects of culture and is all-embracing in its interests, the study of literature properly includes the study of culture. In treating the influence of literature on culture and of culture on literature, comparative criticism is similar to ethnolinguistics; it differs, however, from the latter and from cultural anthropology in general because of a constant concern for questions of aesthetics and values.

Appropriate to an evaluative discipline, comparative criticism subjects to critical analysis the principles, techniques, and results of various methods of literary and cultural criticism, specifies the characteristics and applicability of each, and seeks new standards of evaluation since literature and the life it reflects constantly develop new forms and new purposes. Thus it is not a fixed attitude to literature but a self-adjusting process of understanding, criticizing, and relating literature to other phases of our life-experience. The critique of critical methods is one phase of comparative criticism; another is the analysis and comparison of the value-systems in national literatures of various periods; and a third is the search for basic, supra-national principles of literary and cultural evaluation. Although in reference to specific new trends of literature the discipline remains flexible, it is not formless or purely relative to the material under analysis since its prevailing concern is with the definition and communication of values which have general enduring validity. The values in a given culture are reflected in its literature. A comparison of value-systems will disclose values common to several cultures, and these values can provide the basis for a general theory of evaluation with which present and previous methods of criticism may be compared. The exact nature of the general theory is not so important as is the fact that it serves as a meeting ground—possibly a norm—for specific critical methods, and as a goal for the unceasing search for values. The general theory may well remain an ideal in the service of which the process of comparative criticism is carried on; the main thing is that the search for values remains central in our study of literature and the culture it reflects.

Why exactly this emphasis on values? What of the traditional professional background and training of the student of literature? Must one not read widely in his own and other literatures; be aware of the historical developments preceding a given work; know of the influences from other writers and other literatures affecting it; be familiar with the various classifications of literature in genres, types, schools, and periods; possess a proper grounding in bibliography, philology, prosody, rhetoric, and aesthetics; be able to trace themes, analyze style, and understand the essential relationship between form and content? Must the literary scholar not have at least these competencies to arrive at informed judgments about literature? They are, after all, what provides his expertise; they qualify him to teach and to publish his research findings. Indeed, such knowledge, extensive and practical, prepares one to make instructive, objective, demonstrable statements about literature, to compare literature with literature, and to decide that a work is good or bad relative to other literary works. But it does not prepare one to say that a given piece of literature is good in itself and why.

This, it seems to me, is the task of the humanist. To seek, apart from literary content and form, the aesthetic, social, psychological, and religious values in literature; to state precisely what a writer, representing the style of thinking and expression of his time, finds good and worthy of being acted upon universally; to carry on investigations of this nature with a thorough knowledge of the history and theory of criticism—these are activities which further the humanist's concern for man's welfare, values, and dignity. The purpose of such scholarship is neither moralistic nor didactic; it is, rather, to turn from an ivory-tower conception of literary criticism to an enlarged view of literature in the service of life. Just as the noblest poet is both teacher and prophet, so the finest poetry gives direction to cultural development and anticipates the future; it is the critic's task to recognize these directional and predictive qualities in literature and to relate them to other forms of culture. Similarly, it is the educator's task to transform the study of literature from an historical to an evaluative discipline, to shift the emphasis from specialization to integration, and to train sophisticated evaluators of literature and the culture it expresses. The best student should no longer be the one who has amassed the largest store of information in his area of specialization, but the one who has learned to recognize and respect excellence in his field of competence and to communicate effectively the values he finds there.

In this way the role of the discipline of literary scholarship is enlarged, and the study of literature becomes the study of culture itself. But above all, comparative criticism is concerned with values. This means therefore that it deals with concepts of man transmitted by great literature and that it compares these concepts with those implicit in the major cultures and religions of mankind. It is thus concerned with defining human ideals. With its far-reaching interests, comparative criticism widens our view and our understanding of the most diverse possibilities for the development of human culture and the human spirit.

Perspectives in Literary Symbolism contains a group of studies which examine many facets of literary expression; necessarily they lead to consideration of notions deeply embedded in the language, the lore, the subconscious, the mythology of peoples, in the realm of the irrational and the emotions—in short, they venture into territories that are not usually considered "literary." But in comparative criticism that is exactly what we should do in our search for new evaluations of our experience of literature.

That this first, firm step has been taken to bring about a new orientation and emphasis in the study of literature and thus to begin the work of comparative criticism is the result of the efforts of Professor Joseph Strelka, editor of the new series. With him I wish to thank most kindly the contributors to this volume for their support of a new idea in literary studies. Because of Professor Strelka's wide learning in literature, his keen interest in problems of literary criticism, and his enthusiastic development of the idea of comparative criticism, the creation of this book has been possible. I am glad for this opportunity to express the pleasure I have had from our association in this enterprise. I wish also to acknowledge with thanks the kind financial support our work in comparative criticism has received from The Pennsylvania State University Institute for the Arts and Humanistic Studies under the direction of Professor John M. Anderson.

STANLEY R. TOWNSEND
Head, Department of German
The Pennsylvania State University

CONTENTS

Joseph Strelka

COMPARATIVE CRITICISM AND LITERARY SYMBOLISM

SINCE THE PRESENT COLLECTION OF ESSAYS IS INTENDED AS THE FIRST IN A series of volumes entitled "Yearbook of Comparative Criticism" we should first endeavor to explain what is meant here by "comparative criticism." Neither the word nor the subject is new. In recent literary criticism the expression is found as early as Mercier,[1] where it was used simply as a synonym for comparative analysis.

The subject matter itself, the comparative method, is almost as old as literary criticism. It not only gave the name to one of the most prominent and significant branches of literary speculation, but, as its essential characteristic, assisted it to the great influence which it exerts.[2] Unlike the comparative history of literature, which turns first of all to literary works of art, comparative criticism emphasizes the comparison of various kinds of literary theory and literary criticism. Comparative criticism and comparative history of literature overlap so far as all criticism and theory ultimately serve to comprehend, elucidate, and evaluate literary works of art, and as "they duplicate each other so thoroughly as to make inconceivable literary theory without criticism or history, or criticism without theory or history, or history without theory and criticism."[3]

The justification or even necessity of such a comparative criticism follows from the predicament of literary criticism and theory in our time, described so accurately by a *cognoscente* of the stature of René Wellek, who speaks of an "incredible confusion of tongues . . . a veritable Tower of Babel which seems to me one of the most ominous features of our civilisation." To the Babylonian confusion of tongues within the different national spheres are added other difficulties, arising from strange partitions separating national peculiarities and characteristics from each other even in the realm of literary criticism: "One is struck by the fact that from a very wide perspective a large part of twentieth-century criticism shows a remarkable resemblance of aim and method, even where there are no direct historical relationships. At the same time, one cannot help observing how ingrained and almost unsurmountable national characteristics seem to be: how within this very wide range of Western thought with cross-currents from Russia to the Americas, from Spain to Scandinavia, the individual nations still tenaciously preserve their own traditions in criticism." Finally, however, Wellek summarizes his regret about the situation in these words: "I am not acquainted with any attempt, however brief, to survey the present scene on an international scale. But today more than ever this international perspective is needed in criticism."[4]

Comparative criticism does not presume to be able to provide the overall view demanded by Wellek; rather we hope to supply building stones toward that end in the form of these Yearbooks. The fundamental goal of the Yearbooks is first of all that each will bring observations from various perspectives and from diverse national as well as individual points of view to bear on a central encompassing theme. With some skill of selection and with some luck in receiving the desired contributions, they can be so arranged that their very placement will, without commentary, not only aid in comparing and clarifying the intentions and potentials of recent criticism, but will also help in avoiding some unnecessary terminological contradictions and hence also to discourage the popular disputes about words. It is not only a matter of clarification of terminology but also of basic methodical concepts. It makes no difference whether the papers included here are concerned directly with the critique of criticism or literary theory, or whether they practice one or another method in the interpretation of a literary work of art; what is at issue here is comparative method and comparative criticism. In none of the volumes, however, will there be merely such practical investigations using only one method.

Of course, it is by no means new to recognize the necessity of overcoming all the opinions fostered by a single, narrow-minded approach. No less a critic than Northrop Frye referred expressly to this in regard to the literary symbol:

The principle of manifold or 'polysemous' meaning, as Dante calls it, is not a theory any more, still less an exploded superstition, but an established fact. The thing that has established it is the simultaneous development of several different schools of modern criticism, each making a distinctive choice of symbols in its analysis. The modern student of critical theory is faced with a body of rhetoricians who speak of texture and frontal assaults, with students of history who deal with traditions and sources, with critics using material from psychology and anthropology, with Aristotelians, Coleridgians, Thomists, Freudians, Jungians, Marxists, with students of myths, rituals, archetypes, metaphors, ambiguities, and significant forms. The student must either admit the principle of polysemous meaning, or choose one of these groups and then try to prove that all the others are less legitimate. The former is the way of scholarship, and leads to the advancement of learning; the latter is the way of pedantry, and gives us a wide choice of goals, the most conspicuous today being fantastical learning, or myth criticism, contentious learning, or historical criticism, and delicate learning, or 'new' criticism.[5]

The latter statement does not hold for great and reputable critics of certain persuasions, who, for sound reasons, place the accent on one method or another without, however, deteriorating into one-sidedness. It *is* true for a large number of partisans and blind adherents who are so happy in thus escaping the complexity implicit in any more differentiated critical theory that they reduce the diversity of polysemous literary reality to a narrow theoretical bias. René Wellek is certainly correct when, for example, he declares: "I do not believe that there ever was a single reputable 'New' critic who has taken the position imputed to him," this "position" being to deny "that a work of art can be illuminated by historical knowledge at all."[6] He would be right if the word "reputable" were stressed, but I very much doubt that it is only a fabricated straw man who resorts to such crude narrow-mindedness.[7] I doubt also that the situation would be any different in any other "school" of criticism than New Criticism. If even the greatest teachers of humanity, from Christ to Freud, have had disagreeable experiences with their sometimes very mediocre followers, why should one expect anything different in the discipline of literary theory and literary criticism? Wellek reports of his own experience: "I believe my own *Theory of Literature* (1949) was widely understood as an attack on 'extrinsic' methods, as a repudiation of 'literary history,' though the book actually contains a final chapter on 'Literary History' which emphatically argues against the neglect of this discipline . . ."[8]

Still more striking was the experience about which Northrop Frye reports: "My first sustained effort in scholarship was an attempt to work out a unified commentary on the prophetic books of Blake. These poems are mythical in shape: I had to learn something about myth to write about them, and so I discovered, after the book was published, that I was a member of a school of 'myth criticism' of which I had not previously heard."[9]

Comparative criticism should demonstrate with constantly new examples the so easily forgotten basic truth that different objects, propositions, and problems in literary criticism require different methods. That is no more eclectic than when a bank official uses the method of addition when money is paid in and the method of subtraction when money is paid out, in order to make the balance sheet correspond with the facts.

Comparative criticism should accordingly provide, in the first place, a field of experimentation, open on all sides, for comparative methods, ideas, and conceptions in the area of literary criticism and literary theory. Whatever proves to be fruitful should be preserved, whatever is sterile should be discarded.

Since, however, various methods in the treatment of an object or a problem might not always be mutually exclusive, a variety of combination and integration possibilities can result by using changing groups of methods. There is certainly nothing novel about juxtaposing the most diverse methods of the most disparate national origin systematically and in equality.[10] Furthermore, not even the demand for such an integration of methods both in theory and practice is new. One of the most recent critics, who raised his voice loudly and insistently, is Stanley Edgar Hyman.[11] He named a man who serves as a practical model in American literary criticism: "A substantial and quite impressive amount of integration is possible in the work of one rounded man using a number of methods and disciplines. At one time or another Kenneth Burke has done almost everything in the repertoire of modern criticism, and generally a number of things in conjunction."[12]

Hyman's unattained ideal is, however, a fictitious, hypothetical critic, constructed "out of plastics and light metals," who is "of course nonsense . . . although perhaps useful nonsense as a Platonic archetype." His ideal integration of methods is the direction in which criticism ought to move. The demand for this kind of synthesis or integration of methods has been raised repeatedly in recent years. "Literature appeals to so many values, aesthetic and otherwise, that it requires a pluralistic approach," claimed Harry Levin.[13] From a different perspective, but led by similar considerations, John Crowe Ransom demanded an "ontological critic."[14] And most recently Oscar Cargill suggested a program "towards a pluralistic criticism."[15] These are but a few examples.[16]

Indeed, the fundamental idea of comparative criticism is not new. According to ben Joseph Akiba there never is anything really "new," and even the basic ideas of such a unique achievement as Freudian psychoanalysis were already prefigured in the masterworks of world literature. That the basic ideas are not new does not at all mean that nothing is to be done there.

The first step is a kind of synopsis of each of several topics of criticism. It involves a juxtaposition and comparison, open in all directions, of diverse insights and methods. The second step is an attempt to work out a synthesis, or more precisely, to work out various possibilities and basic forms of syntheses. The transition from the first to the second step may not always be sharply delineated and the two may occasionally flow together, but at the beginning there should be an attempt to make a contribution to the first step only.

Even the realization of the first step is blocked by more difficulties than one would think. The more natural and simple the goal may appear, the more complicated are the obstacles that stand in the way of attaining it.

The first obstacle is that the majority of critics are not conscious enough of their subject, for comparative critique of criticism and comparative theory of literature have been far too slighted for one to simply begin to build from a generally accepted foundation. Northrop Frye formulated the problem polemically:

> Physics is an organized body of knowledge about nature, and a student of it says that he is learning physics, not nature. Art, like nature, has to be distinguished from the systematic study of it, which is criticism. It is therefore impossible to 'learn literature': one learns about it in a certain way, but what one learns, transitively, is the criticism of literature. Similarly, the difficulty often felt in 'teaching literature' arises from the fact that it cannot be done: the criticism of literature is all that can be directly taught. Literature is not a subject of study, but an object of study: the fact that it consists of words, as we have seen, makes us confuse it with talking verbal disciplines. The libraries reflect our confusion by cataloguing criticism as one of the subdivisions of literature. Criticism, rather, is to art what history is to action and philosophy to wisdom: a verbal imitation of a human productive power which in itself does not speak. And just as there is nothing which the philoso-

pher cannot consider philosophically, and nothing which the historian cannot consider historically, so the critic should be able to construct and dwell in a conceptual universe of his own.[17]

Another obstacle lies in the apparent paradox that the work of art arises from an historical and social context and in many cases cannot be understood without knowledge of that context, but that the critic is expected to proceed from an autonomy of art and from the work of art as sole object. The confusions in the face of this problem have led to two extremes: on the one hand the excrescences of pan-estheticism and puristic intrinsic views of art; on the other (among other things) a view of literature as purely an object of moral hygiene and moral utility, no different from religious tracts or party platforms, as well as to an attitude which often obtains both methods and standards exclusively from areas outside of literature and criticism.

Sociological and historical information, psychological and theological understanding, philosophical and ethnological knowledge are often necessities for the critic. Nevertheless he must not forget that his objects are works of art, that he approaches them as a critic and not as a sociologist or psychologist, theologian or philosopher, and that he can commit no greater mistake than to approach them on an empirical level and not on an aesthetic one. In other words this greatest mistake is to reduce the work of art to the material values of another discipline and its methods. The critic then abandons not only his object but also his own discipline—literary criticism and literary theory.

A further obstacle shows up in one of the most significant problems, the problem of evaluation. According to Wellek a work of art is "a totality of values which do not adhere merely to the structure but constitute its very essence. All attempts to drain value from literature have failed and will fail because its very essence is value."[18] Yet Walter Mueller-Seidel gave his basic *Problems of Literary Evaluation* the wary subtitle "On the objectivity of a non-objective topic,"[19] and in Northrop Frye are found such sentences as: "Value-judgments are subjective in the sense that they can be indirectly but not directly communicated," or "The first part of this is a statement of fact, the second a value-judgment so generally accepted as to pass for a statement of fact. But it is not a statement of fact. It remains a value-judgment, and not a shred of systematic criticism can ever be attached to it."[20]

Although a value-judgment and the establishment of facts belong to logically separate orders, the question is raised here whether the difference of opinion between Wellek and Frye is merely a battle about words or whether it involves more. Or in other words: does there exist for Frye another kind of criticism besides "systematic criticism," which in complementing the "systematic" makes up the complete criticism of literature? Apparently it must exist, otherwise one can scarcely understand the following statements from Frye:

> Consequently there is no way of preventing the critic from being, for better or worse, the pioneer of education and the shaper of cultural tradition. Whatever popularity Shakespeare and Keats have *now* is equally the result of the publicity of criticism. . . .
> The present book assumes that the theory of literature is as primary a humanistic and liberal pursuit as its practice. *Hence, although it takes certain literary values for granted, as fully established by critical experience,* it is not directly concerned with value-judgments. . . .
> Comparative estimates of value are really inferences, most valid when silent ones, from critical practice, not expressed principles guiding its practice. The critic will find soon, and constantly, that Milton is a more rewarding and suggestive poet to work with than Blackmore. But the more obvious this becomes, the less time he will want to waste in belaboring the point. For belaboring the point is all he can do: any criticism motivated by a desire to establish or prove it will be merely one more document in the history of taste. . . .[21]

According to Frye this history of taste is the most meaningless thing in existence: it is a mere apparition of short-lived fashion, if not actually caprice. We should, however, keep two words from the last paragraph in mind: "belaboring" and "comparative." To belabor points is what comparative criticism wants to do above all, and Frye obviously ascribes to the method of comparison a fundamental significance. Similarly, Maurice Beebe's conclusions were no mere accident, when he attempted to distinguish from one another the basic types of criticism, which are often more or less thoughtlessly employed as synonyms. He began with the simplest, most fundamental first level and ascended from that to a sixth level. These six levels are in his opinion: (1) exegesis, (2) explication, (3) analysis, (4) interpretation, (5) comparison, and (6) evaluation. Comparison is not merely the method of the second highest level, but it emerges also as the third and highest method in Beebe's sixth and final level, the level of evaluation.[22]

This digression does not indicate the solution of our problems. At the moment we are not concerned with solutions, but only with indicating difficulties and obstacles. The obstacle described above in

Frye's words is certainly not the only one connected with the problem of evaluation.

There is, for example, one further difficulty: if one proceeds from the generally acknowledged fact that the naïve-orthodox standpoint within the bounds of any given historical style (including that of one's own time and environment) has been lost, then all easy orientation, including the possibility of a normative aesthetic, has been lost. Beginning with Malraux's idea of the imaginary museum on one hand and the development of modern aesthetics on the other, Wladimir Weidlé summarizes this development skillfully in a few sentences. Although Weidlé is thinking primarily of the visual arts, what he says is no less pertinent to literary development. After he has set forth his opinion that modern tendencies toward relativity have led to the "death of style," he explains retrospectively:

> Style alone provided the criteria by which it was possible to make a selection among these forms—a selection which was determined solely by the strictly conceived special forces of artistic creation, indeed to a much greater extent than by the taste of the observer who only reflected or interpreted these forces. Though not explicit, there belongs to every style a normative aesthetics, the mere existence of which cannot be reconciled with the existence of a museum in which an unlimited number of works can be found which are not affected by the laws of that aesthetics. The museum notion could not be born until normative aesthetics had yielded to an aesthetics which were not conceived of as a stylistic norm, but rather as absolute aesthetics. This emerged and was given the name 'aesthetics' just when the museum notion was beginning to have impetus, when style was on its death bed and when art history was being reconstructed under the aegis of historical relativity.[23]

It seems to me beyond question that the museum of works of literary art with which comparative criticism is concerned must include works of all peoples, all times, and all styles. However, I do not want to reflect here on how a situation greatly detrimental to the creation of new art can be of advantage to the development of criticism.[24]

It seems equally beyond doubt to me that the standpoint of the critic has to be one completely lacking in prejudices and presuppositions.[25] But which standpoint is that? Even if one suppresses all conscious prejudices, enough are retained unconsciously. What Milton Singer maintains for anthropology is just as valid for literature:

> The pluralistic, relativistic theory of culture was not mistaken in saying that people's ethnocentric bias makes it difficult for them to understand a culture different from their own. The mistake was in

giving the impression that such bias could easily be eliminated through comparative studies of cultures in their own terms. The progress of anthropology during the last thirty to forty years is correcting this impression. Anthropologists, it turns out, are also ethnocentric! They take their own culture with them to the most remote and exotic places. In fact they have no choice: they are like everyone else in not being able to escape from their own culture. And no amount of sympathy or good will can erase the bias of personal interest, outlook, and cultural values which they bring to the field with them. If the values of other cultures are going to be understood, they will have to pass through this screen which every anthropologist carries with him.[26]

That there are many impediments standing in the way of "scientific" criticism is certainly nothing new. Anglo-Saxon literary criticism has systematized both real and apparent obstacles and called them fallacies. There are, for example, the two well-known and time-honored "fallacies" in New Criticism, the "intentional fallacy" and the "affective fallacy." There is the "affective fallacy" of Wimsatt and Beardsley, the "literary fallacy" of De Voto, the "normative fallacy" of Manheim, and the "naturalistic fallacy" of Stephen C. Pepper. There are so many objections that out of such negatives one could construct a theoretical frame of what criticism can and should be. So many potentialities are discarded that those which remain appear to unite of themselves to form the basic outline of what can be realized.

In enumerating some of the difficulties I have unintentionally touched on two problems, that of literary evaluation and that of points of contact between literary criticism and other disciplines. A few words will be said about them since these two problems belong to the least clarified in the field of comparative criticism and will concern it in detail.

With regard to the problem of evalution, there seem to be mainly two reprehensible extremes which lie at either end of a large scale of possibilities: at one end are the theories of those people who through their sectarian or political beliefs have a handy and ready-made recipe for an absolute theory of value; at the other end are the representatives of a subjectivity so broad that it amounts really to an anarchy of values. Indeed, some maintain that one cannot make literary value-judgments at all, which does not prevent them from doing it constantly in practice. But a thing does not become devoid of meaning just because some charlatans and imposters seize possession of it. One should not forego the chance of better though partial solutions just because some unsatisfactory ones have also been

offered. Certainly the necessary requirements are lacking today to
set up normative aesthetics in a short time, as was easily possible a
few hundred years ago. Certainly Frye is correct when he veers away
from the arbitrary fashions of an all too vacillating history of taste.
But before one resorts to sleight-of-hand by denying in theory all
possibilities of evaluation which nonetheless are constantly employed
in practice, everything should be tried that might lead to illumination of this practice. It is even better to set up a comparative history
of normative aesthetics or a comparative history of taste to try to
establish in so doing what is abiding in change and what is consistent in variation. It is better, although not the best. For more than a
hundred years there have been two main currents in aesthetics, one
oriented towards psychology and one towards philosophy. Critics
have attempted to construct just such a purely aesthetic phenomenon
which would be a stable element removed from all historical change,
and they have had no conclusive success. Progress in scholarly affairs
is made, however, when things are made possible for a later time
which were impossible before. It is precisely in this regard that I feel
that hope is the more justified, since Weidlé showed in his intelligent
analysis *why* conclusive success had not been attained. Both main
aesthetic currents have had in common the habit of looking at art
exclusively from the perspective of its effects. But a work of art

is no medicine, whose effects on the organism are to be described.
And it is just as impossible to establish *a priori* in what way this
medicine differs from a chemical compound without medicinal power
(the non-art and non-poetry of Croce) or from a poison (bad art). One
can sooner compare the work of art with a spoken word which has
sound and sense and is chosen by the one who utters it. Even if this
word is the most complicated conceivable, still one single person has
uttered it and has felt the need to express it. A work only satisfies me
if the author has had a different purpose than merely to satisfy me and
the inner poise which I might owe to him can scarcely come about
without assent, understanding and sympathy. Nevertheless aesthetic
assent is not enough: it is merely a beginning, the first supposition for
that which follows, a preamble. If I do not agree, I turn my back; if I,
however, do agree, I must go on immediately in order to enter into the
work and into what lies behind it, for only in this way can it affect the
innermost core of my being. The identity of intuition and expression
which is both point of departure and capstone of Croce's aesthetics,
describes very well the identification that one makes when he is involved with a work of art; the artist, however, still has to grapple for
this identity, for he would not have set out, had he already had it in
his pocket. In order to understand him fully, I, to whom he turns, must
distinguish in the identity the original duality which was not recon-

ciled until the act of creating, an act which preceded the work, but which nonetheless pervades it. I comprehend this act, I intuit it, when I intuit it and understand the work.[27]

Striving after at least relative objectivity by means of aesthetic judgments was, by the way, even for Kant an unquestioned presupposition of such judgments. After he had sharply distinguished the concept of the pleasant from the concept of the beautiful and after he had said of the pleasant that each person has his own taste he wrote of the beautiful:

> The case is quite different with the beautiful. It would (on the contrary) be laughable if a man who imagined anything to his own taste thought to justify himself by saying: 'This object (the house we see, the coat that person wears, the concert we hear, the poem submitted to our judgment) is beautiful *for me.*' For he must not call it beautiful if it merely pleases him. Many things may have for him charm and pleasantness—no one troubles himself at that—but if he gives out anything as beautiful, he supposes in others the same satisfaction, he judges not merely for himself, but for everyone, and speaks of beauty as if it were a property of things. Hence he says 'the thing is beautiful'; and he does not count on the agreement of others with this judgment of satisfaction, because he has found this agreement several times before, but he *demands* it of them. He blames them if they judge otherwise and he denies them taste, which he nevertheless requires from them. Here, then, we cannot say that each man has his own particular taste. For this would be as much as to say that there is no taste whatever, i.e., no aesthetical judgment which can make a rightful claim upon everyone's assent.[28]

This view was soon supplemented and relativized by Herder, when he declared that a philosophical theory of the beautiful is impossible "without history"; still, this does not at all preclude the possibility of objectivity in questions of aesthetic value-judgments. This possibility, however, is without a doubt jeopardized by the contemporary historical situation in a wider sense and the outlines of the danger were sketched only roughly though correctly by the German critic Karl August Horst under the pertinent title: "The Splintering of Critical Standards."[29] Beginning with the demand for universality he disposes of most of the "splintered" standards of egoistic or collectively-egoistic origin, and he names finally the "humanum" as that which is universally binding. The "thing" and the "word," as Horst calls the old concepts of content and outer form, must meet in the "sphere of humanity." Though this may be quite correct from the point of rejecting negative possibilities, still the real problem begins where the essay ends, that is, with comprehending and representing the diverse manifestations in which the connection between "thing" and "word" takes place in the "humanum."

Goethe's familiar, concise concept of "humanity" is still more subtle. In spite of first appearances, it goes beyond what is pure content and provides a true definition.

HUMANITAET

Seele legt sie auch in den Genuss, noch Geist ins Beduerfnis,
Grazie selbst in die Kraft, noch in die Hoheit ein Herz.[29a]

Every experienced critic will recall immediately that there are extremely diverse variations on this concept of humanity within Western literature alone. Some are more individualistic, some more social, some are oriented toward worldly matters, others are pantheistic or platonic or mystical. Here, too, one will have to proceed from a pluralistic standpoint among the separate forms of realization, a standpoint which, nevertheless, does not necessarily contradict the theoretical unity existing behind it.

These brief general remarks about the problem of evaluation are not expected to bring about solutions, nor are they able to even provisionally. The same is true of the following remarks on the problem of the relations of literary criticism with adjacent disciplines. They are meant simply to indicate the concern of the "Yearbook of Comparative Criticism."

Certainly "criticism has a great variety of neighbors" and "the critic must enter into relations with them in any way that guarantees his own independence."[30] The disciplines which are significant to the critic will change from time to time according to his topic and the formulation of his problem. But to treat the work of Chrétien de Troyes without knowledge of medieval knighthood, or the works of Chuang-tse without knowledge of Taoism, or Schiller's work without the philosophy of Kant, or Dante without some knowledge of the history of Florence, and Thomism without knowledge of the gnosticism of the Knights-Templar can simply not be attempted by a reputable critic.

History and philosophy, psychology and sociology, comparative studies of religion, folklore, ethnology, art history, and music history —but also history of natural sciences—will in one case or another play an important role in literary criticism. The literary critic ought never to forget that his object of study is literature and that his methods are those of literary criticism, otherwise he will fall victim to a disastrous methodological confusion. The extremism of a puristic intrinsic literary criticism arises to a great part from the warranted fear of such a confusion and from the hope of averting it. This danger does not exist, of course, as long as the literary critic uses mathematics in order to count verses, but it increases considerably when he employs a computer doing style analysis to attribute a certain work to a certain author, and probably reaches its highest point today when literary criticism is coupled with psychology and sociology. In other words, it is of greatest importance that relations be cultivated with all relevant neighboring disciplines, but not to such an extent that these disciplines take possession of literary criticism or of any of its complexes—rather that literary criticism assimilates the knowledge of the other disciplines and utilizes it with its own methods, these necessarily proceeding from its particular object, literature, and proceeding toward the goal of critical knowledge of literature.

This does not mean that contributions from the representatives of other disciplines cannot be of great relevance to literary criticism. It means simply that the literary critic should use them only as building stones and as material for its own proper activity and that such material in itself usually does not supply critical results for literature.

On one hand the literary critic must be extremely careful in borrowing conclusions from other fields. For example, several decades ago literary criticism in German-speaking areas discovered to what a vast and useful extent art history had developed the concept of historical style as a category of classification and it was altogether understandable that it should try to do the same. It was not the basic idea which aroused a partially warranted attack on such borrowing—even though the basic idea was attacked along with it—it was rather the procedure which had been used and which had tried to appropriate too many of the concepts of art instead of deriving its own from works of literature.

On the other hand, literary criticism cannot possibly function without appropriating results from other areas, for it would also lead inescapably to errors if nothing were taken into consideration except literature itself. Quite rightly, Bernard De Voto alluded to the "literary fallacy"[31] which consists in first deriving sociological facts from literature, in order later to use them for the same pieces of literature as confirmation for the typical social environment which they reflect. This is one of the most unthinking kinds of a *circulus in probando*.

Furthermore, the relation to neighboring disciplines can be of decisive importance for the problem of evaluation. For if philosophy, for example, should succeed in establishing valid epistemological and logical foundations for a general theory of value, it should be possible to deduce from them general principles and methods which would be applicable to individual disciplines, including, of course, literary criticism.[32] Nothing could be more erroneous than raising to a scholarly ideal the principle of paying no attention to other disciplines.

One problematical feature connects all the individual characteristics mentioned. It connects literary criticism with neighboring disciplines in spite of their profound natural differences (works of literature belong to an aesthetic plane, whereas the objects of most of the neighboring disciplines lie on an empirical plane). It connects also the specific characteristics of literary evaluation with literary criticism in general and it coordinates the problem of value itself common to many disciplines. This common feature and mutual problem is the symbol. An imposing although still incomplete cross-section of this problem was offered by the Thirteenth Conference of Science, Philosophy and Religion in New York in 1952. Their findings were also published as a book with the title *Symbols and Values*.[33]

The concept of the symbol is of such eminence in literary studies, that it is sometimes regarded as its constitutive element. Kenneth Burke, for example, viewed literature from a certain perspective as "symbolic action,"[34] and it is probably not a coincidence that Northrop Frye attempts to define his object, that is, literature, in the chapter of his theory of literature which bears the title "Theory of Symbols."[35]

Great writers and poets, too, who have been concerned with the theory or criticism of literature have again and again stressed the central significance of the symbol. William Butler Yeats, for example, speaks of a "continuous indefinable symbolism which is the substance of all style" and continues after quoting and commenting on two verses of Burns: "We may call this metaphorical writing, but it is better to call it symbolical writing, because metaphors are not profound enough to be moving, when they are not symbols, and when they are symbols, they are the most perfect of all, because the most subtle, outside of pure sound, and through them one can the best find out what symbols are."[36]

D. H. Lawrence, moreover, declared: "You can't give a great symbol a 'meaning,' any more than you can give a cat a 'meaning.' Symbols are organic units of consciousness with a life of their own, and you can never explain them away, because their value is dynamic, emotional, belonging to the sense—consciousness of the body and soul, and not simply neutral. An allegorical image has a *meaning*. Mr. Facing-both-ways has a meaning. But I defy you to lay your finger on the full meaning of Janus, who is a symbol."[37]

In spite of that, literary criticism must try to come to terms rationally with symbolism, and indeed with this kind of symbolism, if it does not wish to succumb. It has tried to do just that and in recent literary theory once again it was Frye who made the most extensive and productive attempt. He accomplishes this in his theory of symbols by beginning with the idea that the symbol is of many layers or "levels." One may want to alter Frye's sequence of levels or phases, but one cannot disregard the many-leveled quality of the symbol.

The following remarks—as well as most of the essays in this volume—will not pretend to treat all the levels of the literary symbol. Rather, they will be concerned mostly with those symbols or levels of symbols that would be classed in Frye's fourth and fifth categories: these last two phases he called "Mythical phase: Symbol as Archetype" and "Anagogic Phase: Symbol as Monad."

It is precisely the many-leveled structure of symbols which is one of the sources for the most frequent misapprehension by literary criticism: either one does not see things which are there, or one thinks he sees things which are not there. "Mythical-archetypal" and "anagogic" symbolism have been plagued for decades primarily by the former misapprehension. In recent years, however, very significant ideas and results have been produced partly by outsiders. An impressive example of this is Hedwig von Beit's work on symbolism in folk tales.[38] This study tries to give a systematic cross-section of the folk tale in all cultures, in its nature, structure, and meaning, and it succeeds in revealing unexpected parallels. New knowledge is not only gained about the interworking relations of folk tale, myth and mysticism, but also about the relation of folk tale and popular farcical prose, and of folk tale and the psychological archetypes as expounded by C. G. Jung. The significance of this study for our context is von Beit's persuasive demonstration of how an abundance of symbols is hidden behind an apparently naïve kind of narrative which would be understood in a fantastic-realistic sense by any child listening to it thoughtfully. It shows that this is not simply a swarm of isolated symbols, but rather a unified structure of different symbols out of which the whole shape and course of the story is so composed that not a single symbol can be detached from it.

In the composition of folk tales, mythical symbols are frequent and sometimes predominating. In the literary art of the last centuries we find a similar pattern of frequency, though here we have mystical (anagogic) symbols, not mythical ones. But it would be a grave error to construct a formal opposition out of this difference. For, in the first place, the original unity and purity of the myth are no longer present, even in the versions of folk tales which are available to us. And, in the second place, there is a certain mythical heritage still alive in symbols and even in mystical symbols of literary art of recent times when they are viewed at one of their many levels of meaning.

The terms "myth" or "mythical" will not be used either here or in the following essays simply in the sense of "plot" or "narrative scheme"; rather, they are employed in the sense of those imaginal-anthropomorphic tales of gods and heroes which Frye calls "the union of ritual and dream in a form of verbal communication."[39]

The terms "esoterism" and "esoteric" will be used extensively as synonyms for "mysticism" and "mystical" or "anagogic" and will be understood rather broadly. "Esoterism" will be employed both for the experience of the transcendent in the depths of one's self, and for the expansion of individual consciousness in the wholeness of the undivided supreme being, as well as for those numerous, parallel "secret teachings" which institutionalize the way to mystical experience and try to communicate it.

At this point I will briefly discuss the esoteric or anagogic phases of literary symbolism, since these kinds of symbols belong to the most important but least explored symbols in literature.

The esoteric symbols are mostly connected with esoteric traditions. Through lack of understanding these esoteric or mystical traditions can become superficial; they can be misinterpreted, twisted, and abused. Their use depends finally, as with everything in the world, on who handles them. But unlike many representatives of orthodox or sectarian theology, the leading adherents of esoteric traditions never stand in direct opposition to rational scientific progress; sometimes they are even associated with it and at the outside they may protest its one-sided over-valuation. On the other hand, great poets, writers, and thinkers have always known how to distinguish between the worth and meaning of true mysticism and its cloudy distortion in which boundless blind irrationality takes over. For example, Goethe, who was deeply influenced by the mystical teachings of Neoplatonism, repeatedly expressed the greatest contempt for such cloudy mysticism. He mentioned to Kanzler Mueller in 1825, "the propensity in modern times towards mysticism, because for that one does not have to learn so thoroughly." Robert Musil distinguished explicitly between dark mysticism and "noon-day bright mysticism."

In the following articles mysticism will be used in the latter sense. The same will hold for esoterism, which will be used as a synonym for mysticism and will not carry any of the negative connotations so prevalent in the English-speaking world, where it is often understood as something arbitrarily chosen and then rendered artificial and unintelligible for the sake of being unintelligible. The difference between this kind of esoterism, this sensationalism put forth by exorbitant and naïve snobbishness, and the serious esoteric tradition is as great as the difference between mysticism as an attempt to mystify and real mysticism or that between plain nonsense and the apparent nonsense behind which profundity is hidden. Not subjective parochialism but a universal esoterism is under discussion here, and it is its very universality which connects it with the universality of myths and archetypes. Mysticism and esoterism both find their expression in different levels of meanings or in different phases of literary symbols. Sometimes there are even mythical traces in esoteric symbols. But all this should not obscure the deep difference which separates mythical and esoteric symbolism in literature.

Each of these two types of symbolism is the expression of a fully different stage of human development in life and literature. Myth characterizes the stage of "primitive" oneness and wholeness which became lost in the overdevelopment of human intellect and rationalism. Esoterism corresponds to a kind of sublimated form of myth at a time when wholeness is being sought again. But it would be wrong to see in this necessarily a romantic, Rousseauistic retreat which has contempt for the present stage of human culture and its differentiation or which simply suppresses awareness of it and tries to return to the primitive condition of the mythical stage of development. It is not the question of returning, but of advancing through all the sophistication of rational development without relinquishing an inch of intellectually-attained splendor, proceeding stage by stage, from the *purgatio* to the *illuminatio* to the attainment of that integration and wholeness which all great esoteric traditions describe as a kind of *"unio."* It is true that when one has reached this stage, one might have left the multitude of "realistic" details behind, but only after progressing through them, and above all, never with anti-intellectual disdain but in the course of a development which would not be possible without the participation of the intellect or without its illumination. This is a simplified short outline of one of the basic ideas of esoterism in which no literary critic must believe but which he might find quite helpful to know in some cases.[39a]

We must now touch briefly upon another problem, the difference in attitude between the pure mystic and the poet. Most literary critics, if they write a history of literature, treat the works of the mystics. That is easy to understand because the great mystics were creators of language and poetic imagery. Because literary theory has not reflected enough about its object, this question has been left open and we cannot attempt a clarification here. But it should be pointed out that in a certain sense mysticism and literature move in opposite directions. The great mystic begins from an act of experience which he desires to make known to others. Precisely because this experience is so difficult to make intelligible, he resorts to language which is full of images, metaphors, and symbols. The poet who is interested in mysticism and oriented toward it takes the opposite path: he uses the language and symbols of mysticism in order to approach mystical experience through the act of writing. Of course, the difference is fluid: there have been mystics who wrote poetry and poets who reached a *"unio mystica"* in their poetic accomplishments, at least. But in general the situation of the mystic and the poet is similar to that of the hierophant and the novice in the initiation rites of mysteries. The hierophant uses the symbols to make himself understood to the novice. The novice uses the symbols in order to approach step by step the central acts of illumination and union. No words need to be lost about the unavoidable necessity, the crucial significance, and the universality which parallel symbols have played in all mystery cults of human history. But it does need to be pointed out to what a large extent even the greatest works of literature have been influenced in this direction, and that they cannot be understood except from this standpoint.

Hence we find that many writers have again and again felt an unconscious attraction in mysticism and mystery cults or that they have consciously come to terms with them. This was true not only in antiquity, for which examples are well known, but it is also true in more recent literature. The very greatest authors can be named in this connection and that seems to me to be no coincidence. Of course, it is untrue to maintain that whoever is connected with these things will become a significant writer. But seen from the negative side, it is quite possible to say that the greatest writers would have been less great had they not been so involved.

At the summits of Western literature—not to mention Eastern literature—one finds esoteric symbolism in the most central place. One needs only to remember the rebirth symbol of the phoenix in the works of Dante and Shakespeare, or the symbol of the snake, or the symbols of close relatives of the snake such as the dragon and the leviathan, or the symbol of the whale in the works of Goethe and Melville.

Using Dante's work as an example and especially the *Divina Commedia*, Robert John has shown that a more profound understanding can be reached if one discovers the symbolic meaning behind the text. John traced this in Dante back to the gnosticism of the Knights-Templar, and summarized the results of his book in this sentence: "We recognize that Dante's universal poem with its climb from the sombre valley of misery to the countenance of God, with its journey through all the nether-regions, with its initiations in purgatory, is of a gnostic kind throughout."[40]

In Shakespeare's work it has been Paul Arnold who has shown how often a knowledge of esoteric symbolism leads to a deeper understanding. As John connected Dante with the Knights-Templar, Arnold relates Shakespeare to a group of Rosicrucians around Raleigh.[41]

Jean Paris, who incorporated Arnold's findings in his Shakespeare monograph, apparently wanted to avoid the terms "esoteric" and "rosicrucian" in the title of the pertinent chapter, for he speaks there of the "alchemistic theatre."[42] He seems not to be the only critic who prefers the term "alchemistic" in this connection. Under the title *Goethe the Alchemist,* Ronald D. Gray was the first in recent times to draw attention to and summarize the significance of esoteric symbolism in Goethe.[43] Likewise, using an "Alchemistic" title, Alice Raphael has investigated "symbolic patterns" in Goethe's works as they are related to esoteric traditions and above all to C. G. Jung's archetypes.[44]

Moreover, Raphael is one of the few who points out, marginally but with understanding, the spiritual kinship between literary symbolism on the one hand and the symbolism of initiation found in the orders of the Free Masons and Illuminati on the other hand, from which Goethe gained much. The book that would effectively demonstrate the extent and depth of these influences on Goethe's works has yet to be written.

It is only natural that critics who hold and represent Jung's views would generally have good insight into the relation between literary symbolism and esoteric tradition. In the body of Melville criticism, for example, James Baird's book is more penetrating than others in the field, not only for its insights into "the imagery of Orientalism" and Zoroastrianism, but also for its penetration of the mythology of Oceania, Polynesian fraternity, and Marquesian iconography and tattooing.[45] When, however, one delves further into the history of Melville criticism, one finds the book by Weaver, of whom Mark Van Doren wrote: "His was the first enthusiasm, the first reconnaissance on a broad front, the first outright claim that Melville was what we have come to think of him as being, namely, an author of world importance."[46] Weaver's book has the significant subtitle, *Mariner and Mystic*. As for the "Mariner," Melville had long since found his public and secured his fame in this respect. But Melville's reputation was enhanced by a deeper meaning through the second word of the subtitle, the characterization "mystic." Since then, the references to the relation between his poetic symbolism and esoteric tradition have increased significantly, and Melville's debt to Gnosticism and Manichaeism, Sufism and Neoplatonism has also been established.[47] At first glance, it may not be evident that at the lowest level the individual authors have mutual esoteric goals, because basic esoteric symbolism is early hidden in the abundance of its diverse and colorful forms. This uniformity, however, is more far-reaching than one would think. If one reviews somewhat more closely the different esoteric traditions from which Western literature has drawn throughout the centuries, they can be reduced to three different forms: Christian Gnosticism and Rosicrucianism, Jewish Cabbalism, and Hellenistic Neoplatonism. In contrast to the different orthodox theologies, the leading representatives of these esoteric traditions again and again sought confirmation and a deepening of meaning by comparing their own tradition with those running parallel to it. Hence, at an early date, there arose various combinations of these three main currents as well as versions mixed with Eastern traditions. There was always a far-reaching willingness, if not a tendency, to syncretism.

It would lead us too far astray to investigate here how much great literature and its symbolism has gained from the sources of such esoteric traditions—and only thus would complete understanding be possible—from *Parzival* to the *Fleurs du Mal* and from Pico della Mirandola to John Cowper Powys, not to mention the works of the great Oriental writers from Basho to Mevlana and from Chuang-tse to Nizami. There appear to be several reasons why literary criticism has so readily overlooked these relationships. Along with deliberate prejudice and plain blindness, misconceptions by the critics have also caused antipathy to and rejection of this kind of symbolism. When one reads with what downright fear some authors avoid these relationships in their occasional treatment of them, then one can only assume that they shut their eyes to some of the simplest assumptions, which again Frye formulated so cogently:

> 1.) If men were compelled to make the melancholy choice between atheism and superstition, the scientist, as Bacon pointed out long ago, would be compelled to choose atheism, but the poet would be compelled to choose superstition, for even superstition, by its very confusion of values, gives his imagination more scope than a dogmatic denial of imaginative infinity does. But the loftiest religion, no less than the grossest superstition, comes to the poet, *qua* poet, only as the spirits come to Yeats, to give him metaphors for poetry.
>
> 2.) When the poet and critic pass from the archetypal to the anagogic phase, they enter a phase of which only religion or something as infinite in its range as religion, can possibly form an external goal . . . The literary critic, like the historian, is compelled to treat every religion in the same way that religions treat each other, as though it were a human hypothesis, whatever else he may in other contexts believe it to be.[48]

The description of the close relation between literary symbolism and esoteric tradition, between literature and mysticism, has met with varied treatment and has received as great an acceptance as rejection. One need only think of the famous speech "La Poésie pure" which was read by Henri Bremond more than forty years ago before a joint meeting of the five Academies in Paris, of the storm of indignation and applause, invective and enthusiasm which broke out at that time in France in interested circles. He closed with the statement: "If one is to believe Walter Pater, 'then all arts strive to become music.' No, they all strive, however, each one through the magical medium which is its own—the words, the notes, the colors, the lines—they strive to end in prayer."

Since it was clear to Bremond how problematic these concise remarks had to remain in a short speech on such an enormous subject, he discussed his views in greater depth in twelve essays, which appear as a book with the significant title *Mystik und Poesie*.[49] He explains that the writer can be compared with the mystic primarily in the psychological patterns of his own experiences. Yet beyond this correspondence, he emphasized a profound difference between mysticism and literature which he slanted much to the detriment of literature: "hence the singularity and at the same time the natural imperfection of poetic experience: [it is] the beginning and the point of departure for a higher experience, one which it induces in a certain way; but it cannot of itself lead to that higher level, it rather inhabits it."[50]

Such a conclusion by a critic, who like Bremond also feels himself bound in his literary reflections to specific theological and dogmatic precepts of Christian, and indeed more exactly, Catholic provenance, can be adequately explained. Limitations imposed by the individual denominations had already been surmounted by the words of Franz Kafka when he explained his own writing "as a form of prayer." Our relationship is seen more explicitly in a book by R. H. Blyth where he develops the relationship between the esoteric tradition of Zen-Buddhism and English literature, as for example in Wordsworth and Shakespeare.[51] He does not think for one minute of direct Japanese "influences"; rather, he intends to show the astonishing unity of meaning behind the variety of imagery and symbolism in the literature, as well as the different esoteric traditions. Here one finds no devaluation of literature at all, simply the straightforward equation: poetry is religion. The term "religion" is naturally to be understood here as mysticism, and not as theology. And though the equation is too simplified to be generally valid, it is nevertheless entirely relevant to our context, in which the point at issue is above all the levels of meaning in poetic symbolism.

The unity of meaning beyond the complexity of imagery and symbolism is easy to sketch in a few words, as Ronald D. Gray has done in his book on Goethe, where he simply uses the term alchemy for that which up until now we have described as esoteric tradition. Gray says correctly: "In fact, one is inclined to look for the origins of alchemy not in Christianity but in the Orphic mysteries and their developments in Greek philosophy. Regarding alchemy as a whole, and including the Arabs, Greeks, Chinese and non-Christian Europeans who practice it, it is seen to be an expression not solely of Christianity, but of the so-called 'perennial philosophy,' . . ." and he explains that for Goethe—which is true for all authors, who at any time stood in such a mystical tradition: for them, Christ "is no longer the Son of God but a son of God. Some may revere Christ as the supreme model, others may declare themselves to be the only true Christians, but there is always a tendency to believe that each individual must, like the initiate in a mystery, undergo his own temptation, trial, death and rebirth. Individual experience counts more with them than organized religion . . ."[52]

It is precisely the subjectivity of this "individual experience" which, however, aims toward trans-subjectivism—similar to the symbol in the Goethean sense of going from the particular to the general —which makes the pursuit of mystical traditions so interesting and fruitful for a writer. But though the ultimate meaning behind the variations in imagery is at one with itself with regard to content, the forms can be diverse when these contents are presented in poetic symbols.

In another place, I have tried to show[53] how different the genesis and the function of literary symbols can be at this level. Such symbols are created purely subjectively—no matter how much their creator is consciously or unconsciously bound to a greater cultural tradition which has an effect on him. They can, however, be selected and formed from an equally "objective" consciousness by the writer, but this consciousness again can be of quite different kinds. It can reach from a type of experience, which is released from within, a gnostic "knowledge" in the sense of mystery-initiation, to a lexographic "knowledge," which is acquired by an author who is inclined to flamboyance and who with all his manneristic superficiality still possesses enough instinct to recognize in a purely rationalistic manner the value and meaning in this type of symbolism.

Finally, there are various levels and transitions between forms within individual literary works as well as in the long development of the work of a single author. Roughly speaking, one could say, for example, that Rilke at the beginning of his development made use of a symbolism which he mainly took over from greater historical mystical traditions in order to express his exceedingly subjective feelings, that he later turned from it to create his own subjective symbolism, and that he finally, not without surprise and satisfaction, became aware of how his self-created "subjective" symbolism corresponded to the most remote of mystical traditions.

The meaning of poetic symbols, and particularly those which have esoteric significance, is for many reasons not always simple: first, because of the complexity of the phenomena by which they are able to express themselves, as for example numbers, letters, and colors, persons, animals, and things, forms, gestures, and events; second, because the correct meaning of one or several of such symbols in a work of art discloses only isolated elements and does not reveal the total structure of the work, which frequently is formed by just such a complete structure of symbols; and third, as a result of the fact that this kind of symbolism, like mysticism itself, is subjugated to a historical changing of its forms.[54]

In whatever form and under whatever historical circumstances such poetic symbolism might appear, it is most intimately related to the essence of that which is literature, indeed it directly constitutes that which is literature. Therefore René Wellek was able to write: "In its lower reaches realism constantly declined into journalism, treatise writing, scientific description, in short, into non-art; at its highest, with its greatest writers, with Balzac and Dickens, Dostoevsky and Tolstoy, Henry James and Ibsen, and even Zola it constantly went beyond its history: it created worlds of imagination. The theory of realism is ultimately bad aesthetics because all art is 'making' and is a world in itself of illusion and symbolic forms."[55]

This creative "making," however, that is related to the experience of the mystic, does not because of that have to be unrealistic in any way and the parallelism and the universality of such symbolic concepts is a completely natural process, which has roots in the very nature of man. This was shown by Emerson when he wrote:

> The beauty of the fable proves the importance of the sense; so the poet, and so all others; or, if you please, every man is so far a poet as to be susceptible to these enchantments of nature; for all men have the thoughts whereof the universe is the celebration. I find that the fascination resides in the symbol. Who loves nature? Who does not? Is it only poets, and men of leisure and cultivation, who live with her? No; but also hunters, farmers, grooms, and butchers, though they express their affection in their choice of words. The writer wonders what the coachman or the hunter values in riding, in horses and dogs. It is not superficial qualities. When you talk with him he holds these at as slight a rate as you. This worship is sympathetic; he has no definitions, but is commanded in nature by the living power which he feels to be there present. No imitation or playing of these things would content him; he loves the earnest of the north wind, of rain, of stone and wood and iron. A beauty not explicable is dearer than a beauty which we can see to the end of. It is nature the symbol, nature certifying the supranatural, body overflowed by life which he worships with coarse sincere rites.

The inwardness and mystery of this attachment drive men of every class to the use of emblems. The schools of poets and philosophers are not more intoxicated with their symbols than the populace with theirs. In our political parties, compute the power of badges and emblems. . . . See the power of national emblems. Some stars, lilies, leopards, a crescent, a lion, an eagle, or other figure which came into credit God knows how, an old rag of bunting, blowing in the wind on a fort at the ends of the earth, shall make the blood tingle under the rudest or the most conventional exterior. The people fancy they make poetry, and they are all poets and mystics.[56]

In a few of the greatest formulations, the multiplicity in the whole and the whole as multiplicity become visible, as, for example, in Basho's haikus or more abstractly in Goethe's "Weissagungen des Bakis," or in Spenser when he wrote:

> So every spirit, as it is most pure,
> And hath in it the more of heavenly light,
> So it the fairer body doth procure
> To habit in, and it more fairly dight,
> With cheerful grace and amiable sight.
> For, of the soul, the body form doth take,
> For soul is form, and doth the body make.
>
> [*Translated from the German by Alice Kennington*]

Notes

1. Louis J. A. Mercier, *The Challenge of Humanism. An Essay in Comparative Criticism* (New York: Oxford University Press, 1936). Other critics employed the expression also, although not in such a central way.
2. See: David H. Malone, "The 'comparative' in comparative literature," *Yearbook of Comparative Literature* (1954), vol. 3, pp. 13-20.
3. René Wellek, *Concepts of Criticism* (New Haven and London: Yale University Press, 1965), p. 1.
4. Wellek, *Concepts of Criticism*, op. cit., pp. 2, 345, 364.
5. Northrop Frye, *Anatomy of Criticism* (New York: Atheneum, 1966), p. 72.
6. Wellek, *Concepts of Criticism*, op. cit., p. 7.
7. Wellek, *Concepts of Criticism*, op. cit., p. 6, writes: "A straw man is set up: the New Critic, who supposedly denies that a work of art can be illuminated by historical knowledge at all."
8. Wellek, *Concepts of Criticism*, op. cit., p. 6.

9. *Myth and Symbol,* ed. Bernice Slote (Lincoln: University of Nebraska Press, 1964), p. 3.
10. Recently such methodological clarification has been provided by René Wellek and Austin Warren, *Theory of Literature* (New York: Harcourt, Brace and Company, 1963), Northrop Frye, *Anatomy of Criticism,* op. cit., and Max Wehrli, *Allgemeine Literaturwissenschaft* (Bern und Muenchen: Francke Verlag, 1967).
11. Stanley Edgar Hyman, "Attempts to an Integration," *The Armed Vision* (New York: Vintage Books, 1961), pp. 386-402.
12. Hyman, *The Armed Vision,* op. cit., p. 394.
13. Harry Levin, *Contexts of Criticism* (New York: Atheneum, 1963), p. 257.
14. John Crowe Ransom, "Wanted: an ontological critic," *The New Criticism* (Norfolk, Connecticut: New Directions, 1941).
15. Oscar Cargill, *Towards a pluralistic Criticism* (Carbondale: Southern Illinois University Press, 1965).
16. Other examples from different origin can be chosen at random: we call to mind the book of Marcel Raymond on Paul Valéry, which speaks of "ontological preoccupations" long before Ransom's demand, or the basic theoretical position of another Swiss, Jean Strobinsky in "Les Lettres Nouvelles" (June 24, 1959). Think of the Dane, Erik Lunding's "existential" literary criticism or of the French Jean Pierre Richard's aesthetic-psychological methodology, or of the philosophical integration of methods in literary observation of Julian Maria, a Spaniard. In spite of all diversity, these all lead in the direction of a synthesis.
17. Frye, *Anatomy of Literary Criticism,* op. cit., p. 11 f.
18. Wellek, *Concepts of Criticism,* op. cit., p. 68.
19. Walter Mueller-Seidel, *Probleme der literarischen Wertung.* Ueber die Wissenschaftlichkeit eines unwissenschaftlichen Themas (Stuttgart: J. B. Metzlersche Verlagsbuchhandlung, 1965).
20. Frye, *Anatomy of Criticism,* op. cit., p. 20.
21. Frye, *Anatomy of Criticism,* op. cit., pp. 4, 20 and 25. The first italics are Frye's, the second are mine.
22. *Literary Symbolism,* ed. Maurice Beebe (Belmont, California: Wadsworth Publishing Company, Inc., 1965), pp. 174-77.
23. Wladimir Weidlé, *Die Sterblichkeit der Musen* (Stuttgart: Deutsche Verlagsanstalt, 1958), pp. 179-80.
24. Northrop Frye's standpoint of completion or wholeness, as it were, with regard not only to criticism but also to its object, literature, seems to me to be of special significance. Aside from the arrangement of the four chapters of his *Anatomy of Criticism,* we call to mind two short quotations: "The first postulate of this inductive leap is the same as that of any science: the assumption of total coherence." (p. 16) and: "In other words, there is as yet no way of distinguishing what is genuine criticism, and *therefore progresses toward making the whole literature intelligible,* from what belongs only to the history of taste, and therefore follows the vacillations of fashionable prejudice." (p. 9) The italics are mine.
25. Frye, too, speaks of the necessary independence of the critic and declares in one place: "It is all too easy to impose on literature an extra-literary schematism, a sort of religio-political-literary colorfilter, which makes some poets leap into prominence and others show up as dark and faulty." And: "Such independence of criticism from prejudice, however, does not invariably occur even with those who best understand criticism. Of their inferiors the less said the better." (p. 7).
26. Milton Singer, "On understanding other cultures and one's own," *The Journal of General Education* (April, 1967), XIX, No. 1, p. 5.

27. Weidlé, *Die Sterblichkeit der Musen*, op. cit., p. 181.
28. Immanuel Kant, *Critique of Judgment*, translated with an Introduction by J. H. Bernard (New York: Hafner Publishing Company, 1951), p. 47.
29. Karl August Horst, "Die Aufsplitterung der kritischen Masstaebe," *Zeitwende* (Hamburg, 1964), vol. 35, pp. 103-13.
29a.   Humanity
          It puts soul into pleasure, spirit into need
          grace even into strength and a heart into majesty.
30. Frye, *Anatomy of Criticism*, op. cit., p. 19.
31. Bernard DeVoto, *The Literary Fallacy* (Boston: Little, Brown & Co., 1944).
32. Cf. above all: Viktor Kraft, *Die Grundlagen einer wissenschaflichen Wertlehre* (Wien, Springer-Verlag, 1951), and Stephen C. Pepper, *The Sources of Values* (Berkeley and Los Angeles: University of California Press, 1958).
33. *Symbols and Values*. An initial Study. Edited by Lymon Bryson, Louis Finkelstein, R. M. MacIver, and Richard McKeon (New York: Cooper Square Publishers, Inc., 1964).
34. Kenneth Burke: *The Philosophy of Literary Form*. Studies in Symbolic Action (New York: Vintage Books, 1961).
35. Frye: *Anatomy of Criticism*, op. cit., pp. 71-9. See also the chapter "Works of Art and Literature as Symbolic Creation" in the book by Kurt Mueller-Vollmer, *Towards a Phenomenological Theory of Literature* (The Hague: Mouton & Co., 1963), pp. 156-66, or Leonhard Beriger, "Der Symbolbegriff als Grundlage einer Poetik," *Helicon* (1942).
36. William Butler Yeats, "The Symbolism of Poetry," *Essays* (New York: Macmillan, 1924), pp. 188-202.
37. D. H. Lawrence, "The Dragon of the Apocalypse," *Selected Literary Criticism*, ed. Anthony Beal (London: William Heinemann, 1955).
38. Hedwig von Beit, *Symbolik des Märchens*, vol. 1 (1960); *Gegensatz und Erneuerung im Märchen*, vol. 2 (1965); *Registerband*, vol. 3 (1965) (Bern und München: Francke Verlag). In the meantime she has changed her opinion about archetypal symbolism in folklore, as one can see from her contribution to this volume.
39. Frye, *Anatomy of Criticism*, op. cit., p. 106. The terms "myth" and "mythical" are not used here in the sense Frye uses them on pages 53 or 73 of his book, but only as he does on page 106 and following.
39a. As a kind of comparative outline of the esoteric picture of man cf. the book of René Guenon, *Man and his Becoming* (London: Luzac & Co., 1945). It starts indeed from the tradition of the Vedanta but in its notes it gives comparisons with many other traditions.
40. Robert John, *Dante* (Wien: Springer Verlag, 1946).
41. Paul Arnold, *Esoterik im Werke Shakespeares* (Berlin: K. H. Henssel Verlag, 1957).
42. Jean Paris, *William Shakespeare* (New York: Grove Press, 1960).
43. Ronald D. Gray, *Goethe the Alchemist* (Cambridge: At the University Press, 1952). Cf. also G. F. Hartlaub, "Goethe als Alchemist," *Euphorion*, Folge 3, vol. 48 (1954), pp. 19-40. For older literature, see Gray, op. cit., pp. 299-300.
44. Alice Raphael, *Goethe and the Philosopher's Stone* (London: Routledge and Kegan Paul, 1965). Similar problems are emphasized in the book of Christian Lepinte, *Goethe et l'occultisme* (Paris: Société d'Édition Les Belles Lettres, 1957) and of Friedrich Hiebel, *Goethe* (Bern and München: Francke Verlag, 1961).
45. James Baird, *Ishmael* (Baltimore: The John Hopkins Press, 1956).
46. Mark Van Doren in his introduction of the book *Herman Melville* by Raymond M. Weaver (New York: Pageant Books, Inc., 1961), pp. 13-14. The first edition was published in New York (George H. Doran Company, 1921).

47. Here only a few examples chosen at random: William Braswell, *Melville's Religious Thought* (Durham, North Carolina: Duke University Press, 1943), Dorothea Metlitsky Finkelstein, *Melville's Orienda* (New Haven and London: Yale University Press, 1961) and Lawrence Thompson, *Melville's Quarrel with God* (Princeton: Princeton University Press, 1952), H. Bruce Franklin, *The Wake of Gods* (Stanford: Stanford University Press, 1963).
48. *Anatomy of Criticism*, op. cit., pp. 125 and 126.
49. Henri Bremond, *Mystik und Poesie* (Freiburg im Breisgau: Herder, 1929).
50. *Mystik und Poesie*, op. cit., p. 224.
51. R. H. Blyth, *Zen in English Literature* (New York: E. P. Dutton & Co., 1960).
52. *Goethe the Alchemist*, op. cit., pp. 250-51.
53. Joseph Strelka, "Dichtung und Symbol," *Wort in der Zeit* (June, 1962), VIII, 6, pp. 36-42.
54. See, Paul Böckmann, *Formgeschichte der deutschen Dichtung* (Hamburg: Hoffmann und Campe Verlag, 1949), esp. chapters I and VI, and Friedrich-Wilhelm Wentzlaff-Eggebert, *Deutsche Mystik zwischen Mittelalter und Neuzeit* (Tübingen: J. C. Mohr, 1947).
55. *Concepts of Criticism*, op. cit., p. 255.
56. Ralph Waldo Emerson, "The Poet," *Essays Second Series*, Concord Edition (Boston: Houghton Mifflin, 1904), pp. 1-42.

Helen Adolf

WRESTLING WITH THE ANGEL: RILKE'S "GAZING EYE" ("DER SCHAUENDE") AND THE ARCHETYPE

PRELUDE: WHAT IS AN ARCHETYPE?

In the dim luminosity of a predawn hour he (she or it) suddenly stood before me. I was struck with awe. *"Numen adest!* Leave me!" —"Take it easy," said the monster; "I am only the three-story fountain of energy usually housed along your spinal column."—"But you have feet like a lizard, and a serpent's tail."—"Because I plunge into the arche of things, into the very beginnings of life."—"And why do I see your heart throbbing in your breast, and why is its beat so irregular?"—"Because of the conflict of opposites, because of your complexes, my dear."—"Why can't I see your face? Your head, to be sure, is wrapped in glory, and the eyes, like two stars, emit rays through the mist."—"*Your* stars, *your* ideals!"—"How should I call you?"—"I am an Archetype," said the monster modestly (the voice was coming from the middle story); "the full name is A. C. I., Archetype-Complex-Idea; you may call me Archie."—"You should not have come. Your aspect is indecent."—"Haven't you asked for it? Three are the races of men privileged to see me: those in whose minds the dividing-walls are shattered, those in whom they have become transparent, and those who gaze upon my reflection in the mirrors of the past because they are able to rise on wings. In short,

the alienated, the alienists, and the poets."—"But I am only a critic,"
I exclaimed. "Go and leave me, Archie. All I do is practice for fun
the language of 'as if.' "—"You never can tell for certain where you
belong."

In the preceding serio-comical prelude C. G. Jung's bi-polar[1] archetype has been transformed into a tripartite one—a change that was
prompted to me by the study of a special archetypal image, that of
Jacob wrestling with the angel. A confrontation of the biblical image
with the symbolical use made of it in Rilke's poem "Der Schauende"
should disclose something worthwhile about Rilke's "Gazing Eye"
(as I translate "Der Schauende" since neither "The Spectator" nor
"The Gazer" nor "The Seer" conveys the idea of the steady and dedicated glance peculiar to the painter or to the contemplative).

The story, as told in Gen. xxxii. 22–32, constitutes a tangle of victory and defeat.

22 And he rose up that night, and took his two wives, and his two
    women-servants, and his eleven sons, and passed over the ford
    Jabbok.
23 And he took them, and sent them over the brook, and sent over
    that he had.
24 And Jacob was left alone; and there wrestled a man with him
    until the breaking of the day.
25 And when he saw that he prevailed not against him, he touched
    the hollow of his thigh; and the hollow of Jacob's thigh was out
    of joint, as he wrestled with him.
26 And he said, Let me go, for the day breaketh. And he said, I will
    not let thee go, except thou bless me.
27 And he said unto him, what is thy name? And he said, Jacob.
28 And he said, Thy name shall be called no more Jacob, but Israel;
    for as a prince hast thou power with God and with men, and hast
    prevailed.
29 And Jacob asked him, and said, Tell me, I pray thee, thy name.
    And he said, Wherefore is it thou dost ask after my name? And
    he blessed him there.[2]
30 And Jacob called the name of the place Peniel: for I have seen
    God face to face, and my life is preserved.
31 And as he passed over Peniel, the sun rose upon him, and he
    halted upon his thigh.
32 Therefore the children of Israel eat not of the sinew which shrank,
    which is upon the hollow of the thigh, unto this day: because he
    touched the hollow of Jacob's thigh in the sinew that shrank.

Bible criticism has shed much light upon the story.[3] Our text is a
compilation of two J (Jahvist) versions and an E (Elohist) one, a
process extending over a period of 300 years (from ca. 1,000 to 700

B.C.). According to J 1, Jacob was fighting successfully a night-and-water demon, wrenching from him his blessing and calling the river after the fight (Jabbok). But J 2 replaced the demon by Jahve himself, or by his angel, who therefore had to prevail by laming his opponent. The sun that originally had spelled disaster to the demon, became, in the Elohist version, a symbol of theophany. Clearly there are here, as in the modified Jungian archetype, a mythological, a personal, and a religious level. Fear and desire must be conquered; the will must be "branded," that is, receive the mark of Jahve, God of History and of personality; then the heavens may open. However, there was enough obscurity left, concerning the growth of Jacob and the transformation of his god, to challenge the ingenuity of lay commentators. Böhme, himself a "Jacob," who called his first opus, "Morgenröte im Aufgang" (Aurora) after the sunrise of Gen. xxxii. 31, knew that in his enemies he had been fighting the Dark Fire of God.[4] For C. G. Jung, Jacob's ego is overpowered by his Self, but it must also stand up against the Shadow of the Self, which means universal Evil.[5] A collaborator of Jung, H. Rosenthal,[6] identified, not without rabbinical evidence, Jacob's adversary with the evil in his own character as well as with the evil in the tradition of his people, both of which are Esau, or Edom, who thus evaporates into a symbol. Thomas Mann, on the contrary, needed the very real contrast between the two brothers; the blessing conferred on Jacob is an anticipatory compensation for the deep humiliation Jacob is willing to suffer on the following day.[7]

We may add here the names of three famous painters, Gauguin, Redon, and Chagall. Strangely, Rembrandt who painted, drew or etched quite a host of Old Testament angels and whose genius retold almost the whole of Jacob's story including his reconciliation with Esau,[8] failed to depict the scene at the ford Jabbok.

Gauguin's painting *The Vision after the Sermon* (1888) equals this author's ludicrous "morning vision" by stressing the elements of incongruity. White-coifed Breton girls watch in dumb wonder while a pair of Japanese wrestlers (bodily "lifted" out of a Hokusai picture) perform before them within a circle of stark red—an early attempt at "synthetic" or symbolic painting.[9] Redon, on the other hand, may well be considered a substitute for the lacking Rembrandt, for here in a riot of colors we have everything: Jacob with a dislocated hip straining in the winged embrace of his tall, impassive opponent, whose garb of cool pink contrasts with the turbulent orange of the nascent sun.[10] In Chagall's painting (1955), Jacob and the river are still plunged in darkness, but over them towers, flower-like, Bella-like, the countenance of the Angel.[10a] And Rilke?

His poem, as we read it now, has found a niche of its own in the last section of the *Book of Images* (*Buch der Bilder*). Chronologically it belongs to the first two parts of the *Stundenbuch*, while thematically it foreshadows the *Duino Elegies;*[11] it seems to have more substance than either of those earlier or later ecstasies.[12] Its thirty-four lines, unbridled by any numerical pattern, but melodiously swelling, receding, advancing, form a whole that is as strong as a charm and as effective as a cordial; the one not to have used it in an emergency seems to have been the poet himself.

DER SCHAUENDE

Ich sehe den Bäumen die Stürme an,
die aus laugewordenen Tagen
an meine ängstlichen Fenster schlagen,
und höre die Fernen Dinge sagen,
die ich nicht ohne Freund ertragen,
nicht ohne Schwester lieben kann.

Da geht der Sturm, ein Umgestalter,
geht durch den Wald und durch die Zeit,
und alles ist wie ohne Alter:
Die Landschaft, wie ein Vers im Psalter,
ist Ernst und Wucht and Ewigkeit.

Wie ist das klein, womit wir ringen,
was mit uns ringt, wie ist das gross;
liessen wir, ähnlicher den Dingen,
uns so vom grossen Sturm bezwingen,—
wir würden weit und namenlos.

Was wir besiegen, ist das Kleine,
und der Erfolg selbst macht uns klein.
Das Ewige und Ungemeine
will nicht von uns gebogen sein.
Das ist der Engel, der den Ringern
des Alten Testaments erschien:
wenn seiner Widersacher Sehnen
im Kampfe sich metallen dehnen,

fühlt er sie unter seinen Fingern
wie Saiten tiefer Melodien.

Wen dieser Engel überwand,
welcher so oft auf Kampf verzichtet,
der geht gerecht und aufgerichtet
und gross aus jener harten Hand,
die sich, wie formend, an ihn schmiegte.
Die Siege laden ihn nicht ein.
Sein Wachstum ist: Der Tiefbesiegte
von immer Grösserem zu sein.[13]

Like one of the old Germanic charms (but in the first person singular), the poem begins with the brief narrative report of a harassing situation. Watching the wind lash out against the windowpane and bend the tree-tops outside, the poet is attacked by the fear of unspeakable future ills. But time and place dissolve into timelessness, and the voice of Wisdom, not once but twice, urges him not to hold on to the little things. A second transformation takes place; the vision of the Angel is being conjured and, immediately after him, the figure of him who will rise upright and great from under the hands of his superhuman opponent. Resisting the effect of the charm (that feeling of uplift emanating from its parable), let us weigh what is missing: the victory over the demon, the laming of the thigh, the receiving of a new specific name—in fact, the entire middle (Jahvistic) part. Instead, there is the demand to imitate the pliancy of the things of nature ("liessen wir, ähnlicher den Dingen . . .")—echoes from the *Stundenbuch,* from the vast plains of Russia. Such a doctrine, to put it in a nutshell, is Tao rather than Ya'u (an ancient name for Jahve) . Why then had Jacob's angel to be bothered at all?[14]

At this point a consideration of the biographical circumstances cannot be bypassed.

The poem, as we read it now, is the final version composed in September or October of 1901, whereas its first version, entitled "Sturm," stems from the middle of January, 1901, and was sent, with a string of eight sentimental lines, to Clara Westhoff.[15] The poet lived in Schmargendorf then, a suburb of northern Berlin that faced the woods. He spent sleepless nights, torn by neurotic fears. Unlike Richard Dehmel, whose famous poem "Lied an meinen Sohn"[16] must have been familiar to Rilke, the latter was unable to derive from sight and sound of the storm-tossed tree-tops a triumphant will toward resistance (his abhorrence of violence is even more outspoken in the earlier version). But unlike Dehmel, too, he was able to feel, behind the voices of the storm, a Presence. On December 19, 1900, he had attended with Lou Andreas-Salomé (one of the three "sisters" on whom he could lean at that time, the two others being Clara Westhoff and Paula Becker), a dress rehearsal of Gerhart Hauptmann's play *Michael Kramer*.[17] This play made on him a deep and lasting impression. He wrote into his diary a long and glowing appraisal of it, and he later dedicated to Gerhart Hauptmann the first edition of the *Buch der Bilder* with the words: "In Liebe und aus Dankbarkeit für Michael Kramer."[18] But what concerns us most is the fact that on Sunday, January 15, when Paula Becker came to visit him, he read to her, according to her diary,[19] the last act of Hauptmann's play, which can only have been *Michael Kramer*. And in that last act, the following words are spoken: "Der Tod, sehn Se, weist ins Erhabene hinaus. Sehn Se, da wird man niedergebeugt. . . . Doch was sich herbei lässt, uns niederzubeugen, ist herrlich und ungeheuer zugleich. . . . Da wird man aus Leiden gross . . ." Because his son Arnold had proved to be a misfit, Michael Kramer had argued passionately with his God until the Angel of Death taught him what Life had failed to reveal to him. It is this Angel of Death[20] (in Rilke's own words "ein überlebensgrosser Schmerz") that evoked in Rilke's mind the figure of Jacob's transforming angel and made him perceive, blurred to an extent because of the double reflection (Hauptmann and the Bible), the awesome features of the archetype.

Here we seem to reach the crux of the matter. The biblical fight, the archetypal conflict of opposites, meant something more portentous than what we have gazed on so far: namely, the struggle between Fear[21] and Faith. To cross the Jabbok also meant to choose the right direction.

Why, we wonder, was the poem called "Der Schauende"? It is a participial epithet that applies to Rilke himself but in a three-fold capacity. First of all, he had been the "gazing one" when he moved among the Worpswede painters, learning how to see from the "brown, steady glance of the blonde girl painter."[22] Then, more and more, he had become aware of his distinction as the one lonely contemplative, as brother and redeemer of things within a world that had forgotten the *via illuminativa*, the second phase of the mystical life. Finally, however, this very contemplative attitude no longer satisfied the poet: it became for him a phase to be overcome if ever he was to achieve "union"; "work of the eyes" should be supplanted by "work of the heart," which implied a sacrificial surrender of the will.[23] In our poem the "gazing eye" may have been privileged to see something that in actuality was never to take place.

For there was a rift in Rilke's nature and work, in spite of the fulfillment of his *annus mirabilis* (1922), a problem that remained unresolved.[24] This circumstance accounts for the corresponding rift in critical opinion: to some, he is not only a "Lesemeister," a supreme poet, but a "Lebemeister," a Teacher of the Way of Life; to others he is not.[25] This has to do with the historical moment, the *kairos,* into which he was born. Sensitive to all vibrations transcending this our immanence, he became nevertheless a disciple of Nietzsche, professing a creed that can be reduced to the following tenets: (1) "Bleibe der Erde treu," that is, remain true to Earth, and to Earth only; (2) renounce all consolations (of religion); and (3) accept Existence as it is, with all its ecstasies and all its horrors. How hard Rilke strove to become such a superman![26]

At the turn of the century, in the days of Worpswede and Schmargendorf, all roads still seemed to be open for Rilke. He lived in a kind of happier childhood, "ohne Verzicht und Ziel" (renunciation and goals still equally unknown to him). How lovable he must have appeared to his friends. His heart and mind were equally aglow for the spiritual message conveyed to him by *Michael Kramer,* and for Clara's ethical decision in renouncing, upon her father's request, a projected trip to France.[27] But in reality his choice had been made: Art was to be his religion. Even "Der Schauende" testifies to this inclination—look at its Angel: he is conceived as an artist, men (in the plural) are only his instrument or his material; it is therefore with the Angel that the poet identifies himself. Does that sound fanciful? Then read Rilke's letter of April 24, 1903, to Clara in which he discussed a future prose work that was to surpass his own *Stories of God:* "I will build it with all the reverence I have in my hands, and will not let go of any passage as long as it is less than myself, and will make each into an angel and will let myself be overcome by him and force him to bend me although I have made him . . ."[28] Similar terms are used in a later poem: "Trotz. Der Gebogene wird selber Bieger."[29] (The verbs *biegen* and *beugen* bear witness to the influence of Michael Kramer's *niederbeugen*). This bold and Nietzschean exchange of roles can be met by a bold metaphor: perhaps Rilke had changed horses in the middle of his Jabbok.

For his choice had been made. It would have been inexcusable for him, so he wrote in his diary,[30] to abandon his previous attempts at greatness in order to toil in the service of a lesser man. So he went to Paris, alone; he idolized Rodin,[31] who became a God-Father to him, while he himself, the man with the delicate little hands ("mit den kleinen rührenden Händen"),[32] set out to do the angel's job of handling the granite of experience. It was a truly heroic task.[33] Everything neoromantic was cast overboard, from Botticelli to Heinrich Vogeler, although the ethereal art of Puvis de Chavannes would have been more congenial to him—Puvis de Chavannes whom Rodin adored[34] and who touched Malte Laurids to tears. But Rilke craved the monumental, the whole of reality, not a reality spiritually filtered. This greatness, this monumentality he achieved in emulation of George,[35] Rodin, Cézanne, and Picasso; but the element of transcendence got lost in the process. In order to stay with us, it must be man's only, man's strongest love, his *Amor regnans.*

Rilke, however, like a Prodigal Son ("Verlorener Sohn") turned away in anger from a Father "who chose not to love him yet" and, seeking support from the virile but wayward genius of Rudolf Kassner, not from his own vision of Wrestling with the Angel, he arrived at the formidable gateway of the *Duino Elegies.* There the Angels barred him from entrance. What does that mean?

In the Egyptian *Book of the Dead* we are told that in the House of Osiris anyone desirous of passing the 21 (or 10) pylons had to name the goddess presiding over each of the gates.[36] Rilke failed to know the name of the angel, who therefore remained "full of denial." But Erich Simenauer knew the name of the angel,[37] and so did many an eminent critic after him. It was Rilke's narcissism, his own spirituality forced back into his own system, that was responsible for the "No." So the heavens were closed, but Earth offered ample compensation—Mother Earth, where the dead are and the roots of all things, including those that blossom into vine and into roses. There namelessness is one's lot, for what is Orpheus if not a glorious mask to conceal the loss of personality?

But a memory lingered in the poet (or was it an obsession?).[38] He had, after all, seen the reflection of the archetype. It was not enough to imagine another such encounter with the Angel:

> "sie kämen denn
> bei Nacht zu dir, dich ringender zu prüfen,
> und gingen wie Erzürnte durch das Haus

und griffen dich, als ob sie dich erschüfen,
und brächen dich aus deiner Form heraus."[39]

It was not enough to graft the human-superhuman struggle upon the unsuspecting golden-locked vine of the Alpine south.[40] Rilke was not a Dehmel (whose earthiness he came to acknowledge later),[41] nor was he a Grecian humanist like Paul Valéry. The "dear Earth" Rilke extolled still retained an other-worldly aspect, nor could Rilke forego the most insidious of "consolations," for an absurd hope seems to have loitered in his heart. What his actual career had denied him—the sudden appearance of the *Deus absconditus*—strangely adorns the last line of "Imaginary Career":

Da stürzte Gott aus seinem Hinterhalt.[42]

POSTLUDE

Archetypes are mysterious since they deal, in the language of psychology, with events that may well transcend the realm of the psychological.

Poetry is mysterious since it deals, in the language of symbols, with visions that belong to the imagination, that borderland and no-man's-land, between the personal and the universal.

Dealing with both of them, archetypes and poetry, the critic may well feel that he is wrestling with an Angel. So we are back where we started, but:

Wer spricht von Siegen? Überstehn ist alles.
(Who talks of victory? To endure is everything.)

Notes

1. Cf. J. Jacobi, *Komplex Archetypus Symbol in der Psychologie C. G. Jungs.* Mit einem Vorwort von C. G. Jung (1957), pp. 110 ff., 138; J. Jacobi, *Die Psychologie von C. G. Jung* (1940), p. 74 f.; Ch. Baudouin, *L'oeuvre de Jung et la psychologie complexe* (1963), pp. 143 ff.; on the "transparent dividing walls," see C. G. Jung and A. Jaffé, *Memories Dreams Reflections* (1963), p. 355; on will power in Jung's psychology, see Baudouin, *op. cit.*, p. 273.

2. The New Jewish Version (1962) translates here: "and he took leave of him there," assuming that the blessing accompanied the giving of the new name.

3. This is the modified Graf-Wellhausen theory, as presented in the *Interpreter's Bible* (1952) by C. A. Simpson and W. R. Bowie.

4. See J. Böhme, *Mysterium Magnum* (a commentary on Genesis, chapter 60).

5. C. G. Jung, *Symbolik des Geistes* (Psychologische Abhandlungen, v. VI, 1948), p. 348 ("Vergewaltigung durch das Selbst"); *Symbole der Wandlung* (1952), p. 580 f., with the picture of a Byzantine mosaic, Monreale, 13th century; *Memories Dreams Reflections*, pp. 344 and 242 f.; Fighting the "Shadow of the Self," see Ch. Baudouin, *op. cit.*, p. 359 fn.

6. H. Rosenthal, "Der Typengegensatz in der jüdischen Religionsgeschichte," in C. G. Jung, *Wirklichkeit der Seele* (Psychol. Abhandl., v. IV, 1947), pp. 355 ff.

7. See Th. Mann, *Joseph und seine Brüder*, I *(Die Geschichten Jaakobs*, 1933), chapter 2 (Jaakob und Esau).

8. See especially O. Benesch, *The Drawings of Rembrandt. A Critical and Chronological Catalogue*, vols. V and VI (1957); K. G. Boon, *Rembrandt. The Complete Etchings* (n. d.).

9. Cf. G. Wildenstein, *Gauguin*, p. 90 ff.; B. Dorival, *Gauguin* (1960), p. 89. The painting is now in the National Gallery of Scotland in Edinburgh.

10. *Odilon Redon Gustave Moreau Rodolphe Bresdin*. The Museum of Modern Art, N.Y., in collaboration with the Art Institute, Chicago (1964), p. 82.

10a. Jean Cassou, *Chagall* (1965), fig. 185 *(Jacob Wrestling with the Angel*, India ink and gouache on paper).

11. Cf. E. M. Butler, *R. M. Rilke* (1941), p. 325.

12. Cf. E. C. Mason, *Lebenshaltung und Symbolik bei R. M. Rilke* (2d ed. rev., 1964), pp. 33, 71, 203.

13. *Sämtliche Werke*, eds. Ruth Sieber Rilke and E. Zinn (Weimar: Rilke Archive, n. d.), I:459 f., (henceforth quoted as *SW*).

14. On Rilke and the Bible see M. Sievers, *Die biblischen Motive in der Dichtung R. M. R.'s* (1938), pp. 8, 122; for biographical details see E. C. Mason, *R. M. R. Sein Leben und sein Werk*, p. 11 ff.

15. *SW*, 725 (January 21, 1901).
   Here lines 21 to 26 read:

   > Und der Besiegte von den Beiden
   > (Der Sieg macht leicht verwöhnt und klein)
   > der wie der Sieger ist und rein,
   > verlangt, aus Demut unbescheiden,
   > von immer Grösserem zu leiden
   > das grosse Überwältigstein.

16. The poem was composed in February 1893 (or 1894); cf. R. Dehmel, *Bekenntnisse* (1926), p. 36, and P. Vom Hagen, *R. Dehmel; Die dichterische Komposition seines lyrischen Gesamtwerks* (1932), p. 92.

17. *Briefe und Tagebücher aus der Frühzeit, 1899-1902* (1931), p. 409 ff.

18. Cf. R. Mövius, *R. M. R.'s Stundenbuch. Entstehung und Gehalt* (1937), p. 79 f.

19. Paula Modersohn-Becker, *Briefe und Tagebuchblätter*, ed. S. D. Gallwitz (1957), p. 47.

20. Not the Angel-of-Death motif, but the partiality for the son is usually considered as the reason for Rilke's "gratitude" toward Hauptmann. Cf. E. M. Butler, *op. cit.*, p. 131.

21. On the nature of Rilke's fears see Lou Andreas-Salomé, *Lebensrückblick* (1951), p. 155; cf. also D. Bassermann, *Der andere Rilke* (1961), p. 80 ff.

22. Cf. H. W. Petzet, *Das Bildnis des Dichters. P. B. M. und R. M. R.* (1957), p. 37 ("die so braune schauende Augen hat").
23. See the poems of 1914 "Wendung" (*SW*, II, 82 ff.) and "Waldteich" (*SW*, II, 79 ff.). The contemplative gazing started with the *Stundenbuch* (see St. Steffensen, *R. og Verkeligheden* [1944], p. 89 f., "Den skuende Munk") and climaxed around 1904 (final version of the "Weisse Fürstin," *SW* I, 225). On R.'s meeting with R. Kassner (since 1910) see G. Mayer, *R. und Kassner. Eine geistige Bewegung* (1966), p. 41. "Von der Innigkeit zur Grösse gibt es nur einen Weg: das Opfer" had been the original version of what might be called "Kassner's Jabbok."
24. On this rift or cleavage see F. W. van Heerikhuizen, *R. M. R., His life and work* (1946; 1951), p. 112; E. C. Mason, *Der Zopf des Münchhausen. Eine Skizze im Hinblick auf R.* (1949), p. 82; H. F. Peters, *R. M. R.* (1960), p. 35.
25. The most prominent among them are E. M. Butler and E. C. Mason; see also J. Steiner, *R.'s Duineser Elegien* (1962), p. 8 ff., J. Strelka, *Rilke, Benn, Schönwiese und die Entwicklung der modernen Lyrik* (1960) attempts an absolute as well as an historical evaluation.
26. E. Heller, *The Disinherited Mind. Essays in Modern German Literature and Thought* (1952), p. 105, calls R. "the St. Francis of the Will to Power." Cf. also F. Dehn, "R. und Nietzsche," *Euphorion* XXXVII (1936), pp. 1-21; St. Steffensen, *op. cit.*, p. 35 ff.
27. *Briefe I (1897-1914)* (1950), p. 13 (October 18, 1900).
28. *Letters of R. M. R., 1892-1910*, tr. J. B. Greene and M. D. Herter Norton (1945), p. 107.
29. From "Imaginärer Lebenslauf," *SW*, II, 142 f. (1923).
30. January 8, 1902. Also quoted by E. C. Mason, *Lebenshaltung*, p. XV.
31. R. tended to idolize people. See J. Mendels, *Literarisches Jahrbuch der Görres-Gesellschaft*, IV (1963), p. 227.
32. *Briefe und Tagebuchblätter*, p. 130.
33. Cf. D. Bassermann, *Der andere Rilke* (1961), p. 143.
34. See P. Gsell, *L'Art. Entretiens* (1912), p. 237 f. Puvis de Chavannes' painting "The Christian Inspiration" (Palais des Arts, Lyon), would have been a perfect illustration of Rilke's *Stundenbuch*.
35. See E. C. Mason, "R. und Stefan George," in *Festschrift Korff* (1957), p. 262 ff.
36. *The Book of the Dead (Book of the Gates)*, Theban redaction, ed. C. A. Wallis Budge (1960), p. 409 ff. I owe this reference to my learned friend, Dr. Marianne Beth (New York).
37. E. Simenauer, *R. M. R. Legende und Mythos* (1953), p. 551 ff. But cf. G. C. Schoolfield, "R. und Narcissus," *Festschrift Zeydel* (1956), pp. 197-232; E. C. Mason, *R. M. R. Sein Leben und sein Werk* (1964), p. 92 ff.; H. F. Peters, *op. cit.*, p. 35.
38. Cf. E. M. Butler, *op. cit.*, p. 325 f.
39. "Der Engel," *SW*, I, 508 f., cf. H. Berendt, *R. M. R.'s Neue Gedichte. Versuch einer Deutung* (1957), p. 119 f.
40.   Sowie Jakob mit dem Engel rang,
           ringt der Weinstock mit dem Sonnenriesen . . .
    See *SW*, II, 146 f .("Das kleine Weinjahr").
41. See R.'s letter of December 16, 1923 (*Briefe* II, p. 428).
42. On "Imaginärer Lebenslauf" see J. R. v. Salis, *R. M. R.'s Schweizer Jahre* (3rd ed., 1952), p. 166 ("autobiographic"); E. C. Mason, *Der Zopf des Münchhausen* (1949), p. 84 ("important"); H. Fülleborn, *Das Strukturproblem der späten Lyrik R.'s* (1960), p. 175.

Paul Arnold

CHARLES BAUDELAIRE
AND THE SENSE
OF ENGULFMENT

IN A BOOK WHOSE FIRST VERSION WAS ORIGINALLY PUBLISHED IN GERMAN translation in Berlin in 1958[1] and whose definitive version will appear soon in Paris, I have revealed the true source, totally unknown to date, of the philosophic thought and theme and occasionally even of particular images and locutions of many a poem of Charles Baudelaire. This source is the only French translation existing at that time of the Greek writings entitled *Poïmandrès* (or *Pimandre*) which are attributed to Hermes Trismegistos and which were circulating in Alexandria around the beginning of our era. This rather incorrect translation, elaborated by François de Foix and enriched line by line with his abundant commentaries, had appeared in Bordeaux in 1579. Louis Ménard, close friend of Baudelaire until 1846, cited this very book, today very rare, in the preface to his own translation of *Pimandre* which appeared in 1866. It furnishes us with the key to almost all the enigmas that the supposed textual obscurities or ambiguities posed to the exegetists of Baudelaire, obscurities and ambiguities resulting in extremely contradictory hypotheses which ranged from a Catholic Baudelaire (according to Stanislas Fumet) to an atheist Baudelaire (according to Pierre Flottes).

The following section from my book will show how far from accuracy previous treatments have been and will show why Baudelaire opens his collection of *Les Fleurs du Mal* with an allusion to "Satan Trismégiste."

In these pages, the term "hermetism" will always be used in its pure meaning, that regarding the doctrine of Hermes Trismegistos. This doctrine taught a road to salvation or regeneration of the soul through the rejection of the passions and the rejection of the normal consciousness of the formal world, this normal consciousness being created by the fragmenting of the original Unity into different beings and things, whether Multiple or Numbers. A secret doctrine, it was taught by word of mouth or by writings which were allusive, or "esoteric" (another term whose pure meaning has been deranged in literature). This doctrine was supposed to lead the disciple to a "mystical" state, a state of a higher consciousness transcending that logical or reasonable comprehension which is considered an obstacle to the direct apperception of the divine truth with which the Mystic is supposed to unite.

There has been much discussion about the mystical experiences of Charles Baudelaire. But is the word itself not inappropriate? Certainly, the poet of *Les Fleurs du Mal* recalls, and not without ostentation, his "tendance à la mysticité; ses conversations avec Dieu" and this occurrence "dès son enfance."[2] But the comparisons on which he bases his conclusions on musical ecstasy in *Richard Wagner et Tannhäuser* lead one to believe that he was not taken in by these supposed raptures "faite de volupté et de connaissance."[3] Was he not thinking more of the syntheses and of the relationships between the arts themselves, as Jean Pommier has already very well explained it? And is it not because of these relationships that he formulates in his synthesis the image of "l'espace étendue jusqu'aux dernières limites concevables?"[4] That is, all that can be conceived by the human mind is capable of being defined, and therefore is finite, a position in opposition to the essentially incommensurable mystical conception which is therefore not finite.

In truth, no one appears so badly prepared for the real mystical experience made in the first degree of instinctiveness, of passivity, of humility, and of renouncement. Pitilessly sincere with himself, Baudelaire avows that thinkers of his kind enter into the realm of the infinite only on the day of death.

In addition, it is by an indirect method that he hopes to escape the grasp of our conscious, or reasonable, reality. He tries to "augmenter toutes ses facultés," and through hyperesthetics to become acquainted with the vertigo of the composite. From this aspect, he develops the experience into the very personal form of the "sensation du gouffre." *"Au moral comme au physique, j'ai toujours eu la sensation du gouffre, non seulement du gouffre du sommeil, mais du gouffre de l'action, du rêve, du souvenir, du désir, du regret, du remords, du beau, du nombre, etc."*[5] In what was perhaps only a first manifestation of the sense of evil which was going to carry him off, he believed that he was on the path to transcendency and he cultivated this "hystérie avec jouissance et terreur"[6] in order to escape to the world of "l'infini", to pass from the world of Numbers and of Beings, from

the formal world to the informal and ineffable world. This belief is
one of the themes of his poem *Le Gouffre*:

> Pascal avait son gouffre, avec lui se mouvant.
> —*Hélas! tout est abîme,—action, désir, rêve,*
> Parole! et sur mon poil qui tout droit se relève
> Mainte fois de *la Peur* je sens passer le vent.
>
> *En haut, en bas, partout, la profondeur, la grève,*
> *Le silence, l'espace affreux et captivant . . .*
> Sur le fond de mes nuits Dieu de son doigt savant
> Dessine un cauchemar multiforme et sans trève.
>
> *J'ai peur du sommeil comme on a peur d'un grand trou,*
> Tout plein de vague horreur, menant on ne sait où;
> Je ne vois qu'infini par toutes les fenêtres,
>
> Et mon esprit, toujours du vertige hanté,
> Jalouse *du néant l'insensibilité.*
> —*Ah! ne jamais sortir des Nombres et des Êtres!*[7]

One would be able to dispute the usual interpretation, that the
poet has put a dash at the beginning of the second and last lines,
not in a graphical whim but in order to point out here, as in other
poems, a dialog. Whatever it be, Baudelaire brings to us here the
reflection of a spiritual debate (how can one suspect otherwise?) between the superior aspect of the soul having a presentiment of the
infinite and the essential Unity, and his inferior aspect attached to
the material or multiple; both aspects live together in man, just as
not only Swedenborg but also the *Pimandre* do not cease proclaim-
ing it. And that fact in itself would suffice to explain the marked
indissoluble contradiction between the last line and all the preceding
ones: the inferior soul attached to the material refuses to leave "des
Nombres et des Êtres," refuses to leave the Multiple, the formal
world. It appears to me erroneous to say that this last line expresses
a regret or a wish: it is a refusal made in fear.

One knows—and it is a commonplace in the mystical experience—
that upon approaching the state of ecstasy the mystic is frequently
overcome by an anguish which goes as far as dread and which can be
explained by the fear that the physical being feels upon leaving its
customary element. Did Baudelaire know this only from hearsay?
Had he not lived the experience of it by cultivating "avec jouissance

et terreur" the feeling of engulfment, a description perfectly corresponding to the attraction or to the vertigo in this instant of the great entry? *Le Gouffre* then would be no more than the expression of this personal experience since one finds there the same terms as those in the observation: "gouffre . . . abîme de l'action, du rêve, du désir." The superior soul has a presentiment of the infinite, sees it or rather is just able to see it through all windows, but dreads it; he is seized by fear and horror, but while desiring it, wishing for it. At such a point the soul succeeds in calling forth "l'insensibilité du néant." The response of the inferior soul terminates the struggle and confesses what the poet avowed in *L'Irréparable*: the true ecstasy never visits his heart; it remains on the threshold of the ineffable world which frightens him and which he would like to analyze; thus, the mystical voyage is interrupted.

One could therefore explain the observations and the lines on *Le Gouffre* if he were without doubt that the poet has drawn from his imagination the essential elements of this imagery and their philosophical commentary. But in chapter XIII of *Pimandre*, which, it seems, has already furnished so much material to *Les Fleurs du Mal*, there is a strictly comparable dialog between Mercure (Hermes) Trismegistos in a state of ecstasy, and his disciple Tat who, observing that his own body is affected in the three dimensions (that is, subject to measure, to number, to multiple), feels himself seized with vertigo and fright. Then Mercure incites him to leave the world of reason, the world of numbers, to leave in other manner than through sleeping—that is, other than in a dream.

Before reproducing this passage, I must point out that the text of François de Foix, translated from a variant version, is rather different from the less complete one published in 1866 by Ménard, and that it alone contains several particularities of the Baudelairean poem.

Tat desires to know of what material and of what germinated seed the regenerated man is issue. His limited, or let us say even naïve, intelligence calculates that the regeneration will occur in the corporeal being though it is a purely spiritual transmutation. Trismegistos replies, "C'est par la sapience intelligible en [or, within the] silence"[8] that the regeneration is brought about. And, François de Foix completes it with the following: "La sapience intelligible en silence est la matrice [spirituelle] de laquelle doit naître celui qui sera régénéré." Tat himself disconcerted, Mercure explains to him that man will be like God provided with all powers. But he cuts short some new questions by stating: the doctrine "de régénération ne s'enseigne pas mais [nous est] donnée . . . [étant] ramenée de Dieu en la mémoire des hommes toutes les fois qu'il lui plaît."[9]

He evidently means that this state cannot be described in words but can only be experienced in ecstasy. Then Tat protests with vehemence; he cannot admit that he is excluded from this knowledge so ardently desired. He thus calls forth this profession of faith from Mercure speaking in the state of ecstasy and trying to communicate his vision to his disciple who has remained in his mortal body, or "constructed" matter: "Que parlerai-je, ô mon fils? Je n'ai [rien] à dire sinon ceci: je vois en moi quelque spectacle être engendré par la miséricorde de Dieu, non bâti [that is, without form or substance] et *suis issu* [that is, left or gone out] *de moi-même en mon corps immortel:* et suis maintenant non celui que j'etais auparavant mais je suis né en [la] pensée. Ce fait ne s'enseigne pas et ainsi [il] n'est [pas] permis [de] le voir par ce bâtiment[10] élémentaire, à cause de quoi j'ai méprisé ma forme premièrement composé," the form capable of being measured, that of the Number.

The reader who is not familiar with the language of the mystics will experience some difficulty in penetrating the meaning of these lines. Mercure is aware that he has left his corporeal, formal nature, that he has left the primitive form, "composed in the first place" of matter and not simple like the essential existence. Acknowledging the incomparable superiority of his new state, the state of ecstasy or of union with the divine principle, he "scorns" anew his preceding form as rudely material. In this second state, thanks to the misericord of God, he is permitted to escape from the limitation of the material, of *being,* as the commentary says—"transporté ou changé en un corps immortel" and by the effect of this "grandissime mutation," he "voit en [lui-] même quelque spectacle . . . non composé d'aucune manière de chose corporelle." In other words, he sees the non-multiple, the infinite which in truth is of the same essence as he himself in his immortal body but which he is not permitted to "voir par [that is, through] ce bâtiment élémentaire" that the body is—"*ces murailles de terre que sont les corps humains.*" Note that this image is comparable to the one of Baudelaire who "ne voit qu'infini par toutes les fenêtres."

Having thus transcended the material, Mercure can say in an assertion still in use among the mystics of the Orient who profess to be twice born or reborn in the spirit, "Je suis né du tout [that is, totally] converti en [la pensée]. N'ayant plus [that is, no longer holding] en aucun amour ou estime quelque [that is, not any] chose matérielle,

mon esprit étant ravi de ces divines vertus": in other words, it is the
mind in ecstatic rapture having lost all interest for the material
world, an attitude common to all the mystics. In this expression of
the second state François de Foix adds some comments on transsub-
stantiation, irrelevant to our discussion and also to hermetism, but
which proclaim the inadequacy of the material body in conceiving
the spiritual body, since "notre corps ne peut porter cette félicité de
[la] régénération sans être purifié et mondé [that is, delivered] de
toute mort et imperfection."

Such is the picture of the ecstatic state, or the direct vision of the
divine essence that Mercure offers to his disciple Tat. Immediately
afterwards is situated the following dialog of which Ménard, like the
modern editors of the *Pimandre,* is unaware of the first two responses
so important to this proposal:

> —O mon père, [ne] *suis-je point aliéné* [that is, astonished as far as the
> irrational] maintenant de ces choses [que tu viens de m'apprendre], *à
> cause que je suis taché* [that is, soiled by the evil inherent in the mate-
> rial] *et que j'ai attouchement et mesure en moi* [that is, that I live
> within the world of the senses, of the palpable and of the measurable]?

> —O mon fils, tu me vois des yeux quand tu me considères me regardant
> ferme de ta vue corporelle: mais *je ne regarde pas* maintenant de ces
> yeux, ô mon fils. [That is, you err in believing that you can see with
> the eyes of your body my state of mystical union; I appear to you at
> this time in a form not visible by the physical eye.]

> —O mon père, *tu m'as attiré en une manie* [that is, irrational state]
> qui n'est pas petite, et en un aiguillon de pensée [that is, mental aber-
> ration]: car maintenant *je ne me vois même* [that is, I see myself no
> longer in my habitual, corporeal state, but in the mystical, spiritual
> state].

> —O mon fils, *je désirerais qu'à la manière de ceux qui voient en songe
> tu fusses issu de toi-même* [that is, gone out from oneself] *sans dormir
> toutefois.*[11]

In other words, Mercure wishes that Tat experience by a true rapture and not by a simple dream the mystical ecstasy similar to his
own state at this time.

This little scene shows us then Tat feeling the approach of the
ecstasy but not understanding it. He observes that his judgment is
confused (in the limited sense of the normal human understanding),
or that his intelligence is unsteady, as though he were becoming irrational. He is frightened; the world of reason grips him. "*J'ai at-
touchement,*" explains the commentary, "*et pur usage de ce sens cor-*

porel qui me manifeste avoir corps matériel pourvu de sens, et j'ai mesure en moi, c'est à savoir les trois dimensions auxquelles tout corps est sujet qui est longueur, largeur et hauteur." This world, subject to measure and to numbers, wants to prevent him from passing over the threshold of the ineffable. Reason persists to propose to him some logical notions and lets him believe an instant longer that he can see with the eyes of the body what is forbidden to man to see through the body or "elementary construction." And suddenly the partition is broken through and he catches a glimpse of the second state, however without succeeding in entering completely into ecstasy, the state of which he has the presentiment of the related nature of the dream. The body resists and the experience ends with the wish of Mercure who would like to see him achieve the rapture in the state of wakefulness. *"Et cette manière de ravissement ou extase,"* adds the commentary, *"advient à ceux qui d'un désir ardent et volonté fort résolue se retirent de tous bruits, de toutes occasions d'être recherchés soit pour négociations ou tous autres empêchements, recherchant tout repos en corps que les sens lui demeurent oisifs."*

It is certainly this same vein that *Le Gouffre* indicates to us. On one hand the soul feels the approach of the second state with all the symptoms that Mercure and François de Foix enumerated: the end of the formal and of the three dimensions, of space, of action, of movement, of sound, of the word, of the dream; on the other hand the body resists, being caught up in its world of the palpable and of the measurable and resuming its anxiety in this cry: "Ah, ne jamais sortir des Nombres et des Êtres!"

And in the same way that Baudelaire feels the engulfment "en haut, en bas, partout la profondeur . . . l'espace affreux et captivant," Mercure points out in another passage that in his ecstasies, the man purified by the abandon of the senses *"monte au ciel et ainsi le mesure et sait quelles hauteurs il a et quelles profondeurs. Et qui plus est . . . tout en délaissant la terre il est en haut, si ample est sa grandeur à s'étendre."* The commentary explains that *"Son âme* pourvue de la divine pensée, cependant que son corps est tenu ici-bas, *a liberté de se promener en ses connaissances et intelligences non seulement à . . . traverser les murs, pénétrer un feu ardent, visiter les abîmes, courir tous les arts et sciences . . . mais passer outre vers le ciel auquel elle monte sans difficulté* et se trouve non comme y allant mais comme y étant."[12]

The Count de Foix, concluding then his long commentary on the ecstasy of Tat, underlines the importance of the mystical experience to which Mercure had just urged his disciple: "Et c'est la vraie entrée [that is, beginning] de la régénération."

Such was also the value that Charles Baudelaire attached to his "sentiment du gouffre" which he considered related to his "conversations avec Dieu." This relation is why, in *L'Aube Spirituelle*, in the intentions at the same time hermetic and mystical, the poet mentions that the spiritual Heaven "s'ouvre et s'enfonce avec l'attirance du gouffre."[13]

[Translated from the French by Phyllis C. Brooks]

Notes

1. Paul Arnold, *Das Geheimnis Baudelaires,* trans. G. Henniger (Berlin, 1958).
2. Charles Baudelaire, *Oeuvres Complètes,* Bibliothèque de la Pléiade (Bruges, 1961), p. 1299.
3. *Ibid.,* p. 1214.
4. *Ibid.,* p. 1214.
5. *Ibid.,* p. 1265.
6. *Ibid.,* p. 1265.
7. *Ibid.,* p. 172.
8. The literal and irreproachable translation conforms to that of Festugière, whereas Ménard commits here a contrary sense by writing, "La sagesse idéale est dans le silence."
9. Hermes Trismegistos, *Pimandre,* trans. François de Foix (Bordeaux, 1579), p. 565.
10. One can notice in the passage the preference of François de Foix for the term *bâtiment* (building, construction) designating the human body, just as Baudelaire uses it in *L'Irréparable.*
11. *Pimandre,* p. 584.
12. *Ibid.,* p. 411.
13. *Ibid.,* p. 44.

Hedwig von Beit

CONCERNING THE PROBLEM
OF TRANSFORMATION
IN THE FAIRY TALE

FOR MODERN MAN ONE OF THE MOST BEWILDERING AND AT THE SAME time fascinating fairy tale motifs is transformation, especially the transformation of an animal into a human being or of a human being into an animal. The transformation can also happen between a human being and a plant, a human being and a stone or even an object, between two different animals or also between plants and objects with each other; thus, for example, a deer turns into a horse, a cooking spoon turns into a fan, flowers into weeds. Demons and gods, in like manner, appear in different shapes. The transformation of an animal into a human being and vice versa can result from laying aside or, as the case may be, putting on an animal skin. The human shape or the bird shape of the swan-maiden, for example, depends upon whether the hunter is able continually to hide from her the feather garment which she temporarily laid aside. This garment came into his possession and the question is whether or not she can regain her animal covering.

In most European fairy tales transformation is the result of an enchantment or a curse, from which the one transformed should be released; in other fairy tales the hero is granted as a precious gift the capacity for transforming himself, the gift often coming from thankful animals whom he had spared. He also can attain this capacity himself through special effort, and then is able, thanks to this capacity, to overcome a demon or to escape from him.

Since it is not possible within the scope of this short investigation to discuss the numerous forms of the transformation motif, two well-defined types will be chosen for consideration: first the transformation contest and then the type which involves the animal-prince who needs release.

Transformation Contest

In the first type the transformation develops in intensity to a vital moment, to the point of a contest of transformation. A characteristic example is the Russian fairy tale, "Och" (*Russische Volksmärchen* No. 6),[1] the content being the following:

At a time when the world was different than it is now and all kinds of miracles occurred, a poor man had an only son. He was not well-mannered, rather he lay lazily upon the oven. Since he did not wish to know anything about work he ran away from all instruction; as thrashings also did not mean anything, his father decided to hire him out to the first person he came across in another kingdom. On the way in a dark forest he sat down upon a tree stump and sighed: "Och! how tired I am!" Then there appeared out of the tree stump a little old man with a long green beard who introduced himself as the king of the forest, Och, who would be prepared to take the son as an apprentice. If, after a year, the father could recognize the son when he came to get him then he could take him home, otherwise the son would have to serve another year. Och took the son into a hut in which everything was green. The lad fell asleep when he was chopping fire wood, whereupon Och burned him upon the pile of wood, but he brought him to life again; thereby the son became more nimble. After Och had repeated this process twice the lad had grown quick and handsome. When the father came after a year's time he could not recognize his son, who had assumed the shape of a rooster and was among many roosters. Thanks to an old man's advice the father, however, did recognize his son after the third year. Consequently, the son in the shape of a dove was the only one among many other doves which was not eating. On the way home with his son the poor man complained about his poverty. The son devised a clever plan: he would transform himself into a greyhound in order to catch a fox whereupon some hunters would buy the greyhound. The father should demand three hundred rubles but only sell him without a collar. The father acted accordingly, the son returned to the father, and transformed himself back into a lad. When the father needed money again, the son changed himself into a falcon and was sold without a hood to the quail hunters. As before, he returned to his father. When, however, the son permitted himself to be sold as a horse, the father gave the halter as well to a gypsy for extra money. The gypsy, however, was Och, who thereby had the son again in his power. When Och then led the horse to the river to drink, it changed itself into a perch. Then Och turned into a pike and chased the perch which was swimming away. On the shore the daughter of the czar was doing her laundry. The perch changed itself into a garnet ring, which the daughter of the czar slipped onto her finger. Och appeared at the czar's palace as a merchant and inquired about the lost garnet ring. Since the czar supported the merchant, but his daughter wanted to keep the ring, she threw it upon the ground, so that from then on it should not belong to anyone. Then it broke into grains of wheat and the merchant changed himself into a rooster, picked up the grains and flew away. The daughter of the czar had set her foot upon only one grain of wheat and this turned into the lad, whom the daughter of the czar married.

Other versions of this motif deal with a master and his pupil. The latter learns self-transformation from the master and overcomes him in a contest of transformation. In "The Story of Ali Dschengiz" (*Türkische Märchen* No. 12), for example, a youth, beset by dangers and despite thrashings, undertakes to master the Ali-Dschengiz game through a dervish in his cave for the benefit of the Padishah. When he is once again with his mother she sells him transformed as a horse without a bridle. On the following day he should be sold as a ram. Since he notices, however, that the buyer is the dervish, he changes into a bird, whom the dervish follows after changing himself into a dove. The bird changes into an apple which falls into the Padishah's lap. The apple changes into millet and the dervish as a hen begins to pick it up. The millet changes into a marten, who strangles the hen and then changes back into a youth again, who enlightens the Padishah about the Ali-Dschengiz game and is rewarded.

In another variant, "The Arts of the Devil," (*Lettisch-litauische Volksmärchen,* Lettland No. 13), a peasant sends his son to the raven school and the son wins the contest of transformation—ultimately as a hawk—against the teacher of the school. The teacher is the devil in "Apprenticeship with the Devil" (*Finnische und estnische Volksmärchen* No. 5) and a tailor and black magician in "The Sorcerer's Apprentice" (*Italienische Märchen* No. 27). In "The Master and His Pupil" (*Kaukasische Märchen* No. 4) the list of transformations is especially long: the horse which again falls into the master's power flees out of the dark stable as a mouse, the master becomes a cat, the mouse becomes a fish, the cat changes into a net, the fish changes into a pheasant, the net into a falcon, the pheasant into an apple which falls into the king's lap; the falcon becomes a knife in the king's hand, the apple becomes millet, the knife changes into a hen with chicks, a millet grain becomes a needle, the hen and chicks change into the thread in the eye of the needle, the needle bursts into flames, the thread burns up, the needle changes into the lad.

Not only must we forego investigating all motifs other than that of transformation, but also unfortunately we must disregard the intermingling of the transformation-contest motif into such motifs as that of the contest of concealment or the motif of the hidden life. Furthermore, the literary development of the apprentice figure to the "master thief" and even to the cunning little tailor cannot be dealt with here.

One meaning of transformation in this type of fairy tale is only partially discernible, that is, when the lad in "Och" grows more proficient and more handsome. In this case the transformation works like a marvelous acceleration of development. The final transformations are quite different. The transformation contest has an almost playful, sporty character. The exciting effect springs from the constantly arising danger, but no logical line running through these repeated changes of shape can be detected.

From the standpoint of symbolism a consideration of the transformation motif, which is so essential in this fairy tale, brings to mind the question: was the popular fairy tale also enriched or even formed by symbolism which is so often and consciously employed in literature for a deepening effect? Was the story perhaps symbolically fashioned by the naïve narrator as Goethe does, for example, with his *Faust* or *Wilhelm Meister* or as Hermann Hesse with his *Glasperlenspiel?* The fantasy of these poets is clearly supported by a conscious and definite need for verbal expression. In regard to Goethe, especially, there are comments about his underlying purpose. Faust, Mephisto, Euphorion, Mignon are images of fantasy which express a clearly defined idea for the consciousness; accordingly they are symbols because the symbol is an image for a meaning which is not otherwise apparent. In this "symbolic image" the meaning and the image permeate one another; they become one. "Symbolism," says Goethe (in "Maximen und Reflexionen" No. 1113), "transforms the appearance into an idea, the idea into an image . . ." Are the fairy tale figures really images for "ideas" or are they symbols? Are they the masks of thoughts and do the motifs "mean" something deliberately concealed? Is the transformation in the above-mentioned Russian fairy tale and its variants a symbol perhaps for a transformation process within the soul?

In order to answer these questions it is necessary to observe the figures intensely, to attempt a symbolic interpretation, and furthermore to determine whether a solution to the problem can result from investigating other fairy tales and from ethnological observations with the help of a psychological approach.

In all the variants the apprentice is a naïve, occasionally lazy, but nevertheless basically capable lad. The master is a demonic father-figure pitted against the simple personal father-figure of the lad, or against the Padishah, or he complements the latter, if one regards both "fathers" as a single figure. The psychological fairy tale interpretations, therefore, can regard the transformation contest as a reckoning of the son-image with the father-image because they employ methods of dream interpretation and see in the shapes and processes which arise out of the unconscious and fantasy, *grosso modo,* personifications of forces, drives, and tendencies in one's own soul. This does not mean just the "problem of generations," but the confrontation of everything which the image of the father signifies for the son and that of the son for the father. The father can be the image for physical and spiritual superiority, wisdom, and creativity. He can be honored like a god, but also hated like the devil; he can be the "master" and sovereign and at the same time the tyrant, who, on the one hand, provides restraint as master of the situation, and on the other hand, always embodies the challenging force.

For the father the figure of the son represents the future one through whom the father will continue. The son is a renewer, but also he replaces the father, hence he is the one who deposes and overcomes, who no longer understands or desires that which is old, and he is the one to whom the father endeavors to remain superior.

The father can be considered the symbol of a condition of consciousness to be overcome, be this condition represented by the somewhat foolish, naïve, natural father of the fairy tale hero, or be it by the overwhelming demon, master of magic, nature spirit (therefore in "Och" with a green beard in a green hut), which manifests as the demonic and instinctual in the human soul. Both figures taken together correspond to "the father" and form a given condition to which the human being at first is delivered up. The son, on the other hand, stands as a symbol of a freer being, of a conscious ness, which adopts the capacities of the "father" and then enhances them, finally to make free use of them from a higher standpoint, no longer as the dismal "master" living in obscurity, but in a more human way. The son represents a positive force; he has the capacity to differentiate, thus he frees himself from the darkness and confu- sion of primitive dullness and at the same time from the pressure of demonic powers, thanks to his courage, strength, and intelligence. The fairy tales in which the son is victorious and even marries the princess produce a mood and presentiment of a brighter future. The son in the fairy tale could be symbolically equated with human consciousness which overcomes the predominant incalculable danger of unconscious powers which appear in most diverse forms. This development occurs more or less in the course of each person's life, hence we may recognize a reflection of this process in the struggle between the father and the son.

The struggle of the sorcerer and the pupil leads to the trans- formation contest which has the character of an archetypal battle, in which archetypal figures, namely the demonic father and the conscious son, contend for power. The antagonistic archetypes as- sume different shapes one after another. They traverse the various kingdoms of nature and change into animals, into fruits, and even into jewels, then again into grains and into a hen, until the battle is decided in favor of the son, either with or without the help of a princess. Each of the different transformation shapes is, to a certain degree, a defining factor from which a meaning can be derived; for instance, parts of the plant or animal kingdoms may be traced or precious man-made things chosen, or even a disintegration into many particles may occur until a new germ unfolds from one of the particles. Despite these defining elements the essential question re- mains unanswered, namely: to what can the idea of transformation per se be attributed? Furthermore, undoubtedly our sympathetic understanding of the fairy tale can be deepened through becoming aware of the numerous connections between this kind of plot and other related motifs. Again, however, nothing is said thereby about why it is precisely transformation which becomes a method of ex- pression in so many fairy tales. Where does this motif come from, which only in myth and fairy tale can be found as the intellectual basis, and which is used in the more developed forms of poetry and narration as a consciously employed artistic device? We are not familiar with the idea of transformation today. We experience it only in dreams. Therefore it is obvious that modern man must approach the fairy tale motifs, which present the miraculous, by means of the dream and the 20th century psychological method of dream interpretation. Only the child accepts transformation without astonishment.

Release of the Animal Prince

Before we take our investigation any further, the second transformation motif chosen will be illustrated, namely the release of the animal-prince.

> In "The Forest House" (*KHM* No. 169)[2] a prince is enchanted by a witch and has to live in the forest as a hoary old man. Only his three servants in the forms of a hen, a rooster, and a cow, may be with him. The stipulation for release is that a maiden first would care for the animals, then for the old man, and only lastly for herself. The two older sisters of the heroine fail. She herself wins the prince through her care and friendliness towards the animals. In "Hans My Hedgehog" (*KHM* No. 108) a farmer's wife wishes so much for a child that she goes so far as to say: "I want a child even if it is a hedgehog." The child which she receives has the torso of a hedgehog and the limbs of a boy. He is freed later because a princess takes him as her bridegroom and during the wedding night the animal skin which had been laid aside is burned.

In both fairy tales the transformation shape is the result of a spell. In the first fairy tale the hoary old man, who sits at the table in the hut and has such a long beard that it flows onto the ground, produces more the effect of rigidness, whereas the servants in their animal shapes appear more mobile. Hans is half-human and half-animal. Indeed, as a hedgehog he belongs to the porcupine family. Both princes through their enchantment are imprisoned in matter. The release succeeds in the one case through the humble devotion of a human being to the animal, in the other through the destruction of the animal skin, that is, of the animal aspect. In other words, the human being, in the fairy tale the princess, recognizes the bright core of being hidden by the animal skin. (To this group belongs the well-known fairy tale, "The Frog-King or the Iron Henry" (*KHM* No. 1).

Among the various versions of the release-motif of the prince banished into an animal shape, the story of "Amor and Psyche" in Apuleius' *Metamorphoses* is one of the best known. It also appears, although in a more popular folk version, in a structurally identical form in several European folk tales, such as in "The Singing Springing Little Lion Cub" (*KHM* No. 88) as follows:

> Before setting out on a journey a father asks his three daughters what he should bring back for them. Whereas the two elder daughters ask for jewelry, the youngest wishes for a "singing springing little lion cub." After a long search the father sees such a little lion cub in a forest not far from a castle. But a father lion jumps up and threatens with death everyone who wants to steal his little lion cub from him. The father can only save himself by promising to grant to the lion whatever meets him first upon reaching home. This proves to be his youngest daughter, who is gladly prepared to marry the lion. The lion is the enchanted son of a king, who is a lion during the day but a human being at night. Later, when one of the sisters is to celebrate her wedding, the young wife is instructed by the lion to participate alone, because if a ray of light were to hit him he would be changed into a dove and would have to fly about in the world for seven years. The young wife wants to protect him from this fate and has a room with thick walls built in her father's house. Nevertheless a beam of light only the breadth of a hair shines on the prince through a crack in the fresh wood of the door and as a white dove he immediately vanishes. During the seven years at each seventh step he lets a drop of blood and a white feather fall as a signpost for his young wife. When after seven years neither drops of blood nor feathers fall any longer and yet her loved one still is gone, she travels up to the sun. The sun had not seen the dove, but he gives the young wife a little box, which she should open in a moment of need. The moon gives her an egg which should be broken open when she is in distress. The southwind saw that the dove flew to the Red Sea and the king's son was fighting there as a lion against a king's daughter who was in the shape of a dragon. The night-wind advises the seeking wife to beat the dragon from the shore of the Red Sea with eleven rods so that the lion could conquer the dragon. Then the griffin would carry her and her loved one across the sea and back home. But the king's daughter, freed from the dragon shape, takes the prince herself away on the griffin, so the deserted young wife must resume her symbolic search. She reaches the castle where her husband, the prince, and the king's daughter wish to celebrate their wedding. There she opens the little box and takes from it a splendid dress like the sun. The bride wants it and obtains it for spending one night in the chamber of her bridegroom. First, however, he is given a sleeping potion so that he does not hear how his wife tells of her laborious journeys. On the next day she takes from the egg a golden hen with twelve chicks, which she sells to the bride during a second night in the chamber of the bridegroom. Since, however, the prince had heard a murmur the previous night and learned everything which had transpired from his servant, he poured the sleeping potion

out under the bed so that he could recognize his wife. Then he is liberated. Immediately they secretly depart from the castle, because the king is a sorcerer. The griffin carries them over the sea and back home.

In a Swedish variant, "The Lame Dog" (*Nordische Volksmärchen* Bd. 1, 2. Teil, No. 13), the animal-husband is a lame dog; in an Irish fairy tale, "The White Dog from the Mountains" (*Irische Volksmärchen* No. 38), he is a white dog; in a Norwegian version, "The White Bear King Valemon" (*Nordische Volksmärchen* Bd. 2, No. 29), he is a bear, and in "Pain and Suffering" (*ibid.* No. 25), a squirrel.

The possession of the loved one or of the desired precious object is plainly connected with the taking on of the animal form, hence with the valuable animal strength as well as with the domineering animal emotion. If the loved one needing release can be conceived of as the masculine image, that is, the spiritual impulse within the soul of the woman, she must recognize him in every shape if the blending of both is to attain a higher psychic image. Moreover, to the extent that the heroine represents the ideal image of the feminine essence within the soul of the man, to which he is bound by his feeling and which helps him to free himself from so many entanglements, this type of fairy tale reflects the reciprocal interplay between masculine and feminine within the psyche. If the shapes are regarded as images of forces of the psyche, as enchanted portions which have fallen into distress and are rooted to nature in her overwhelming demonism, the release from enchantment means transformation to a free self-determination, to an attainment of the human condition, so far as it is superior to the demonic. The recognition of the woman in her sacrificial humaneness resembles a clearsightedness, an overcoming of illusion. Seen in this way, the above fairy tale, like all the others which deal with the release of the animal-bridegroom or bride, is a story whose details can be understood when elucidated symbolically.

The essential moment in the course of the action is the undesired illumination. In the fairy tale from classical antiquity, "Amor and Psyche," the heroine is induced by her jealous sisters to let the light from a hanging lamp shine upon her husband. A drop of the hot oil falls on him and awakens him. He then disappears. This occurs in like manner in "The Lame Dog." In "The White Bear King Valemon" the mother incites the heroine to disobey the commandments of the magical world, and in "Pain and Suffering" the heroine accomplishes the calamitous deed by herself. The "taboo" is broken because a rational attitude gains the upper hand. The "magical marriage" between human being and animal, a harmonious and enrichening condition of the psyche, becomes disturbed through tendencies which are peculiar to the profane sphere. A higher comprehensive consciousness does not work destructively upon the unconscious occurrences and connections, but a consciousness which only discriminates does. "A light is cast" too soon with its harshness which disturbs and profanes the tender beginning of inner development, so that the clear perception of the animal-shape, which is regarded as inferior by the rational tendencies, results in a flight of psychic value into distant—hence unconscious—darkness. From here he can only be won back through great effort. The lack of respect for the taboo-commandments of the magic world and an inquisitive desire for its precious things destroy the hidden germ of evolution. Only deep respect and gentle, loving acceptance on the part of the consciousness can abolish the demonic magic of unconscious powers. This attitude is represented in the heroine's resigned and sorrowful search into the beyond and leads, although the details are different for each version of this theme, to the goal, to the emancipation of the prince from the animal-shape to which he was bound by enchantment. In the Swedish version, "The Lame Dog," the inhibition, which comes to expression through being imprisoned in the animal-shape, is characterized as a chain. A nightingale sings to the heroine: "Maiden, unfasten the chain, unfasten the chain!" She unfastens the chains that had bound a terrible lion (previously the lame dog) and when the last link falls the lion becomes a handsome young prince.

Since the civilized human being of the 20th century does not believe in the concrete "truth" of such transformations as occur in a matter-of-fact manner in "Och" or in the fairy tales about the animal-prince, where they are something "special" but still possible, a question arises: how is it that myths, fairy tales, and sagas employ the motif of transformation as self-evident, whereas transformations hardly ever appear in formal literature and then only as quite amazing (so far as the transformation motif does not just revert back to fairy tales, as is the case in many medieval epics). Modern adults read or tell fairy tales quite seldom; they do not take animal transformations seriously. They try, on the contrary, to "explain" the fairy tale happening in a reasonable manner from a supposedly higher standpoint, for example, as a mirroring of a process of the psyche, as was mentioned above. A symbolic interpretation results which, as far as possible, ascribes an intentional meaning to the image of transformation. It is interpreted as an "inner transformation" of the one enchanted. The bearer of the animal-shape is seen as the only one who experiences the transformation. A symbolic interpretation, on the other hand, wants to comprehend all the characters of the fairy tale together as a unit.

In contrast to adults it is striking that children, until about the age of eight years, relive stories intensely and are not disconcerted regardless of how strange the motif may be. Furthermore, ethnologists report that for primitive man the idea of transformation from man into animal and vice versa is self-understood. Some fairy tale interpretations attach an abstract meaning to the events in the fairy tale, and by doing so they supplement the events, they stress the curse and release as causes of the transformation, and they draw in mythological, moral, or psychological explanations. Basically, however, the fairy tale uses throughout images which are intended to be "concrete." In this respect the transformations also mean nothing other than that which is presented. We observe the same seriousness when the child is playing who experiences the actions within his fantasy spontaneously and concretely. The action and its unfoldment are not a "thinking about" a theme, not a concealment of a deliberate assertion, but concrete happenings. This is so much more the case since the elements of fantasy, in the final analysis, depend upon actual experiences,[3] where outer or inner perception or observation are concerned. What is presented pictorially, narratively, or even dramatically is experienced as reality by the child who cannot experience other than in a concrete manner.[4]

It can be assumed—as far as contemporary research is able to fathom the mental structure of early man—that he behaved in a similar fashion. If the human being stems from the animal, his feeling and perception must be related to that of the animal. Hence, under certain conditions he also will regard objects as active beings and will experience their mode of expression as delightful or fearful. When the development of the human being proceeds away from the animal an inner connection between the being of early man and of animal still remains from this relationship. This has been depicted so often that one can assume that it is known. For the present study the belief is important that the hunter, who in animal dress carries out the hunting rituals, transforms himself into an animal in order to make the magic of the hunt more effective. In cave drawings from the glacial period these assimilations taken on in the ritual are depicted through dancers who are disguised as animals.[5] In the mythical thinking process of early man there exists a magical association between man and animal. Their "magical effect" constantly permeates one another. "But"—we read from Ernst Cassirer[6]—"this unity of the *effect* would not be possible, seen from the standpoint of the mythical thinking process, if a unity of *being* were not the basis." In the course of time this feeling of relationship, or at least of an inner connection between man and animal, leads to the idea of the descent of a human being or an entire tribe from one animal. With this observation the basis of totemism is founded.

In the fairy tale of "Och" the difference between the human being and animal is indeed clearly stressed, but is not experienced as important. Self-transformation is no longer possible for everyone; nevertheless it can be "learned." For the human being the animal is of value as it is equipped with special magical forces, according to the view of uncivilized peoples, so that possessing the animal means, consequently, an increase of power. The capacity of transformation, of changing shapes, brings the power of the human being closer to that of the demons and renders possible a victory.

In contrast to the above, the transformations in "The Singing Springing Little Lion Cub" depend upon a curse. The one who is transformed is passive. In a large group of fairy tales a "magical marriage" occurs with a being which from the beginning was not human, which only occasionally has the form of a human being. Usually it is an animal but it can also be a nature spirit. The presupposition of this marriage is that every allusion to the non-human origin of the magical partner is ignored. For the mythical-religious consciousness of early man the boundaries between him and his world remain fluid. "For early stages of the mythical world conception a clearly-defined silhouette does not yet exist, which severs the human being from the totality of everything living, from the animal and plant world."[7] Nevertheless it happens in the stories of primitive peoples as well as in the European fairy tales—with isolated exceptions—that the non-human origin of the marriage partner is divulged and consequently the marriage is ended. Hence it is to be assumed that a separation of the sphere of magic and of the profane gradually was prepared. The time is past in which the connection between animal and man was so intimate that "one became now man, now animal," as it is told in an Eskimo fairy tale.[8]

Due to the development of human self-consciousness, the magic and the profane spheres become separately distinguishable. Thus, for early man impressions and sentient experiences change into the idea of concentrated power in the shapes of individual demons; this idea replaces the feeling of general, unspecified forces. Such personifications of individual demons presuppose a thought process which makes it possible to come to grips with the power vis-à-vis. This stage is delineated in the above-mentioned type of fairy tale about the release of the animal-prince, since a demon is presumed in the figure of the father of the dragon-princess, who casts a spell. Sorcery, in the sense of a curse or a blessing, is an expression of will strengthened by passion, a magical force, which in a negative or positive sense is emitted by the magician and this force overpowers those who are struck by it. If the magician is recognized as a demon, as a concentration of forces, then it is possible to deprive him of power. Whereas previously the general forces which were present everywhere could be appeased and propitiated and their laws accepted, the thinking which was evolving toward a rational state disentangles the net of forces and points the way to freedom, to conscious action.

The process of entanglement is revealed clearly in the fairy tale · about Och. In the mythical thinking process a mystical partaking of all beings one from the other, and secret connections and ties between natural beings and objects, are taken for granted. Since the as yet intellectually undeveloped person is impressed in his sentient nature by objects, the experience is felt as a force which issues from the object he encounters. There is a secret oneness of all forces; or better, there is a oneness of power, which governs everything, which is experienced by feeling. In as much as objects share in this general force, the most diverse beings and objects are clearly felt to be identical by the man engaged in a mythical thinking process. The idea of the *"pars pro toto"* arises from this idea of identity. That means that the parts of the body or things which belong to a human being or an animal—such as hair, nails, feathers, clothing—are the same as he himself and symbolically stand for him as a whole. The feathers of a bird or the scales of a fish bring about magically whatever the entire animal could do. Consequently the heroes of various fairy tales with the help of a feather given by a thankful bird or a scale from a grateful fish can change themselves into these forms and thereby acquire their capacities. From this it becomes understandable how in "Och" the one who is in possession of the collar, the falcon hood, or the halter always has power over the lad. These articles are a part of the being of the dog, the falcon, and the horse and as such, the part equals the whole. It is obvious that this principle of the *pars pro toto,* which is founded upon the idea of identity, makes transformation easily possible, because it deals with a change in shape of the general core of being. Even though the character of those transformed assumes a new shape (the prince turns into a dangerous lion), an identity nevertheless results because the same being is a lion by day and a human being at night. The mythical mode of thinking does not see things next to and after each other, but as interlaced and simultaneous. Thus a lion can be a human being at one and the same time or vice versa. This identity is a basic mental supposition about magic, as are for us all the strangely flowing boundaries between things, beings, happenings, conditions of life and death, and the realms of the Here and the Hereafter.

A reciprocal effect of both worlds exists in which the kingdom of magic to begin with is infinitely superior to the kingdom of the profane. The kingdom of magic becomes the world of the "holy" (means "taboo") whose commandments must be respected. The "holy" places, things, and even times are "taboo," that is, especially mana-laden. They conceal within themselves a magical-religious power. The "taboo" commandments must be observed most explicitly. The heroine of the animal-prince fairy tales (the fairy tales concerning the deliverance of the animal-prince) has to make good again her errors through great effort since she allowed herself to be tempted by the profane world to disregard the "taboo" commandments. Since, on the one hand, the profane world has sufficient strength and on the other hand, the animal-transformation depends upon a curse, it follows that the possibility of transformation and the predominance of magic no longer exist as foregone conclusions. Rather the profane *will* tries to achieve its own end; for the human will too—carried by passion—operates magically. Whereas before a valued magical power was attributed to the animal, now the human aspect is more highly esteemed. He who was enchanted as an animal must become a human being again. Worldly, "profane" thinking acknowledges less and less magical happenings for the reason will not accept them. (The contrast between the mythical and the rational process of thinking becomes obvious through the work of Ernesto Bozzano.[9]) The reports of these phenomena come from astounded Europeans. More and more the magical word grown powerful through passion and will changes into a mere magic formula.

In the course of the development sketched here, the feeling for the power of magic grows increasingly cooler. Those fairy tales, therefore, in which the magic world still is a self-understood force permeating the profane-human realm begin with indications of bygone times. The long beard of the old man who is to be freed in the Grimm fairy tale "The Forest House," indicates that he has been in the enchanted condition for a long time. Also the Russian fairy tale, "Och," begins: "Earlier it was not like it is now: earlier all kinds of miracles happened in the world, and also the world itself was not like it is now. In our time there is nothing left of all this." There are many fairy tales which begin in such a manner. They introduce the incomprehensible by pointing to it in the past. For when contemporary man wishes to have a connection with an experience —be it an inner or an outer one—a concrete or a narrated one, if he wants to feel an experience as appertaining to himself, then he must have "understood" it. He does not always succeed in this, because he can only seldom "understand" as an adult even what he experienced as essential in his early childhood, or seldom comprehend magical ideas, which then were self-evident for him. He begins to interpret and to look for a seemingly "logical" meaning behind the images and to regard the motifs symbolically. He derives his interpretation from his present inner and outer experiences. Frequently he overlooks the fact that in interpreting the meaning of other literary works he takes into consideration the spiritual life at the time when these works were produced. In order to comprehend the spiritual background of a primitive work of art, from which a magic-mythical mode of thinking speaks, an attempt should be made to become familiar with the mentality of men in their early stages of development. For even if many European fairy tales appear to take place in the Middle Ages, they contain so many strange motifs that it cannot be assumed that these motifs actually stem from the Middle Ages with its knightly culture and its ingenious theological teachings; rather, they could be considered relics of an earlier epoch. The crux of the matter then is to acquaint ourselves with these relics of the past and especially with the reasons behind their origin, furthermore with their emergence in the mentality of the contemporary child as well as in that of the adult. Only then can we determine whether these forms of thinking which we meet as fairy tale motifs lend themselves to symbolic interpretation.

To what extent this is the case can be deduced from developmental psychology. The question is: to what extent can an explanation for the change of the transformation motif be gleaned from developmental psychology. From Heinz Werner's *Einführung in die Entwicklungspsychologie*[10] we find a confirmation of the preceding statements. His work is founded upon observations of the animal, the primitive man, the modern child, and the modern adult, healthy or sick.

Even as the embryo genetically progresses through earlier stages in becoming a human being, it seems that modern man relives psychically in childhood earlier stages of human existence. In comparing the soul life of the primitive man, the animal, and the contemporary child with that of the European adult, we must first be clear about whether the image-world of psychic conditions which can be interpreted symbolically and which "in the sense of psychiatry is abnormal" may be taken into consideration. Here two types come into question: those mentally ill on a permanent basis and those who through dream-like conditions sink below their normal level of development into childishness. This question can be answered in the affirmative for developmental psychology, but with reservations in regard to fairy tales, so far as childish thinking on the part of the patient results from changes due to illness. For this childish thinking is not the result of a mental maturity not yet attained, but of an incapacity to retain this maturity.

The observation of animal, primitive man, modern child, modern adult, and patient from the point of view of mental *development* leads to the cognitions of developmental psychology. The question here, among others, is concerned with establishing the special structure of developmental stages and "of determining the relationship of these stages in their superposition, their genetic homogeneity, the direction of development and the meaning, that is, the tendency of this direction." To be considered are the organic stages of development, the development of the child into adulthood, as well as the development of mankind in general. Previously the childhood stage of the individual as well as that of primitive man was regarded as a "not yet," that is, the will governed by the passions of the moment and the thought processes "not yet" logically organized. Furthermore no effort was made "to comprehend this stage as an organically homogeneous one." The more modern developmental psychology tries "to detect the mental construction plan on the basis of which the modes of behavior of the primitive man or the child of a certain stage are uniformly understandable in all parts: the voice of memory, the special nature of willing and feeling and of thinking and acting." Every stage is, of itself, a whole. The uniqueness of the

childhood stage is not that the characteristics of a higher stage are
lacking; characteristic for primitive man is not that he does not
think or do what the contemporary European, for instance, thinks
or can do, but both, each on its own level, are a *rich organic whole,*
with values unique to it alone. Hence the primitive man does not
think less logically than the European, but his thinking is logically
different. For him not only can a demon transform himself into an
animal and at the same time remain a demon, but, for example, for
the Mexican Indians, in connection with a specific cult, grain, the
stag, and the *hiculi* plant are identical. Generally for the mythical
mode of thinking the most different things can be one and the same.
(Compare the transformations within the transformation contest!)
The idea that the same person in transformation can be different
creatures is a conception which has as its basis an entirely different,
but in itself completely logical, mental attitude than that of civilized
man, without thereby being "less significant." Thus, also the mental
structure of the child (and especially that of the animal) is subjected to other laws than those of the modern adult, and a different
world of ideas results, based upon a special nature of feeling and
willing. But even then, when the manner of behavior issues from
the same psychic structure, a difference nevertheless exists between
the animal and the primitive man on the one side and the child
of the modern civilized world on the other. This difference is that the
animal and primitive man have reached a determined, insurmount-
able peak of development, whereas this peak of development for the
human being surpasses that of the animal even if the actions of
the animal let us assume a complicated structure. The child of the
civilized world, however, is able to cross these boundaries so far as a
certain predisposition gives him the possibility of advancing. (This
possibility is not inherent in the psychic instability of the mentally
ill. The related structure of the mentality of the latter with that of
primitive man or with that of the modern child does not result from
the fact that the mentally ill person likewise belongs to an earlier
stage, but results from his sinking down from a certain height due to
changes brought about by illness.) The genetically different levels of
consciousness become obvious through the comparative contemplation of animal, early and primitive man, and the modern child, but
also in the developmental phases of the individual. Moreover, it
follows that a human being of the European culture does not possess
only one mental mien, only one level of experiencing and reacting,
but at different moments in one and the same person a plurality of

levels becomes discernible: he "appears to belong to genetically different stages."

The "augmentation of hierarchical centralization" belongs to the mental development from a lower to a higher stage, which has been mentioned. New mental functions "of a higher centralizing force" appear, "feelings come under the domination of intellectual processes, perceptions become increasingly dominated by concepts and thought processes." In the animal world, on the other hand, especially with primitive organisms, there is an inner inseparable connection of the animal with his environment, only an "insignificant differentiation exists between object and subject, between matter and condition, between perception, feeling, and active movement." Details and environment form, as it were, a unity. Moreover, in a certain stage of development it occurs that things in the environment, even if they no longer induce automatic reactions, nevertheless are not perceived objectively by the naïve human being, but are experienced according to their mode of expression—physiognomically. This kind of observation is the result of the strong participation of passion with a mental comprehension of an object. From this kind of observation the demonization of things arises. Added to this is the fact that for primitive man these mode-of-expression experiences are "concrete," for with him (as with the child), thinking has a purely "object" nature (that is, based on objects and not abstract) in contrast to higher scientific thinking. This "naïve, object-thinking [is] not separated . . . from the shapes in material nature, from perceiving; *primitive* thinking means always *perceptual shaping.* Characteristic for every type of naïve thinking is the clinging to the sensual-object, from which the primitive person can sever himself either not at all or only with difficulty." Thus everything which is seen, even when it is subjectively influenced, that is, when it depends to a certain degree upon mere semblance, is "truth," a tangible fact, and abstraction is impossible. The more advanced an individual is, the more distant and impartial he is and, above all, he recognizes that which is opposite to him in a more differentiated manner. The more primitive—as especially the lower animals are—the more the object viewed forms a unity with the environment; things are imbedded and disseminated into the environment, they blend, as it were, with the environment. This produces a vagueness, a variableness, in the manifestation of the environment. Modern man also experiences a diffused kind of perception. "The development towards an unvariable shape . . . is connected with the increasing extrication of matter-of-fact reality from a state of expression." With reality follows the knowledge of centers, which are accents in the unity of perception. These centers are more emphasized, the other parts less. How such units of perception lacking center, so to speak over-all perceptions, "are represented by primitive man can be seen, for example, with the Melanesians of the Bismarck-Archipelago. For them the expression *'ciki'* does not just mean drop, a little drop of water, but the idea of the spot which it leaves behind also. Furthermore it includes the sound of the dripping, the idea of the regular periods of time between the drops falling from the roof and finally, also that of the unexpectedness of sudden dripping." For primitive man the vague, the diffused perception experienced as "a mode of expression," leads to viewing the world as "dynamic and continually changing." He knows only the instability of things, as things are dependent upon the magical connection in which they momentarily exist, hence their manner of appearance and their "mana-radiation" fluctuate. This instability of appearance results not so much from the forms of the environment which are viewed as objectively centralized but much more from those which are subjectively felt. This instability, furthermore, has as its result the possibility for easy transformation. Therefore, also the transformation of details commensurable with the above-mentioned principle of the *pars pro toto* means for primitive man a revolutionary conversion of the whole, because the detail as such is not judged in relation to a center, but *is* the whole as well, which results from the dispersion of impression. When, therefore, in many fairy tales a king is saved, "his entire kingdom" is saved with him. The child of the civilized world rejects every alteration of detail in the *narration* of a fairy tale, because with this alteration—even if it is only in the form of an expression—the entire impression, the entire idea becomes strange.

As in the mythical thinking process the perceptions are diffused and consequently variable, in like manner are also the names of things. They do not express "sharply limited objective details, but total situations." As a result of this indefiniteness of perceptions and definitions the belief in the capacity for transformation is established. Because a single being or thing can simultaneously be one thing as well as another and can change itself from one into the other, both conditions are retained. In the cases in which, for example, a dancer assumes an animal shape through a mask, he not only represents the animal, but he *is* the animal, and yet remains at the same time who he was. Primitive man does not see unity *in* multiplicity but the unity *of* multiplicity. Hence also the name based on the principle of diffusion, is a "name for the totality of units," whereby various facets are comprised by one general expression. Just as the word *ciki* is employed by the Melanesians for various impressions concerning the drop of water, the Baïri have a single word *yélo* for "lightning" and for "thunder" and for similar phenomena. In a similar way small children today refer to the most different things and beings with the same word, so far as they experience a seemingly common impression from them. From such a similarity of meaning and vagueness of ideas it is obvious for primitive man that transformations are not to be doubted. Feeling is the basis of identification and the identity is affirmed or denied according to emotion. "In the magical sphere, which becomes ever more conscious, things and persons of the environment are comprehended as demonic powers whose final condition lies in the part which the passions play in shaping the environment. The world turns into magical entities, which are the counterparts of the fears and wishes of the human being . . ." The perceptions therefore are completely subjectively colored.

Summing up, it can be stated: the naïve "thinking which unfolds in unorganized totality" is indefinite and variable. Contrary to this, mature thinking has centralizing tendencies. It "attempts to move beyond the ambiguity of the world of appearances" and to attain clarity. In consequence of the experience of iridescent impressions for primitive man, various facts which contradict one another can be simultaneously true and correct. Gradually the human mind overcomes the limiting entanglement with the magic and the profane environment. The more clearly formed attitude taken up by the human being at first is, as yet, undifferentiated as compared to that of the demonic world. It does not correspond to the "feeling-attitude of the advanced religious person," but rather "to an inconclusive experience, in which the contradictory feelings of inclination and horror . . . fuse into a unity." At first there is no conscious ethical humanity pitted against the contradictory world of demons. The possibility of magical transformation depends upon the minor importance of the individual. At a more advanced stage of development concentrated, overwhelming powers are usually attributed to the medicine man or magician, who has the power to bring about transformation.

If we turn again to the fairy tale our consideration shows that in the transformation contest of the Russian fairy tale, "Och," the transformations indeed are "learned" but occur with the obviousness of mythical mentality. Contrary to this the animal-transformation in the animal-prince fairy tales becomes a problem and counts as a misfortune which is attributed to a curse. The transformation from the animal shape back into the human shape cannot succeed without the help of those called from the profane world and it is a very laborious process. It is conceived as a "release" from captivity, indeed from an "inferior" condition. Hence a change of evaluation is manifested. (This conception was still found during the Middle Ages in the belief in lycanthropy.) All genetic stages of the human psyche are mirrored in the stories of primitive races which are still vitally experienced by them as true and in the popular fairy tales of the European culture. Here they are presented in a somewhat cautious manner as part of the distant past. In the earliest stages of human existence an identity of man and animal, that is, the simultaneity of existence of a human being as animal and as man, was assumed. In ensuing stages of development the occasional self-transformation from one condition into another was understood as self-evident. In a further development the human being withdrew also from this way of viewing things: in "Och" only the demon is accomplished in self-transformation, the pupil must "learn" it. The fact that the pupil is able consciously to learn this and in addition surpasses the master, distinguishes him. The next advanced stage of human self-consciousness takes for granted that animal transformation indeed is possible, but not desirable.

The gradual loosening of the growing consciousness from a feeling for life in which the general environment flows into a unity is mirrored in myths and fairy tales through the appearance of a savior, that is, a hero, who acts independently and conquers the mystical parts of the environment, the demonic world. Like the diffuse perceptions, the ideas of fantasy of primitive man, which were "of an undifferentiated totality" and "little organized according to the essential and non-essential moments," become more centered, because the developing mental functions operate as a centralizing force. It is, moreover, not strange that occasionally early and later ideas intermingle. The old survives and at the same time the new prepares its own way.

If we make a survey of the stories of primitive races which have been handed down to us and a study of our own fairy tale literature, we see that the art form corresponds to the manner of thinking, gives expression, so to speak, to this manner of thinking. As stated above, the stories of primitive races with which we are familiar have indeed a hero, who more or less has the character of a savior, but the depiction of his deeds, especially in the stories of very primitive races, is mainly a uniform recitation of various victorious adventures, a string of scenes without essential accents. In contrast to this the highly evolved popular fairy tale introduces a hero whose deeds are dramatically depicted in actions which become intensified up to a culminating point. Then the lysis of the conflict follows: the hero, for the most part, becomes the "inheritor of the kingdom" and, as such, the sovereign authority with superior strength. The "genetic multistratification" of contemporary man is reflected in the various forms as well as in the content of the fairy tale.

Historically viewed, it can be stated that the fairy tale motifs go back to a basic meaning which, at the same time as the development of rational consciousness, sank into oblivion more and more in the course of centuries. With time the structure of the human brain and man's mode of thinking have changed and probably also the fairy tale motifs arising out of memory have so changed that only a symbolical type of consideration transmits an approximate comprehension. Nevertheless, a translation of the images and events as well as a translation of the symbols into 20th century concepts does not correspond to the impulse of their genesis, nor to the basic principle of their original formation. In contrast to the literary works of modern man who creates consciously, we find here not a hidden message behind the image, but the image itself speaks, it *is* the message, because its origin depends upon the feeling-experience and this experience is not precise.

It is tempting to interpret the hero and heroine of fairy tales as symbols of the awakening of self-consciousness with its independent thinking process, because, as stated above, the figures of savior and hero emerge with the mental capacity for centralization in the stories which oppose single demons. In the myths, that is, in early times, the savior usually disappears at the end of the account but his deed continues to be effective. Contrary to this, the hero or heroine of the European fairy tale becomes the ruling power. They do not come from the Beyond like the savior nor do they vanish afterwards; rather, they are human beings, even if they are exceptional. The instability of the mythical-magical "feeling-thinking" process does not permit forms to be transposed into definite concepts. The figures are unconscious-sentient and straightforward, characterized as for example "formidable" or "beneficent." In like manner the fairy tale manages with few ideas. The figures are "beautiful" or "ugly," "lazy" or "diligent," in short, pleasant or unpleasant. In the archaic-magical conception of reality folk belief lived on in the fairy tale, hence the principle of identity gave the value of reality to things which we regard as symbols. (The blood with which the pact with the devil is signed does not "mean" the bearer of the psyche, but it *is* this bearer, which as *pars pro toto* falls into the hands of the devil.) Thus we realize that we must apply symbolic explanations to fairy tales with great caution. Adolf Bastian[11] calls the motifs "elementary thoughts." Thereby their archaic nature, which does not correspond to more modern symbolic interpretations, is clearly indicated. These interpretations, nevertheless, in the appropriate place and limited to the right epoch, can disclose a fascinating double standard. The meaning concluded about the fairy tale motifs through more or less arbitrarily selected and transmitted explanations is indeed similar to the original meaning, but not the same, because the original meaning is derived from the immediate experience. In modern consciousness the mirroring of impressions imbedded and preserved in the deeper psychic levels does not correspond to the archetypal images. Thus it is not the same if transformation is concretely experienced, or relived through narration or lastly, viewed symbolically, even though an approach in a symbolic way can be vital for modern man since he lacks any other means of approach.

The interpretation of the elementary thoughts in conformity with their original meaning calls for a deep penetration into the mythical thinking process. Certain fairy tale motifs are clearly stamped by the epoch of their origin and are recognizable as expressions or "elementary thoughts" from a period or stage of development, when thinking, which was already becoming conscious, comes to terms with the origin and nature of beings. Such motifs are the question about descent *(Lohengrinmotif)* or the guessing of a name such as in "Rumpelstilzchen" *(KHM* No. 55). We have lost the natural relationship to such mythical thought forms.

Perhaps, however, the knowledge about magical life and essence which once existed should not be entirely forgotten. A thorough study of the ideas of illiterate peoples and of children, an investigation of the details and the change in meaning of images in the time up to their emergence in the dreams of contemporary man undoubtedly would be illuminating for an understanding of the human psyche and consequently for understanding fairy tales. What were the impressions and experiences or memories—it could be asked—which, when assimilated, led to fairy tales with motifs like that of transformation? How did the strange ideas, of which transformation is but *one* example, arise? The entire fairy tale literature would have to be quoted in an investigation because, from the viewpoint of historical development, the change in direction in the thinking of the human being, in his experiencing of the world, is mirrored in this literature. Could the tension brought about through it have been the impetus for forming? Should one of these two ways of looking at the world be the only valid one?

[*Translated from the German by Virginia Sease*]

Notes

1. From the collection, *Die Märchen der Weltliteratur,* ed. Fr. von der Leyen and P. Zaunert (Jena, 1922-29), cited in the text according to specific volume and number for the non-German fairy tales.
2. The fairy tales of the Grimm brothers are cited from the classical edition: *Kinder- und Hausmärchen der Brüder Grimm,* edited by Friedrich Panzer (Wiesbaden, n.d.). Abbreviated here: *KHM* with the specific number.
3. Cf. William Stern, *Psychologie der frühen Kindheit bis zum sechsten Lebensjahr* (7th ed.; Heidelberg, 1952), p. 233 ff.
4. Cf. ibid. p. 23 and pp. 63-4.
5. Cf. Johannes Maringer, *Vorgeschichtliche Religion. Religionen im steinzeitlichen Europa* (Einsiedeln, Zürich, Köln, 1956).
6. Cf. Ernst Cassirer, *Philosophie der symbolischen Formen* (Oxford, 1954), II, 218-19.
7. Cf. ibid. p. 213.
8. Cf. Knud Rasmussen, "Die Gabe des Adlers," *Eskimoische Märchen aus Alaska,* trans. Aenne Schmücke (Frankfurt A.M., 1937), p. 142.
9. Cf. Ernesto Bozzano, *Uebersinnliche Erscheinungen bei Naturvölkern* (Bern, 1948). Epilogue and index by Gastone de Boni.
10. Heinz Werner, *Einführung in die Entwicklungspsychologie* (München, 1959). The quoted matter on pages 63-69 is taken from this source.
11. Cf. Adolf Bastian, *Beiträge zur vergleichenden Psychologie. Die Seele und ihre Erscheinungsweisen in der Ethnographie* (Berlin, 1868). Also see Bastian's lecture, "Die Verbleibs-Orte der abgeschiedenen Seele" (Berlin, 1893).

Kenneth Burke

WORDS ANENT LOGOLOGY

HERE, I THOUGHT, WOULD BE A CHANCE TO GET IN SOME PARTING WORDS Anent Logology, using as point of reference the Empson book on *Milton's God*.[1] A most convenient way in is provided by these lines from Milton's *De Doctrina Christiana*, quoted in one of the papers:

> "For Granting that both in the literal and figurative descriptions of God, he is exhibited not as he really is, but in such a manner as may be within the scope of our comprehensions, yet we ought to entertain such a conception of him, as he, in condescending to accommodate himself to our capacities, has shewn that he desires we should conceive."[2]

With regard to the epic of the Fall, a Logological counterpart of this statement would involve, first of all, considerations to do with the "temporizing of essence." That is, the nature of narrative will require that non-temporal relations be treated in temporal terms (logical priority in terms of temporal priority). We could also speak of this as a problem of "dramatization," if one uses the term loosely enough to cover the epic. Thus, though the dialectics of Christian theology must necessarily treat of God in terms of a divine *personality,* and though the divine personality must be conceived after the analogy of the human personality, the two kinds of personality must be so essentially different that any attempt to "dramatize" God must involve a contradiction in terms. An intuitive grasp of this dilemma may have figured in the proscription against depicting God on the stage. The mere fact that theology is *dramatistic* does not make it a perfect fit for the *dramatic.*

Consider, for instance, how the temporizing of essence is related to Arianism. Arianism carried into theology itself the temporizing of an essential relation (since it treats the Son as coming *after* the Father). Hence, the more thorough a poet is in proposing a *narrative* view of relations in "Heavenly eternity," the more likely he is to adopt narrative devices that can be analyzed for traces of "Arianism."

Further, inasmuch as Christian monotheism was proclaimed in the midst of pagan polytheism, during its formation (particularly with relation to the Bible, whose first word for the *one* God is a *plural*) there was a transitional tendency to admit the reality of the pagan gods, but to put them in a subordinate role by treating them as "demons." God tended to be the "one" god in the sense that a monopoly might drive out or swallow up small competitors, or might tower above any that were allowed to survive. As Milton's epic makes apparent, this tradition makes for a dialectic that lends itself well to narrative. But whereas theories of Redemption (or "ransom") present no great logical problems for polytheism (the ransom involving merely the sacrifice of something deemed precious in return for the release of something else deemed precious), there are obvious difficulties for monotheism, inasmuch as the one God's power is absolute, so that no "demon" can operate except by that one God's permission. Obviously, a much more complicated theory of "justice" and "mercy" is needed, to rationalize the one God's sacrifice of great treasure in a transaction involving a demon whose power is wholly dependent upon the will of that one God.

Over the centuries, the theories invented to meet these requirements have undergone many developments. But I might cite this quotation from a letter of St. Ambrose, where the pattern is stated in something of its early simplicity:

"The devil had reduced the human race to a perpetual captivity, a cruel usury laid on a guilty inheritance whose debt-burdened progenitor had transmitted it to his posterity by a succession drained by usury. The Lord Jesus came; He offered His own death as a ransom for the death of all; He shed His own Blood for the blood of all."[3]

It is not our task, or within our province, to attempt assessing the validity of Christian monotheism's theory, or theories, for the rationalizing of ransom (or whatever else the operation may be called) in connection with the explanations for the Father's concurring in the sacrifice of the Son. Our task is, simply, to see how Milton's relation to the issue looks, as viewed purely from the standpoint of verbal symbolism (or "symbolicity"), its resources and embarrassments.

To this end, as in our *Rhetoric of Religion,* we must focus attention not just upon the narrative of the Fall (not mythologically) but also upon a cluster of terms implied in the idea of Order (logologically). And whenever we do turn to the narrative, we must always keep on the look-out for ways in which its temporally irreversible treatment of such terministic relationships differs from their nature as a sheer cluster devoid of temporal sequence.

Though I shall touch upon the line of analysis I used in my essay on "The First Three Chapters of Genesis," I certainly don't want to write that all over again here. But I do very much want to add some further steps along those same lines. For instance:

In the Chart,[4] we align "Promise" and "Reward" on one side, against "Threat" and "Punishment" on the other. From the standpoint of sheer symbolicity, we could also have added the two terms traditional with rhetoric, "Praise" on one side and "Blame" on the other *(laus* and *vituperatio).* In class, I referred to "Praise" as a basic "freedom of speech." There is great exhilaration in being able spontaneously to praise, since "Praise" is in the same bin with "Love." Hence, as I note in my essay on Augustine, a great sense of freedom becomes possible when one hits upon the idea of God as an absolute Principle of Laudability. In being able to admire something unstintingly, one is released—and the greater the burdens of Order, the greater will be the exaltation of such release.

So far, so good. But once the Principle of Perfect Laudability is endowed with the kind of personality needed for a narrative, at that point a vexing problem arises. What of the august Person's attitude towards such praise? Is he to be a veritable glutton for flattery? Is he to show signs of a Jehovah Complex? Or if he considers the praise negligible, coming as it necessarily does from such petty sources (and what other sources but petty ones could there be, since he is the all-powerful?), could he say as much without being mean in another way? For would it not be unkind of him to belittle his praiser, who is working so hard to transform the dignities of emergent worldly empire, to make them serve, however insufficiently, the needs of a "sublime" Protestant theological epic?

Under the circumstances, Milton uses two fairly good narrative devices: First, there is God's plan to give over the powers and honors of supreme office to his Son. This is a personalized analogue for the step from Judaism to Christianity. It automatically cancels tendencies to think of God as greedy for authority and adulation. Empson himself treats of this point (on pp. 124, 137, and 144); but in his very enthusiasm he ingeniously contrives to undervalue its function as poetic tactics. And of course, this arrangement supplies a personal (human) motive for the revolt of Satan, who saw his own high office threatened. Satan's revolt, in turn, could be treated as motivation for the *obedient* revolt of the angels immediately under him. For if this work is to be sublime, it must above all stress the motives of *hierarchy*. And Satan's high position in the hierarchy can be cited as sufficient explanation for the revolt of his underlings (quite as many a drafted man goes to war, not because he would fight, but because he is obedient to the authorities who have drafted him). See the all-important lines to this effect in *Paradise Lost*, V, 704–710—and note how Empson dodges them, in his quotations on pp. 71–72. Indeed Empson's way of ending in the middle of a sentence (on 72) can easily give the impression that the words "but all obeyed" have much the same meaning as they would have in the sentence, "The gunman said 'Hands up!' and all obeyed." As for another risk, that the Son in turn might present the same problems besetting the portrait of the Father, this is adequately solved by a stress upon the Son's total deference to the Father's judgment.

But the main point I was after is: The delight in the giving of praise is as good a trait as the human animal is capable of. And in the search for an ultimate ground that most absolutely justifies such praise, the human person tries to picture a divine person who would be the perfect recipient of the praise. Whereupon, there arise such problems as we have mentioned. And I question whether Empson is sufficiently secular in his views of the Miltonically epic theology that arises from such quandaries.

I think I can now say what I primarily have in mind:

Consider the war in Heaven. If you simply start with that, on its merits, you can't get very far beyond the kind of texts which Empson cites in his ambiguous role as "mediator." That is, you infer that there must have been something radically wrong with God's governance, if one-third of the angelic population was ripe for revolt. (See p. 95 where, incidentally, Empson comes closest to the kind of approach needed by Logology. I refer to his remark that the critic he is citing "does not discuss how Milton could have avoided this effect.") God, in his omnipotence, must seem tyrannous to many; and if he lets the battle surge indecisively for some time before victory, either he must be scheming or he must not be all-powerful.

However, if you start from the logological angle, the issue looks quite different. First, the revolt of the angels is seen as a function of

Adam's fall, which was in turn a function of the idea of Order. That is, implicit in the idea of Order is the principle of Temptation, which was stated narratively in terms of the "first" man's sin. But beyond that, in turn, there could be a kind of ultimate "pre-first," to personalize the *source* of Adams' temptation (deriving it not logologically from the nature of Order or Law in general, but mythologically from some *prior* happening that prepared for it, and thus "implicitly contained it"). Thus, an epic account of a Grand Angelic Revolt would be a "thorough" way of finding a narrative equivalent for the principle of division that my Chart in *The Rhetoric of Religion* treats purely schematically in terms of "classification-negation; the 'set-apart.' "

However, once you translate this principle of division into terms of an epic war, certain purely formal conditions begin to make their claims. First of these is one I considered in my article on Joseph Fontenrose's discussion of the "combat myth" (in his volume, *Python*). Here, I recalled the Aristotelian observation that the form of a perfect contest, or agon requires a peripeteia. It's a poor game, if the winner starts winning from the very start, and simply goes on piling up a bigger and bigger score. And it's a much better game, so far as sheer formal appeal is concerned, if the tide of battle wavers, and there is a change of fortune whereby the roles of victim and victor ultimately become reversed. And so far as sheer games are concerned, we most intensely enjoy a game in which "our side" breaks through to victory, just when we had nearly given up hope. Milton's epic contest is constructed along these "natural" lines.

Try to "dramatize" the principle of division in terms of such "primal" combat (a basic resource of narrative), and do you not *inevitably* confront the problems that Milton confronted? In solving the problems at one point, you raise problems elsewhere. You can't have a big combat at all, for instance, without raising the question: "What's wrong with the Heavenly Administration, when so many angels are ready to wage war in the Home of Perfect Peace?" You can't possibly prolong the war and delay the victory without implying either that the Ruler was not so all-powerful as he claimed to be, or that he was not playing straight with his own followers.

Under polytheism, the traditional "combat myth" does not raise these problems. A hero is fighting a dragon, or a new god is seeking to displace an older god. Neither side is all-powerful, since the myth itself concerns a struggle for supremacy. The battle can quite "naturally" be prolonged. And so far as trickery is concerned, either side is expected to use any resource at its command.

But as soon as you transform this polytheistic design for use in an epic of Christian monotheism, the motivational problem becomes much like that of a man trying to build a perpetual motion machine. He necessarily finds that his model of such an "absolute" machine won't work. So he thinks of adding at some point a new device to correct an obvious shortcoming in his present model. However, as soon as he builds this correction into the machine, he discovers that it in turn has raised problems which need correcting elsewhere. And so on, *ad inf.*, as befits a perpetual motion machine.

Again, so far as a sheer Cycle of Interrelated Terms is concerned, it's quite easy to show how, implicit in the idea of freedom there is the idea of temptation, etc. But once you start translating these "timeless" interrelationships into terms of a narrative, and begin setting up appropriate "personalities" which variously represent such ideas in the motivational form of actions and passions, you are like the man trying to patch up his perpetual motion machine.

Consider, for instance, the notion of the "Fortunate Fall," which Empson can use as a way of indicting the Father, on the grounds that it proves Adam's fall to have been in the cards from the start, and thus to have involved the collusion of God. In my *Rhetoric of Religion* I have given a Logological account of the "Fall" itself. We should now add a Logological discussion of the adjective, "Fortunate." In itself, this adjective is designed to interpret and reinterpret the implications of the Fall in such a way as to lay primary stress upon the redemptive role of the Son (an emphasis natural to a specifically Christian terminology). Similarly, in keeping with Christian notions of Christ as the "Word," Christian theologians could "Christianize" the very beginnings of the Old Testament, by viewing God's creative fiat as operating through the power of the Word, that is, the Son. (See Empson, p. 92.)

But while such "solutions" serve well enough certain particular needs of Christian apologetics, their translation into an epic narrative involving specific personal motivations raises problems at other points, implying the Father's collusion in the Fall, along with the notion that the Son, as distinct from the Father, had been the creative power. (A mild logological counterpart of this notion would stress the fact that any particular terminology for the sizing up of a situation is "creative," since it leads to related kinds of observation.)

Logologically, one should *begin* with the thought of such sheerly terministic resources and embarrassments, rather than beginning with their manifestations in Milton's epic. In brief, rather than beginning with the portrait of God in *Paradise Lost,* one should begin with a Logological frame in terms of which one would "derive" or "prophesy" certain unresolved and unresolvable problems of the epic, which translates these purely terministic relationships into the images of *personal* motivation. (From the sheerly Logological point of view, the so-called "impersonal" or "absolute" nature of God is seen to have its analogue in the non-temporal relationships implicit among the moments of a terministic cluster or cycle.)

Just where, then, are we?

So far as terms merely imply one another, they are in a state of directionless "interpenetration," the Logological analogue of "eternity" and "infinity." (Since angels are etymologically "messengers," Logology finds it particularly apt that they are said to take delight in "interpenetration," as their equivalent for sexual communion.) So far as some terms are subsumed under others, they are arrangeable in a hierarchal relation leading up to a "god-term." But so far any such terms attain quasi-temporalized counterparts in the form of narrative or dramatic personalities or personal motives, the "heavenly" peacefulness of their relationship to one another is disturbed by such accentuating of their possible *division* from one another as gets its fullest or most characteristic dramatic expression in terms of *revolt* or *combat*. The *term* "Disobedience" doesn't "rebel against" the *term* "Command," but a dramatized representation of their relationship in terms of personalities *does* involve such destruction of the terms' mutuality, or angelic "interpenetration."

As with problems that confront the U.S. Supreme Court whenever the various clauses of the Constitution are brought to bear upon some particular temporal situation, several clauses may be found to conflict variously with one another in this particular case. And the Judges must decide which ones shall have precedence. Milton's "dramatizing" of the "dramatistic" Christian theology involves a corresponding problem. (For Empson's treatment of this ambiguous relation between the "personal" and the "impersonal Absolute," see p. 93.)

Next to the initial distinction between logical priority and temporal priority, we should list these related considerations:

(1) There is the idea of Creation, something out of nothing. Such "derivation" is complicated, or further defined, by the fact that in the Bible, the Creation is called "good." So, telescoping, we get: Creation equals good out of nothing. This in effect equates Ontological Derivation with Moral Derivation. (On pp. 140–141,

Empson gives reasons for doubting that Milton subscribed to the *theological* notion of Creation *ex nihilo*. However, the *principle* is implicit in the idea of an act. For an act cannot be an act unless it has novelty. And the idea of Creation *ex nihilo* "perfects" the principle of novelty.)

(2) There is Transformation. Here belong variously ideas of biological generation, the making of artifacts, and natural evolution. This notion ranges from the idea of "like producing like" to the idea of something giving rise to its opposite. Thus, the possible range of moral "derivations" is: Good out of good, good out of evil, evil out of evil, evil out of good.

(2a) There is an intermediate step: the orthodox Christian idea of the Father as generating the Son, a biological (*temporal*) analogy that is to be conceived in terms of *non-temporal* derivation. (Logologically, the situation might be stated thus: If you "begin with" the idea of the Father, you find implicit in it the idea of the Son—and implicit in both terms taken together is the idea of their perfect correspondence, or love, which is the Holy Spirit.)

(3) But in both the dramatic and the dramatistic, there is the sheerly Grammatical tangle whereby Action implies Passion and Reflexive. Such a grammar centers theologically in the idea of God as Pure Act, hence as impassive. Aristotle's God, wrapped in enrapt self-contemplation, is probably the most perfect instance of the Ultimate Reflexive. And the doctrine of the Son's Incarnation most thoroughly represents the principle of the Divine Passion. Monarchian and Patripassian heresies (representing the one God as offering himself for the redemption of mankind) are interesting variants of this grammar on one side; on the other side is Subordinationism, which rescues the logic of the Father's impassivity by too clearly differentiating him from the suffering Son. The Trinitarian relation between Father and Son allows for a divine self-sacrifice without Patripassianism. (Empson considers the same grammar without benefit of Logology on p. 208 thus: "What Milton is thinking has to be: 'God couldn't have been satisfied by torturing himself to death, not if I know God; you could never have bought him off with that money; he could only have been satisfied by torturing somebody else to death.' ")

At various points in Milton's text and Empson's comments, you will see these terministic trends manifesting themselves, though Empson does not approach them thus "prophetically." And things became still more complicated when, as Empson does effectively point out (and as I stress in the opening discussion of *Samson Agonistes* in my *Rhetoric of Motives*), the translation of Milton's theology into terms of narrative personality is further complicated by the fact that it was interwoven with current political motives, even regicidal ones (a confusion that one might expect to find operating in the paradoxical transformation of Satanic evil into the good of God's plans).

We might add a note on the question of predestination and free will. Theologically, it is said that Adam was free either to sin or not to sin. Logologically, Adam *necessarily* sinned—for only if the *first man* sinned could the story of Genesis say in effect that the *principle* of Order implies the *principle* of guilt (or, in St. Paul's terms, that the law makes sin). Thus, when Empson says, on p. 145, "the poem, to be completely four-square, ought to explain why God had to procure all these falls for his eventual high purpose," we must recall that, as viewed from the standpoint of Logology, no narrative could possibly have met this challenge by providing an adequate set of *personal* motivations. For personal (narrative, temporal) terms are not competent to solve this purely technical problem in the construction of a terministic perpetual motion machine. Such translation of non-temporal "essences" into terms of poetic "existence" is of itself a kind of Creative "Fall," with corresponding imperfections.

Since, in a monotheistic scheme, the one God is the over-all term for all responsibility (to which any other responsibilities would by definition be subordinate), it is Logologically in the cards that Empson could say (p. 93): "Milton steadily drives home that the inmost counsel of God was the Fortunate Fall of man; however wicked Satan's plan may be, it is God's plan too." Or he can rightly say (p. 95) that God "could have convinced Satan, because he actually does it when he reduces Satan to despair on Niphates' top." Or there are opportunities to feel scandalized (p. 151) by such remarks as these in the argument of Milton's Book V: "God to render man inexcusable sends Raphael to admonish him of his obedience, of his free estate, of his enemy near at hand." And obviously God must not endow Raphael with the ability to do a wholly adequate job of admonition. For if God had endowed Raphael with perfectly persuasive eloquence, Adam of his own free will would not have fallen. And by failing to fall, he would have made it impossible for the book of Genesis to say, in terms of narrative firsts, that the *principle* of guilt is intrinsic to the nature of Order.

(On the side, we might recall that Raphael's limited prophecies also serve three specifically poetic purposes: to produce an effect of mystery in general; to produce an effect of mystery as belonging particularly to the top rung of the heavenly hierarchy; to employ mystery as a storyteller's convenience, since it enables Milton to dodge problems of motivation, unless importunate critics arise who point out that such evasions can be shown to have troublesome implications.)

All told, once you begin with the Logological fact that the *principle* of the law's negativity is to be stated narratively in terms of Adam's (the "first" man's) disobedience (with corresponding guilt), you have set up the conditions for a motivational regress, to Eve, the serpent, the revolting angels, Satan in particular, the nature of things (the principle of division intrinsic to "Creation"). And thus ultimately, in a monotheistic system (however complicated by the triune grammar of active, passive, and reflexive), if you but have the will, you can find theoretical ways to blame this Logological problem on God himself.

Why, then, did God "have to procure all these falls for his eventual high purpose"? So far as Logology is concerned, the answer is: Language is based on the negative. ("Reason's sense of right and wrong" is a special case of symbolicity's distinction between Yes and No.) And so far as Order involves the protection of property by law (which in turn involves the principle of the thou-shalt-not), here again we confront the negative. And the "fall" is the mythic, or narrative way of *personalizing* such prime negativity. Accordingly, the more assiduously a narrative attempts to build and revisionistically alembicate the perpetual motion machine of Ultimate Motivation, the greater the need for "all these falls." The idea of the fall is but the idea of Order translated into terms of the prime problem inherent in Order.

A couple of odds and ends now, and we're through:

One paper referred to the charge that Milton was a "Subordinationist." That was an interesting contribution to the cause. I would link it with the thought that Milton's cult of the "sublime" (as the *effect* aimed at in his epic) is the stylistic counterpart of his feeling for the mysteries of "degree" (a kind of "social divinity" variously discussed in my *Rhetoric of Motives*.) And this Principle of the Ladder (intrinsic to both social and linguistic Orders) gets its ultimate over-emphasis in "Subordinationism" (a theological doctrine that brings out, too thoroughly for the orthodox view of the Trinity,

the distinction between Father and Son). The subject is treated by
Empson on p. 109.

Finally, in paying particular attention to the epic's use of the word
"fall," as noun or verb, note how it also includes the quite differently
tempered idea of falling in obeisance. In "befall" it takes another
turn. I have the vague impression (which I cannot check on at this
time) that "fell" is somewhere used as an adjective, akin to "foul."
I'd certainly treat "fail" as a tonal variant of "fall." And in Book
IX, 644–645, the fatal word appears enigmatically: "the Tree/Of
Prohibition, root of all our woe." Would that I could claim credit
for this last ingenious observation, but it was originally suggested to
me by Empson himself.

As regards its application to life in general, Logology's main stress
should be placed upon this thought: Inasmuch as *substitution* is a
prime resource of symbolism, the tendency to employ the sacrificial
principle of the scapegoat for "purgative" purposes is continually
born anew in human relations.

Notes

1. William Empson, *Milton's God* (New York: New Directions, 1961).
2. John Milton, "The Christian Doctrine," *Complete Poems and Major Prose,*
   ed. Merritt Y. Hughes (New York: The Odyssey Press, 1957), p. 905.
3. Saint Ambrose: *Letters.*—Letters to his sister Marcellina, no. 62: "A brother
   to his sister," December 388. In the edition of the translation by Sister Mary
   Melchior Beyenka, O.P. (New York: Fathers of the Church, Inc., 1954), p. 387,
   the sentences differ in some words from the quotation above.
4. Kenneth Burke, "Tautological Cycle of Terms for 'Order' ", *The Rhetoric of
   Religion* (Boston: Beacon Press, 1961), p. 183. For the discussion of the
   "combat myth" in Joseph Fontenrose's *Python*, see my "Myth, Poetry, and
   Philosophy" in *Language as Symbolic Action* (Berkeley: University of California Press, 1966).

Walter Hinderer

THEORY, CONCEPTION, AND INTERPRETATION OF THE SYMBOL

Theory of the Symbol

THE QUESTION ABOUT THE CONCEPTION OF THE SYMBOL HAS LED TO many and sometimes contradicting answers. Friedrich Theodor Vischer complained,[1] "The conception is difficult, a shape-changing Proteus, hard to handle and to arrest." However, what does symbolic mean? What is a symbol? The old Greeks understood a *symbolon* to mean: "a preconcerted secret sign by which friends, married couples, kin, or members of a society recognized each other. . . . Such a symbol was, for example, the *tessera hospitalis;* it consisted of the halves of a ring or cube which guest and host exchanged and bequeathed to their children. The meeting parties held their respective halves up to one another and the interlocking proved the authenticity of their old friendship."[2] But the symbol was not only a sign of recognition, a sign which meant that which was put into it, but it pointed, especially in the relation of *religio* and *pietas,* to a sacred being; it attained a numinous character. We speak here of the mystical, archetypal, or religious symbol. In the span between worldly and religious function "nest the possibilities of symbolic art."[3] Most critics justified this simple scheme by attempting to arrest the symbol through historical categories or by dividing it into different strata and phases.

Hegel distinguishes in his *Ästhetik* the "unconscious symbolism" (the religion of the Persians, Indians, and Egyptians), "symbolism of the sublime" (Indian and Moslem poetry, Christian mysticism), and the "conscious symbolism of comparative art forms" (forms of poetry such as the fable, parable, metaphor, image, simile). These three phases are again subdivided by Hegel into three subphases. Since the main conceptions are placed above the rest, the second part of the *Ästhetik,* which deals with "the development of the ideal to the specific forms of artistic beauty," has as its foundation the three art-forms which, according to Hegel, present themselves in their historical sequence: (1) the symbolic art form, (2) the classical art form, and (3) the romantic art form. For Hegel the focal point "toward which the symbolic art form aspires and in whose attainment it dissolves symbolically," is represented by "classical art."[4] Vischer criticized this conception as a mixture of historical and logical argumentation.[5] Departing from the fact that the symbol is first of all only "an extrinsic entanglement of image and content through a point of comparison,"[6] Vischer arrived at a definition of three major types[7] of connections between image and meaning: (1) a dark and unfree one, (2) a middle one lying between "free" and "unfree," and "light" and "dark," and (3) a light and free connection. The first type naïvely confuses meaning and image. The second type, which Vischer sees lacking in Hegel, is marked "symbolism as emotional penetration." The third and last type is constructed according to Hegel's arrangement, as is the first. In this last phase, we find then the insight "that image and meaning are only connected through a *tertium comperationis.*"[8] Hegel, who considers "symbolic art as a constant struggle between suitability and unsuitability of meaning and form" expresses it this way:

> der bisher *an sich* seiende Kampf [ist] jetzt ins Kunstbewusstsein gekommen und das Symbolisieren [wird] deshalb zu einem *bewussten Abscheiden* der für sich selber klaren Bedeutung von ihrem sinnlichen, mit ihr verwandten Bilde . . . jedoch in dieser Trennung zugleich ein ausdrückliches *Beziehen bleibt,* das sich aber, statt als *unmittelbare* Identität zu erscheinen, nur als eine blosse *Vergleichung* beider geltend macht, in welcher die früher ungewusste Unterschiedenheit ebensosehr hervortritt.[9]

After Hegel and Vischer many critics of the Symbol adhered to this basic historical conception. Emil Ermatinger still distinguished four phases in his book *Das dichterische Kunstwerk:*[10] (1) naïve symbolism or the symbolism of folk-belief (folk-mythos), (2) the rationalistic-teleological symbolism (allegory), (3) pantheistic (ideal-rationalistic) symbolism, and (4) characteristic or psychological symbolism.[11] All these corruptions, more or less coined by the historical point of view, show with a varying arrangement and definition, different phases of the relationship of "meaning and image or thought and form,"[12] of the "connection between image and meaning,"[13] the relationship of import and form,"[14] and "meaning and expression."[15]

The result of the various stratum-theories, as different as they may be in particular, is basically the same. It tells us that the forms of the symbol are in immediate connection with the forms of thought and consciousness, and that like them they are subordinate to historical changes. Symbols express foremost the relationship of a subject toward the world. From the mythical symbol the path leads to the poetical symbol, which still sees its leading feature in *Weltbewältigung*.[16] However, the question arises here whether the conception of the symbol can be used for the mythical phase at all. When I speak of the symbol, of symbolic, when I say I mean this or that symbolically, or that I do this only symbolically, then this means *per definitionem* nothing else but: I do not actually mean and do this in reality. The symbol has thus a different plane and, as Käte Hamburger has shown so expressively in her book *Die Logik der Dichtung*,[17] a different structural constitutionality. The basic attribute of the symbol is that it "means" something.

Ernst Cassirer[18] understands symbolic form to mean "every energy of the mind, . . . through which an intellectual content of meaning is connected to a sensuary sign and becomes inwardly a part of it." Cassirer finds such forms in language, mythos, and art.[19] In these three areas, respectively, the relationship of the I and the world is delineated. Cassirer[20] shows mythical thinking and consequently the mythical symbol through the principle of *pars pro toto,* the precedence of intention over extension, of quality over quantity. To mythical thinking also belongs the precedence of spatial over timely reflection, the *coincidentia oppositorum*,[21] the principle of analogy. Mythical thinking could accordingly be defined as "metaphorical thinking"[22] where "imaginative content through the name of another content"[23] is replaced or "transferred." Between a *terminus a quo* and a *terminus ad quem* a conceptual movement takes place. Here the symbol would not only become an expression of that which is thought, but of "the inner movement of thinking itself."[24] For the construction of form-values of language, and with that of the symbol indirectly, Cassirer names "a threefold gradation."[25] First, the sign

which points to something aligns itself as closely as possible with that
which it signifies. To this phase belong imitations of sound and
sound-metaphors of the different onomatopoietical types. After that
follows the second phase, analogical relationship. The relationship,
which is arrested between sound and meaning, goes through the
subjectivity of thinking or feeling.[26] In the third phase the function
of meaning becomes particularly conspicuous. Now the form of
language does not want to be a direct image of the world or to
identify itself with the meaning of that world. In the form of language and symbol, *Sinn* or meaning is especially emphasized. Instead
of the mimic or the analogous expression, which Plato discussed
ironically with the image of the mirror[27] in the tenth book of his
Politeia, "the phase of symbolic expression"[28] was reached which,
on the side of language, equals the phase of *Stil.* One could enter
here and assert that next to personal style there is the personal
symbol. Every author has access to a personal, individual symbolism
and a symbolism which belongs to the style of his epoch. It is not
always easy to keep apart the structural forms of epoch and individuality, especially in modern literature.

However, with such conjectures we have already left Cassirer and
we now approach a conception which maintains that the artist creates the symbol. Susanne Langer, in her book *Feeling and Form,*[29]
has dealt with this aspect thoroughly. Symbolic art would not be an
early form of art, as Hegel maintained, for example, but a constant
phenomenon which from the very beginning belongs insolubly to the
essence of art. Art has its own mode of being which distinguishes it
from the empirical as well as the conceptually real mode of being
in that it is symbolic, that it not only "is," but above all "means."[30]
Conceptual reality, the theory of ideas in Plato, for example, implies
besides the real thing (apple, table, house) only that which they or it
in itself *is.* Particularly the fact that the work of art "points beyond
itself in two directions: to the [concrete or ideal] object, which is its
substance, . . . and to the conception, which has created it as a work
of art,"[31] constitutes "the inner structure of the symbolic form of a
work of art." The fictitious character of art determines also its symbolic mode of being, so that its "closed, mimetic structures" already
contain the "full power and function of the symbol."[32] Art and symbol stand in the "reciprocity of object and conception"[33] and in the
"variable tension between that which means and that which is
meant." We identify the conception of art and symbol here according
to modes of function and existence, out of the cognition of their

mimetic structure, whose essence does not consist in imitation, but in a creative act, which as the "constituent element contains that of abstraction."[34] The degrees of symbol-connection, or the fictionalization, are hereby different: they extend from tendencies of faithful pictorial reproduction to illustrating allegory and to the conscious destruction of reality and coercion of the symbol. To determine these degrees of symbol-connection will be one of the tasks of interpretation. More recent efforts[35] have shown that research of myths and interpretation of the symbol do not necessarily profit from each other. The theory of archetypes, begun by Jung and continued by many of his students, lures toward free association and brings, without doubt, options into the symbolic game. Yet one should not practice total abstention and close one's mind to the ideas of these theories. Even if the symbols in Goethe's works[36] may stem predominantly less from archaic-mythical roots than out of a specific, psychic-noetical situation and out of the reservoir of a general body of knowledge, it should not be overlooked that arch-symbols do exist as "archetypal patterns" and "emotional patterns" which express an inner basic structure and which bridge the gap from the mythical to modern thought and experience. Such archetypal symbols, even if they have to be translated into a modern function, can be detected in the poetical works of the 20th century.[37]

However, we must ask ourselves again in this connection, whether we can at all talk about symbols in the realm of the mythical. F. Th. Vischer realized that the mythical is symbolic only for the "educated, free conscience."[38] Like religion, mythos takes that which is stated literally, that is, factually. That which is expressed in the mythical phase does not stand for or mean the other, but *is* the other. They are transubstantiations such as in the proceedings of the Eucharist, where "wine" and "bread" do not *mean* but *are* the "blood" and the "body" of Christ. Such transubstantiations or identifications are found in mythos and religion. The image is confused with meaning, the symbol with reality.[39] For the interpretation of the symbol this is, however, a false problem, since it can understand "mythical imagery" only as a type of fictional mode of being. Whoever is under the spell of mythos will hardly practice mythology, and even the practicing mystic is not necessarily the ideal interpreter of mysticism.[40] The discrepancy between "being" and "meaning" and the awareness of it creates only the supposition for interpretation. In other words, the fictional character, the mode of being of the symbol, which is divorced from reality, must first be recognized before one has the desire to explain the suspected meaning of the image through concepts.

Northrop Frye combines several different methods in his book *Anatomy of Criticism* and does not shy away from starting with an "assumption of total coherence,"[41] a "coordinating principle,"[42] in order to determine out of this principle the constituents of the organism. His book consciously builds upon the ideas of antiquity. Besides a "theory of modes" and a "theory of myths," which represents a typological view of imagery, his work contains a "theory of genres" and, above all, a "theory of symbols."[43] Here, Frye points expressively to the reference-character of word, sentence, and image and to their symbolic function or their function as symbols. He differentiates various relationships and interlocking of connections according to phases, to which again belong certain forms of *dianoia* (meaning), *mythos* (narrative), and *ethos* (characterization)—all elements of the rhetoric tradition. The phases Frye names in the following manner: (1) literal and descriptive phase—symbol as motif and as sign, (2) formal phase—symbol as image, (3) mythical phase—symbol as archetype, (4) anagogic phase—symbol as monad. With this stratum-theory, Frye attempts to outline the complicated web of relationships of the symbol in a work of art. He does not limit himself to one aspect, but with the strata he works out the manifold meanings of the components. The conception of the symbol is not narrowed down, but unfolds; it is not isolated but is seen in its appropriate context. Frye knows how to connect the different results, to which other methodical essays have led, into a unified system.

From the first phase of his theory of the symbol, Frye departs from the word-sign, or from word-unities, which stand for objects or point to them.[44] He distinguishes between assertive and discursive writing (whose aim is agreement of the word-sign) and the real phenomenon; and between poetical literature, whose criteria cannot be truth, since its basic structure is hypothetical, or, as we say with Käte Hamburger,[45] fictitious, that is, mimetic. "The real core of poetry is a subtle and elusive verbal pattern,"[46] and so the symbol expresses itself first of all on a literal level. Here the symbols are motifs and every insight down to the letter may be relevant to our understanding.[47] As I will illustrate in the interpretation of Ernst Barlach's drama *Die Sündflut*, conspicuous substantives and verbs[48] are, next to phrases constructed out of core passages,[49] especially important for critical conjecture on symbolic form. Reaching beyond Frye the field of the symbol builds out of the field of the word, so far as the field of the word is structured by a definite meaning.

Frye clarifies the difference between naturalism and symbolism through the comparison of centrifugal and centripetal forces. In the formal phase Frye begins with Aristotle's conception of *mimesis praxeos* and identifies it with *mythos,* the secondary imitation of action.[50] Mythos is, for Frye, more philosophical than history and describes only particular action. *Dianoia* is, in his opinion, a secondary imitation of thought, a *mimesis logon* which is concerned with "typical thought, with the images, metaphors, diagrams, and verbal ambiguities, out of which specific ideas develop."[51] With symbols we mostly think in terms of meaning, since we do not have a word for the imagery which moves within the literary work of art and which, in my opinion, structures and organizes the word-field. According to Frye, the formal critic considers especially images. Frye deals here with allegory, metaphor, concetti, objective correlative, the heraldic symbol, and subjective associations as various modifications of the symbol. This way of looking at the problem seems so much more emancipating, since in Germany, for example, Goethe's definitions of the symbol and the easy distinction[52] between allegory and symbol were, for a long time, decisive.[53] Apart from whether one deems it relevant to differentiate in this connection between "idea," "conception," and "thought" or not, for practical reasons alone one is compelled to consider differentiations of conceptions like "allegory", "emblem", "metaphor", and so on, as modifications of the symbolic, since the symbolic meets the mode of being in poetry. A few examples will illustrate that, in spite of the obvious differentiation between symbol and allegory, the latter was always subordinate to the first, sometimes consciously-direct, sometimes unconsciously-indirect. Ermatinger, for example, understands allegory as a kind of flattened out symbol, "eine wenig tiefe Schale mit flachem Boden."[54] Hiuzinga[55] terms it in one passage as "symbolism projected onto surface-imagination." Karl Vossler emphasizes the dogmatic character of allegory, the tendency "to poetically unfree, half artistic, poetically deprived and didactic inferior or peripheral forms of symbolic art."[56]

The fourth phase concerns itself, according to Frye, "with the social aspect of poetry, with poetry as the focus of a community."[57] The predominant symbol of this phase is the "communicable unit," which Frye, who deviates here from the definition of C. G. Jung, terms archetype. Archetypes are for him conventional symbols with

history. Every phase of the symbols is, in a specific manner, concerned with meaning and narrative. In the archetypal phase the
meaningful content would be the conflict between wish and reality,
whose basis is the dream, and the narrative, the ritual, or the imitation of human action as a whole.[58] In general, Frye[59] terms the archetypal symbol as natural objects with meaning to man. The last phase,
which Frye mentions in his essay "Theory of Symbols," is the anagogic phase. Here remains to be added as a supplement, that the specific phases run parallel to the analyzed modes of expression in the
first essay of *Anatomy of Criticism*. The division and outlines also
allow conclusions to the respective epochs. So the center of gravity of
the archetypal phase seems to rest, for Frye, on the "romantic" mode
of expression, and in the last phase on the "mythopoeical aspect".[60]
As mythopoeic writers, Frye names Dante, Spenser, and also poets
of the 20th century such as Henry James and James Joyce. While in
the archetypal phase the literary work of art is mythos and combines
ritual and dream,[61] literature of the anagogic phase imitates, according to Frye, "the total dream of man, and so imitates the thought
of a human mind which is at the circumference and not at the center
of its reality."[62] It would, therefore, according to Frye's terminology,
be apocalyptic, whereby he understands apocalypse to mean "primarily the imaginative conception of the whole of nature as the content of an infinite and eternal living body."[63] Anagoge, a conception
which is also used in the hermeneutics of theology, is medievally
understood in this context, as the universal, that is, the "ascending"
to the universally absolute. The symbol in this kind of poetry is a
monad; "all symbols" are, according to Frye, "united in a single
infinite and eternal verbal symbol which is, as *dianoia,* the logos
and, as *mythos,* the total creative act."[64] The anagogic symbol mostly
leads the observer into religious associations.

We interrupt here the extremely differentiated investigations of
Northrop Frye which, at least in their systematic entanglement,
stand up to the complexity of the whole phenomenon. We ask for
the utility of his theory of the symbol in practical literary interpretation. It will be seen here, that up to now the most differentiated
analysis is, in spite of all caution, still based on cultural history.
The interrelationship of modes of expressions, phase-sequence, and
formal and narrative categories, together with historical excursion,
are somewhat like a labyrinth, so that at times we suddenly stop in
the middle of a partially clear analysis in order to search for Ari-
adne's thread. Like all phase and stratum theories, whether they

are founded historically or systematically, Frye's theory, too, is only useful in view of a broader context for the practical symbolic interpretation (which has to isolate out of the word-field of the particular literary work that which is symbolic, that is, that which symbol "means").[65] Next to a theory of the symbol which he understands first of all quite generally as "any unit of any literary structure,"[66] Frye intended to introduce to literary criticism "a theory of criticism whose principles apply to the whole of literature and account for every valid type of critical procedure."[67] These are the words Frye uses to describe that which, in his opinion, Aristotle meant by poetics. Like Aristotle, Frye seems to approach poetry as the biologist approaches a system of organisms to determine genera and species, "formulating the broad laws of literary experience, and, in short, writing as though he (Aristotle) believed that there is a totally intelligible structure of knowledge attainable about poetry."[68] This, according to Frye, is poetics as well as aesthetics "as soon as aesthetics becomes the unified criticism of all the arts." The theory of the symbol stands here as an overlapping conception and can, out of necessity, represent the different strata of meaning, functional properties and reference-attributes of the symbol itself only in a systematic abbreviation.

Conception of the Symbol

As some examples in the first part of this essay have shown, theory and interpretation of the symbol obviously go in different paths, since they aim for different objectives. Even such a matured and integrating representation of this stratified phenomenon as Frye's *Anatomy of Criticism* delivers, for an interpretation of the symbol, less of a basis than a stimulus. This is in part caused by a diversified method of categorization. Categories or conceptions of the symbol which are forged for systematic reasons and out of the realization that a work of art consists of different strata and phases, may be appropriate for a general view, but for the interpretation of the symbol they give few points of departure. Therefore, one would say that the interpretation of the symbol cannot build upon the theory of the symbol; on the contrary, the theory of the symbol must rest upon the interpretation of the symbol, which works out through micro-analysis and in the word-field that which the theory of the symbol then outlines and simplifies and casts, so to speak in a rough model, in a more general context. The symbol, the mode of the symbol, its locations and strata, its mechanics or technology, its spheres of function and meaning, and its place within the context, all this can only be worked out by the respective analysis of the poetical work of art itself. This analysis must consider the self of the author, which not only creates the symbol more or less unconsciously, but which also structures the symbol through respective noetic or emotional intentions. Since these phenomena show themselves only in the field of word and language, the analysis of the symbol will simultaneously have to be an analysis of style and language, and beyond that, an analysis of the motif. Only from these directions can the respective symbol be delimited and determined, and which peculiarly seems to change and transform immediately as soon as it is taken out of its system of reference, disconnected from its context, isolated, marked as the carrier of an idea, and compared and classified with carriers of ideas x or y. The conception of the symbol is thus shortened or mutates. Just as certain chemical substances easily change their properties if they are exposed to changing conditions or are brought into different reactions, so the symbol seems to change its nature easily in other circumstances and connections. This may in part be determined by the fact that the symbol, on the one hand, represents certain conditional qualities, that it only exists in function or reference, and that on the other hand it shows itself as a visible evident image, as a perceptual medium. If the sentence gives "an image of reality," a "model of reality"[69] as we understand it, then the symbol is a sign with indicating functions which point to a reality which we perhaps *think*, but which we certainly are not always able to explain conceptually. Viewed in this light, the conception of the symbol would almost be a kind of model for a second conception of reality, for which the property of the sentence is insufficient. While the sentence still delivers "an image of reality,"[70] since it copies reality and represents the possibility of existing and non-existing conditions, the symbol represents only that which it indicates. But already the principle of representation seems to be misleading here. The symbol can definitely be of multivalent character, so that one can recognize the indication function, but not the objective referred to. The interpretation may here only introduce possible potential objectives which could definitely have unreal characteristics. This principle of inexhaustiveness or incommensurability of a certain kind of symbolism leads also directly to the problem of value, the question of value-growth, as René Wellek[71] asks it, for example.

For the time being the theory of the symbol seems only to be able to present conceptually some major directions and distinguishing marks. Nevertheless, it gives interesting insights into the historical change and epochal typology of the conception of the symbol. In order to grasp somewhat such a differentiated and to such a degree immanent "conception" within the organism of art in its manifold functions, conditions, and forms of presentation, many more individual investigations are necessary. Especially investigations which trace a certain symbol[72] in different works of different epochs. In spite of a number of excellent works, we should not let ourselves be deceived, for we still stand at the beginning in this area. The third part of this essay, especially, calls attention to a phenomenon which I would, to begin with, call "symbolic formality,"[73] since language, as formula, takes over certain qualities of the symbol here. Such individual investigations would have to show whether there exists next to a personal style a personal symbolism. In reference to the literature of the 20th century, whose distinguishing mark seems to be that every poet has developed his own style and symbolic forms, one cannot discuss epochal style anymore.

The conception of the symbol can without a doubt be defined as a modern phenomenon if one looks at it and understands it with the eyes and the mind of the literary historian, that is to say, as a phenomenon which obviously runs parallel to the increasing complexity of the proceedings of the conscience. But even the most abstract and complicated symbol can, as Hermann Broch correctly remarks, be traced back to a "natural and naturalistic nucleus."[74] This natural nucleus of the symbols can also be termed the "banal nucleus." To continue one of Broch's conceptions, I would, with allegorical, metaphorical, or parabolic forms, speak of "banal symbols," since they have a broad basis of understanding and are less individualized. The original symbols were no doubt natural symbols which were in time more and more de-naturalized, patterned, and outwardly simplified.[75] This process of abstraction signifies at the same time an enlargement and widening of the content of the symbol. The original symbol, which stood on a broad basis and in a greater social and religious-mythical connection, became more and more a seal, a sign of almost formal character. Yet, in spite of this formality, it kept its imagerially-natural nucleus, and with this double characteristic, as a sign of image and thought, it seems to emerge in the empiric world as an expression of something ideal,[76] as a carrier of meaning for an idea. But the reason that this and nothing else is experienced, that the symbol has especially this content of meaning, must lie in the field of references of the artistic work itself.

The fact that a symbol makes sense, that its allusion "ignites," precludes, of course, a certain receptiveness. If one can speak of *Wertblindheit* (Max Scheler), we can also talk of "blindness" toward symbols. This conception would at the same time imply that the experience of the symbol, even if it is guided by connections in the artistic organism, takes place in an emotional sphere, in the very depth of personality. A symbol can have evidential character within a particular constellation and yet be without rational, conceptual explanation, although the founding of the symbol and its placement, as well as the experience of the symbol itself, did not exclude the noetic-spiritual realm. That symbols are nevertheless transferred into conceptions but are not exhausted lies therein, that they direct toward the fact, that they mean, but that they do not fully explain what they mean. "Symbolized forms are irreversible processes of reproduction."[77] They represent, as H. Broch says, an arch-image but this does not allow "a point for point isomorphic reproduction, but necessitates on account of its 'abundance of contents,' a differently modulated 'insinuated' representation."[78] If we concentrate on the general sign-meaning and function-character of the symbol, rather than on the character of "reproduction" and "arch-image," we will plainly see that in the symbol there is laid out in its directing function a meaning (be it noetic or emotional), which is, however, not fulfilled or completely delineated. In short, the meaning surpasses the symbol, at least a specific kind of symbol. In the place of "abundance of content" one could also speak of "abundance of meaning," or better yet, of "receptiveness of meaning," since symbols which are open to meaning can experience a growth in meaning and value.

Broch[79] pointed to the fact that man owes his "eidetic pre-knowledge of the diverse combinations of thing and property in the world" to the "cognitive sphere of the unconscience" which in structure is akin to the mathematical sphere. This sphere should yield, according to certain sequences of associations, striking possibilities of combinations whose evidential character we then experience in the conceived symbol. But it would be wrong exclusively to connect the birthplace of the symbol with such a "sphere of the unconscious," because unconscious, as well as conscious powers, take part in the formation, placing, and coordination of the symbol, whereby we have, of course, a different ratio of components or gradation. On this dual property rests, nevertheless, the possibility of interpretation for the symbolic mode of being. As the interpretation of symbols attempts to translate the symbolic mode of being into the world of concepts, or to lead to a different structure of reality, one could say to the contrary that the symbolic reality strives for a kind of hermeneutics or art of translation, but on a mimetic, fictional plane through imagerial, delineated relationships. With that, we would maintain that symbols not only give a model of reality but above all an interpretation, a clarification of their meaning which is infinitely richer and diversified as the meaning of the conception.[80] This again does not take place on the conceptual-logical plane, but on the mimetic plane. Here, however, some doubt arises. Did we not say that the symbol means more than it says and that it, above all, has a directing function? The question is actually directed toward the answer which we already know, and which at the moment seems questionable and demands an explanation. That the symbol points beyond itself depends on the mode of being which, if it means, does not become meaning, but keeps this kind of conditionality. And especially as such, in its conditionality, this mode of being cannot be defined on the mimetic plane; the rules of analytic logic are less valid than the principles of analogy and correlation. While the object is limited and defined in conceptual interpretation, the mimetic-functional interpretation broadens it and lifts the borders. The latter creates infinite connections, a web of meanings and relations while the first excludes and narrows down. The symbolic mode of being, one could infer, aims for totality, for the total sum of meaning and cognition, while the other, above all, aims for detail. Northrop Frye would mention this kind of symbol in his anagogic phase. I want neither to narrow down the conception of the symbol here through categorizations, nor to abstract or outline it through a theory, but merely to recognize again its multiple stratification.

Above I have made the assertion that the field of the symbol becomes only concrete in the field of the word. This would meet Hermann Broch's formulation which says: "the symbol of art and language belong together archetypically."[81] Although this seems to be almost self-evident, there is reason to emphasize that literary symbols are primarily symbols of language. First, language is an artificial system of signs which carry, negotiate, and accumulate meaning. The language-sign can also be a sound-sign, it can negotiate and portray stimuli of sound as it can trigger stimuli of memory and perception. The heard and spoken sign of language (*species audibilis*) also corresponds to the world of the senses as often, to the contrary, the language sign is an expression of parts of a physical reality. In this connection the use, length, and brevity of the vocal, and the timbre of the word, play an important part. The smallest components of the symbol are the substantive and the verb. The next biggest unity is the sentence (or the period.) A sentence — a thought — a symbol: with this sequence the correlative structure can be determined. Out of the sentence, the correlation of words among themselves, the field of words which is more or less consciously structured by meaning (behind which stands, of course, the poet as the asserting subject), the symbolic mode of being builds itself.

The symbol can also be designated according to its object which it irreversibly represents (for example, thing-symbol, personification), according to a medium in which it articulates itself (language-symbol, gesture), and according to ideally conceived intentions toward which it points (a mythical, mystical, religious, magic, realistic, and so on, symbol). But with such more or less external designations, even if they still include various forms and grades of composition, not much has been gained. The different symbols must first of all be worked out of the respective work of art, out of the pattern of words which in this case almost always is a pattern of correlatives. *Quod non est in verbo non fuerit in symbolo*, one could sum up in a formula.

The multivalence of the symbol results from the principle of the analogy, out of the manifold correlative chains which accumulate meaning. The character of the analogy is thus still strengthened through the mobility of the world of images. Yet, within the flowing relationships there exist fixed points which give the symbols their directing or aiming function. Symbols only "mean," if they stand in a correlative point of function which, however, can again become the correlative point of another point, and so forth. The continuous change of the meaning object and point of correlation, which can almost be compared with an endless mathematical series, lies in the analogous character of the symbol. On the basis of this tendency of enlargement or totality, one can consider symbols "windows into the absolute" (Hegel) as well, whereby the absolute seems to rest quite generally in the perception or in the relative conscience of a sphere which cannot be determined or fenced in. Although the symbol no-

where denies the relationship to reality, it only represents reality by
"interpreting" it, or it even creates it anew in a certain way and in a
flash-like intuitive realization, which is already built into the symbol
and which it passes on as a representational sign. This representational sign triggers feelings and associative thinking and addresses
the senses, sets into action and ties together all or particular basic
human abilities. As symbols trigger movements of feelings and
thoughts, so they are themselves often expression and result of movements of feelings and thoughts. As in human gestures and in mimi-
cry, an inner process is reflected outwardly, so in certain symbols
certain feelings are reflected. For this we have sufficient examples
in dream symbolism. But one does not have to leave the field of
literature, because in lyricism particularly, in the occasional poem
or the poem based on actual experience for example, the emotion is
only communicated in or through the symbolic. The minnesinger
used the image of winter to illustrate a mood which was anything
but cheerful. In the lyric of nature itself, the poet connects processes
of nature with those of the psyche;[82] the image of nature actually
becomes a mirror of psychic events. One does not intend to describe
nature objectively or copy it, but primarily feels its forms, colors,
and emotional values, which very often are only the outpourings of
one's own momentary inner state. Or one views nature as a personality whose different conditions of the soul express themselves in
gesture and mimic. From these emotional attitudes, as they are interpreted into the evident forms of nature, we let ourselves be contam-
inated. To this kind of symbolic formation there is yet added the
association which ties together images with feelings and feelings with
images in the realm of imagination and recall.[83]

Basically the process of symbol-formation does not solely depend
on the style of epoch and time but particularly on the personal point
of view, the world view and style and the personal interests and intentions of the poet. A lyricist, dramatist, or novelist, for example,
who treats the theme of death will use different symbol forms than
the lyricist, dramatist, or novelist who treats the theme of love. In
the treatment of the themes of death or love, it is also of basic significance whether the respective poet follows more mystical, mythical,
or even naturalistic-realistic tendencies. Generally it can be ascertained by the enumerated example, that there is a specific death and
love symbolism which is shared by different cultures and which, in
a certain way, confirms Jung's archetypes.

The symbol is formed by two directions of meaning, which again are connected with the emotional-noetic intentions or the make-up of the respective author. The direction of meaning can be "centrifugal" or "centripetal,"[84] that is, it moves to the outside or the inside, whereby we have to distinguish whether the directions of meaning are led more by intellectual or emotional endeavors. It was mentioned above[85] that most of the symbols stem from the realm of nature, which does not mean, however, that such symbols have to be nature-symbols. This is pointed out especially clearly by external symbolism, which has more of an illustrative and ornate tendency or which shows less content of contemplation and more ideality with less meaning. This kind of symbol we find in the *topoi* and images of minnesang and baroque, or in the less valuable world of formulas used by epigonous symbolists.

It should be the task of the interpretation of the symbol, I repeat, to analyze the field of the symbol of the respective work of art in the field of language and to show the manifold associations. Out of the core and guide symbols, which are at the same time the "key" of the poet,[86] and out of the accidental, co- and subordinated symbols, we uncover not only the directing and meaning function, but also the message and the meaning itself. For that reason, an interpretation which wants to approach especially the themes and intellectual tendencies of a work of art, must seek a way through the analysis of style and symbol. The material of the symbol as such is structured, organized, and polarized within the organism of the linguistic work of art. The smallest unities, from the metaphor to the single word, can yet be important hints. For that reason the analysis of the symbol must be joined by the analysis of the motif, subject-matter, and style. The next part of this essay will show this tight connection, the multiplicity and the manifold stratification of the conception of the symbol in an example—the drama *Die Sündflut* by Ernst Barlach.

Interpretation of the Symbol

In Barlach's *Die Sündflut*[87] we have a model configuration of archetypal symbolism. The plot itself is at least predetermined by old testimonies like the epic of Gilgamesh and the account of Noah's ark. A modern poet, who, to speak with Frye, is in the anagogic phase, no longer stands in the center of the mythical realm to which he refers; rather, he takes up a model which has already been coined by archetypal symbolism. A change of the old symbolism must result out of the changed constellation and the different modes of the conscience. It changes its function, is differently aligned, and receives other tendencies and conceptions at which to aim. Here we see that the asserting subject[88] is, in spite of the independence and spontaneity of the work of art, the *conditio sine qua non* of the reference points. The old testimony is loaded up with a new meaning, and that means that in our connection Barlach changed the symbolism. One could already work out, through a comparison of the symbol, the different intentions. In the case of Barlach, however, we nevertheless know definitely that he did not want to identify himself with the traditional story because he, on the contrary, found this "old story utterly absurd."[89]

With the symbols, the motifs obviously change their function, are tailored to the new intentions, and are aligned according to new horizons of meaning. From the biblical source, Barlach took "external things like landscape and names, the dimensions of the ark,"[90] and, of course, larger parts of the narrative. The drama begins with the conviction of man by God ("And it repented the Lord that he had made man on the earth, and it grieved him at his heart," Genesis 6:6) and ends with the flood. In between there unfolds in the foreground the fight between Calan, the adversary and tempter of Noah, who was invented by Barlach, on the one side and Noah and God on the other. The plot, the external narrative, limits itself, as far as biblical tradition is concerned, to singular assertions, which stem from Chapter Six of the Book of Genesis. In spite of that, the world of the symbol in the drama conveys the impression of almost mythical totality. The reason is not to be found only in the archetypal structure of space and time, in the archaic simplification of horizontal and vertical conceptions of space, in the mythic-schematic division of above and below, heaven and earth, mountain and valley, desert and tent area, barren land and oases, animal and God, far and near, old and new time, in the four arch-elements, water, fire, earth, air, and so on, but also in a style which renders all things "archaic" and which reminds us of the *Edda*[91] and frequently of the Old Testament. It is an "abstract-metaphorical,"[92] an allegorizing style, as Walter Muschg believes, in which is reflected the "dissonance between being and the reflection of being."[93] Correctly observed characteristics of Barlach's language are doubtless the "tendency to

abstraction,"[94] the "abstracting metaphor,"[95] the "allegorical character of images,"[96] the "stylization,"[97] a "style of pure meaning,"[98]
augmentation of the word to *"Inbegriff"*[99] and "plays on words."[100]
Barlach himself spoke about this in view of one of his dramas, that he
had lifted it "out of a low-German Edda-mood."[101] In another letter
he says, "If I am supposed to relive an inner experience, it must speak
a language in which I can relive the deepest and most hidden, . . .
since my artistic mother tongue is the human figure or the milieu,
the object, through which or in which man lives, suffers, enjoys himself, feels and thinks."[102]

This sounds all a bit general and does not describe the specific
quality of Barlach's language achievement. In a superficial observation of the word-field, we notice already the alliterations, the many
abstract formations in "*-ung,*" "*-heit,*" "*-keit,*" the mystic lines of
style, and the predominance of the substantive, that is, the preference of the nominal style. All this points to the fact that language is
here an expression of *essentia* and that it aims toward the essence.
Behind this stands the endeavor, which, through the loss of individuality of the concrete and the material, wants to arrest the idea
of both creativeness and reality. Especially since Barlach, like the
mystics, has experienced the limits of the word—the word is "a
wretched substitute, a shabby tool, and the essential and last wisdom
is wordless . . ."[103]—he proceeds like the mystics "to transform the
language out of himself: he becomes the word-creator."[104] Besides
the transformation of the word-medium, we have the "accumulation
of linguistic means of expression,"[105] the style of language which is
formed by the style of thought, the "augmentation," "hyperbole,"
and the "paradox."[106] Substantives, formed with the abstract suffix
"*-ung,*" which render concrete all action, becoming, and happenings,
are peculiarly enough relatively rare in the *Sündflut.* More so we run
across "*-heit*" and "*-keit*" in formations like *"Herrlichkeit," "Heilig-
keit," "Traulichkeit," "Getrostheit."* Barlach too does not want to
seize "living beings in concreto, but in abstracto, in their idea" and
wants them to express themselves through the "given means of abstraction,"[107] but in the process of abstraction he does not predominantly use the mystic technique. This results again out of the style of
thought, which is actually not mystical throughout. In *Die Sündflut,*
the mystical means of language becomes clear only in the last act,
especially in the last scene when Calan speaks of the "shapeless God"
(p. 382f) and his identification with him. This *unio mystica,* which
is then experienced by Calan as such, is described by Barlach with

means of language, which we can definitely consider as mystical. *"Glut ist Gott, ein glimmendes Fünkchen, und alles entstürzt ihm, und alles kehrt in den Abgrund zurück"* (p. 383). In this example we have the technique of "accumulation" and "augmentation" which enlarges the properties, the metaphorical parable (*"Glut ist Gott"*) and the prefixes *"ent-"* (*"entstürzt"*) and *"ab-"* (*"Abgrund"*), which characterize the mystical process of the return to chaos.[108] Images like barren land, desert, which express a horizontal conception of space, change with the image of the abyss, which expresses the vertical conception of space. Besides, the conception of the abyss expresses something eternal, mainly the actually indescribable mystical experience in connection with the "emotional moment of a staggering height."[109] Mystical tradition is also shown when Barlach calls God *"winziger als Nichts"* (p. 383). God is expressed in negations, since he is "ineffable," *"als in nichts Bestehendem."*[110] *"Nichts,"* *"Abgrund,"* and *"Fünkchen"* are also, in *Die Sündflut,* essential expressions which are closely connected among each other. The little spark, *scintilla animae,* is the godlike nucleus of the mystics, the foundation of the soul which is, like the foundation of God, without *"zuovelle,"* without chance, just pure being, *actus purus.* Here the process of becoming one with God takes place, and that *"in einem bild-und weiselosen Geschehen, in dem der Erfahrende alles Wissens und Bewusstseins 'entsinkt.' "*[111]

With Barlach, God and man are, at least according to Calan, the *"glimmende Fünkchen,"* out of which everything *"entstürzt"* and in whose *"glühenden Abgrund"* everything returns. Calan becomes *"Glut und Abgrund in Gott,"* *"Er ist ich geworden und ich Er"* (p. 383). The cessation of the object-subject cleavage, which Karl Jaspers[112] names as the typical feature of the "mystical orientation," the final union in which the absolute *coincidentia oppositorum* is experienced, is preceded by the "loss of the self," the "crushing of the self." Calan experiences the mystical unity only in the lowest phase of his existence, at a point of utter reduction. But this "mystical orientation" is only valid for Calan, and the mystical field of word and thought shows itself only[113] where Calan, in an inner vision, mystically perceives of the mystery, the secret— ("*myein*" means "to close the eyes"), that is with closed eyes (*"Als die Ratten meine Augen aus den Höhlen rissen, Noah, bin ich sehend geworden"* p. 382). Here and only here the mystical style of thought determines style, motif, and symbolism. In other places, we have forms of style and thought which yet serve the purpose of destroying reality, that is of abstraction, but these may not be considered typically mystical. It would be incorrect to view Barlach exclusively as a mystic and just as misleading and inappropriate to interpret the abstract qualities of his language only through mystic-allegorical forms. It is just as valid here, that the modes of representation depend respectively on the object.

Generally we can say that Barlach's word-field is determined by the substantive and that he tends toward nominal style. The sentence is based on the substantive and augments in it. The adjectives have pointing and directing functions; often they give a formalized competence and property (for example, *"handloser Hüter," "brechende Brunnen," "zorniger Flug," "widerhaarige Kunst," "linde leise Lust"*) or they render the abstract into the concrete or into an image (for example, *"fingerlanges Vertrauen," "aufgekeimter Dank," "saurer Mut"*). In spite of that, the adjectives in Barlach have, in comparison to the substantive, a subordinated function. The verb exhibits an imagerial tendency; it actualizes, personifies, and gives dynamic proportions to the more abstract substantive, as the following examples show: *"Schwere schleicht auf leisen Füssen"* (p. 363), *"Leid hat mich eingeschaufelt, Bitterkeit hat mich begraben"* (p. 340), *"Lass die Lust auf deine Seele hauchen"* (p. 333).

We already see in these few quotations that Barlach's style is determined by two opposing movements: first, the negation and establishment of images; second, the loss of reality, and the establishment of concrete form. These two movements cross one another. Barlach again and again jumps directly from the concrete state of imagery into the utmost abstractness and vice versa. Often the abstract and the concrete are insolubly connected with one another. One has talked about Barlach's "will towards allegorical expression"[114] and herewith pointed to the fact that the linguistic image in Barlach has an intellectual basis and thought, on the other hand, an imagerial core. The different interpretations of *Die Sündflut*[115] show which problems are inherent in the conception of "allegoric" in symbolic interpretation. Here we must, nevertheless, consider that thought and image do not stand in a clear relationship, in the sense of the old conception of allegory, but that this relationship is constantly dissolved. One could sooner talk of a continuous motion, in which substantive language, image, and thought stand, a motion which beyond reality leads to thought and from thought leads back to reality. This motion obtains through the substantive points of orientation. The alliterations give rhythm to the material of the language and fill the alliterating substantives simultaneously with meaning.[116] The word becomes thus the carrier of meaning and idea, the formula to imagery and, at the same time, to thought. This formula, which can mostly be understood as symbolic formula, characterizes the style in Barlach's *Die Sündflut*. A striking example out of the drama[117] should show how these formulas, in variation, transformation, and change of function, become signs of images and signalling sequences of images, in which is expressed a totality of action and meaning.

God has come to Noah as a beggar. In order to tempt Noah and his God, to provoke a somewhat reversed ordeal, Calan had the hands of the young herder cut off and had them nailed to a post as a clearly visible sign. We shall return later to this core-symbol of *Die Sündflut*. Calan's bloody deed, the bleeding herder who screams in his thirst and pain, the beggar worried about Noah, and the God who was wounded and maltreated by the wolf-like children are presuppositions for the scene which unites several typical motives (for example, *"Hände," "wölfische Kinder," "Bluttat," "Wassernot,"* and so on) and symbols that are connected with one another. In the actions and the words of characters their true being finds expression: the indifference towards Calan's bloody deed. God says only, ". . . *in meinen Tagen schlug man den Menschen nicht die Hände ab"* (p. 346) and then lets Noah bathe his feet. To what extent this indifference inflames Calan's derision and how this fact remains determining for the direction of the scene, we can see in the field of the word, the rich web of associations of symbolic language-formulas, and in the fact that especially Ham, who is described as anything but sensitive, asks for the one who had so drastically mutilated the bleeding man in the forest (p. 347). The irony of the scene augments into the grotesque when Noah tells the beggar (God), in simply overriding the question, about Ham's children, a technique in which Noah proves to be an unsurpassed master during the play.

The *"teure Wasser"* and *"Blut"* are now set into relationships by Calan. He coins them as formulas in the scene: *"Weisst du, dass das Wasser teuer geworden ist, du Schmutzfink? Für jeden Tropfen, den er [Noah] an dich verschwendet, beten die beiden blutigen Hände, dass er wiedererstattet werde . . ."* (p. 347). Calan condemns God because of the waste of the *"teuren Wassers"* that is brought into connection with the *"blutigen Händen"* which are exhibited as a reproach. The bloody deed committed by Calan directs itself in this formula against God: the *"blutigen Hände"* pray for *"Wasser"* which Noah wastes for the beggar. The *"blutenden Hände"* stand as

synecdoche or better as *pars pro toto* for the herder who sighs and
screams for water. The formula *"Blut-Wasser"* is taken by the beggar (God) and its meaning reversed: *"Für jeden Tropfen Blut wird
ein Meer aus den Brunnen der Tiefe brechen, für jeden bangen
Hauch des klagenden Mannes wird ein Schwall aus den Schleusen
des Himmels niederschlagen"* (p. 347). The formalized character,
which is strongly coined through alliteration, shows itself also in the
verbs *"brechen"* and *"niederschlagen,"* which have less optical and
imaginative than acoustical functions, if they do not stand altogether under the formalized systematic constraint of alliteration. The
ocean which breaks *("bricht")* out of the well does not appeal
to the imagerial ability; it awakens only the strong impression of a
"Gewaltsamkeit," an action intensified into excess. The *"nieder-
schlagende Schwall"* is similar. Here it is plainly shown that the substantive with Barlach is more a sign of meaning than a sign of an
image, although it still remains in the realm of the concrete, even as
a sign of meaning. Herewith the concrete remains general; it has
formalized character.

Calan changes the blood-water formula by shortening it. The result is a contraction which ironically alludes to the flood-prophecy:
"Oho, was für eine überfliessende Erfüllung" (p. 347). God (beggar) broadens the formula in the same sense as before: *"Calan täte
gut daran, die Seufzer des Mannes* (here Calan's expression is placed
in a different context) *in Barmherzigkeit zu ersäufen."* The *"Gewalt-
tätige, Rohe"* which finds its expression in the verb, is contrasted
with subject and object. The same is the case with the final clause
which forms a kind of mental chiasmus: *"für seine Seufzer werden
die Bäuche des Himmels sich erbrechen."* (p. 347). The verb *"ersäufen"* is in strength yet surpassed by the verb *"sich erbrechen."* Both
verbs point almost onomatopoetically to the terrible occurrence of
the flood, which again is announced and that in a parallel juncture.
To these prophetic words, when they are fulfilled, Calan will later
refer and again vary the formulas. He says to the herder: *"Deine
Blutstropfen haben sich in Meere verwandelt und mir Herden und
Herrschaft ertränkt. Deine Seufzer zogen alle Wolken der Welt über
uns zusammen . . ."* (p. 369). This formula which Calan has played
into the scene is, like several such formulas in *Die Sündflut*, determined by the archetypal scheme of space. Calan's formula is yet
simple; it connects the bleeding hands with the herder who pleas for
water and can be formulated in this manner:

(a) *Für jeden Tropfen Wasser beten Hände* (later repeated).
(b) *Nach Wasser schreit der Hirte.*

The"*Hände*" are nailed on in front of the tent; the herder (his screams penetrate across) is in the grove. Points of association are "*Wasser*," "*Hände*," "*Hirte*." The formula is changed by the beggar (God):

(c) *Für jeden Tropfen Blut wird ein Meer aus den Brunnen brechen.*
(d) *Für jeden bangen Hauch wird ein Schwall aus den Schleusen des Himmels niederschlagen.*

The points of association are here "*Blut*," "*banger Hauch*," "*Meer aus Brunnen*," "*Schleusen des Himmels*." In formula (c) we have the conception of the lower realm, the "*Brunnen der Tiefe;*" in formula (d) the conception of the upper realm, the "*Schleusen des Himmels*." The same is the case in the next formula:

(e) *Die Seufzer des Mannes sollen in Barmherzigkeit ersäuft werden.*
(f) *Für Seufzer werden Bäuche des Himmels sich erbrechen.*

The scheme of the equation is broken in (e), but again (e) and (f) are contrasted. The points of association are "*Seufer*," "*Barmherzigkeit*," and "*Bäuche des Himmels*." In the formula (a), (b), (e), and (f), the respective point of departure—"*Wasser*" and "*Seufzer*" —is the same. The last variant we have in the fifth part of *Die Sündflut* (p. 369). It says:

(g) *Die Blutstropfen haben sich in Meere verwandelt (und Herden und Herrschaft ertränkt).*
(h) *Seufzer zogen alle Wolken der Welt zusammen.*

The future tense in the prophesy is replaced by the past tense of fulfillment. The points of reference "*Blutstropfen*," "*Seufzer*" and "*Meere*," "*Wolken der Welt*"—here again the contrast of below and above—are related to each other like cause and effect. The equation in the formula expresses a causal relationship. The formula itself was fulfilled and flows into the leitmotif of this scene which carries and symbolizes the action: "*die Zeit ist reif*." In the second part of *Die Sündflut* this sequence of formulas is concluded with the variants (e) and (f). Calan's next answer takes up the verb "*ersäufen*" (p. 347) and turns it into a substantive. Calan denotes it as his word and asks: "*Wie kommt mein Wort in deinen Mund?*" In fact, previously Calan said, in regard to God, when he had the hands of the herder cut off and Noah complained about the screams: *"Das Opfer ist getan, mag er sich sättigen am Schreien, denn es schreien viele, ohne dass er ihr Schreien in Gnade ersäuft"* (p. 343). Calan demands here an answer from Noah's God, an answer, which the beggar, hinting at this formulation of Calan's, later gives: *"Du tätest gut, die Seufzer des Mannes in Barmherzigkeit zu ersäufen"* (p. 347). However, the beggar (God) too had already used the verb *"ersäufen,"* which Calan cannot know. He uses it when he decides to inflict the flood upon man—*"ich will sie ausraufen und ersäufen"* (p. 336) —since he regrets the whole of creation. This verb connects as a motif, with symbolic functions, Calan's bloody deed with God's decision for the flood as it connects evil with judgment, whereby Calan turns around the relationship of cause and effect. The bloody deed is committed to prove God's indifference and impotence. Calan operates with the concept of divine *"Gnade,"* the beggar (God) with human *"Barmherzigkeit"* in which the *"Schreie,"* that is the sighs, are to be *"ersäuft."* The words, the language-signs, and formulas thereby gain a double meaning. In them is reflected the dialectical train of thought typical for Barlach. The thesis becomes antithesis, through the shifting of the aspect. Calan, who recognizes his provoking word *"Ersäufen,"* is surprised at the knowledge of the beggar. The beggar takes advantage of this surprise and connects to Calan's previous formulation. In the latter it said: *"Wenn deine Ohren nicht zu faul wären."* The first one meant: *"Meine Ohren sind nicht so faul, wie du dachtest"* (p. 347). Here remains to be added, that Calan's formula aims for the deafness of the beggar (God) against the screams of the herder, while the beggar associates it with the *"Wort vom Ersäufen"* spoken by Calan. In the background of this con- trapuntal play of formulas, however, stands the bloody deed in whose connection the specific word—*"es schreien viele, ohne dass er ihr Schreien in Gnade ersäuft"* (p. 343)—was coined by Calan in order to tempt God. The formula *"Meine Ohren sind nicht so faul, wie du dachtest"* does not only mean *"ich höre alles, was du sagst,"* but also *"ich habe das Schreien des Hirten gehört, ich weiss um die Bluttat, und ich werde sie rächen."*

The web of image, motif, and symbol in Barlach's *Die Sündflut* is extremely tight. The allusions, changes, and different associations unfold only with careful reading. To the spectator, that is the listener, these connections must remain shrouded. "Language does forge meaning into the scene,"[118] yet it is not going to be easy for the one who hears and sees the drama, to understand the subtle connections of meaning, since they are integrated into the field of language.

In the beginning of the scene, which was mentioned as an example of formality in style, stood the motifs *"blutende Hände"* and *"blutender Bettler."* These motifs or signs of meaning are followed by Calan's allusions to the *"teure Wasser."* Throughout the whole scene *"Blut"* and *"Wasser"* are constantly brought into connection with each other. This repeats itself even at the end of this scene when Ham reports: *"Der Fluss versiegt, die Tiere erliegen und die wilden Kinder mit Wolfszähnen trinken ihr Blut."* (p. 347). The *"wölfischen Kinder"* also, who have *"zerschunden"* the beggar (God), appear here again in a variant. They drink *"Blut,"* since there is no *"Wasser."* *"Blut"* becomes here *"Wasserersatz"* and later on, in a *"überfliessenden Erfüllung,"* an ocean of water will be spilled from above downward, in order to revenge the *"vergossene Blut."*

The subtle relationships that dominate the above scene, which is symptomatic for many others, make evident that Barlach's language is principally a language of meaning, a symbolic language.[119] Yet, that seems too general a definition and it merely repeats Ermatinger's conclusion[120] on a different level; "All poetry is in essence symbolic." This sentence, whose validity was first proved by Käte Hamburger, must be somewhat broadened here. Language of meaning, symbolic language, means, in Barlach, a specific language whose different particles and eidetic unities are, more than in comparable works, endowed with "guiding functions." Here especially, the abstract character is formed; the specific points of meaning, which mediate and lead the direction of the action, the "symbolic action,"[121] become sign-like formulas out of which come, in a symbolic indication, modes of feelings, the thinking of a person, and the meaning of the particular scene. The symbol-abbreviations[122] make evident in the whole work the persons, the intellectual tendencies, and the processes of an inner, noetic nature as well as those processes pertaining to the action. Heinz Schweizer[123] has observed Barlach's typical tendency "to describe actions of people . . . only rarely as real processes" but to reduce them "including their objectives, to a moveable structure of conceptions," also in Barlach's novel *Der gestohlene Mond.* Instead of the "structure of conceptions," we must here again speak of symbolic formulas, which maintain a close relationship to the intellect in their stylized imagerial quality, so that they were often taken for conceptions. Through these formulas or symbol-abbreviations Barlach dissolves reality. His intellectual objective is like that of the mystic: he would like to penetrate to the essence of things via the process of dissolving reality. This stylistic attitude can also be observed in Barlach's plastic works. Barlach himself pointed to this parallel quality in a letter to Friedrich Düsel[124]: "I obviously have no idea about my dramatic aloofness. I only know, that within me there exists the longing to capture the simple line of my plastic work and the simplicity of feeling in my wood carvings, in order to say that what I can only say in the drama." Although he doubtless threw down "blocks" into his dramas which he left "unhewn,"[125] in the analysis of the symbol the impression is dominant that he "chiselled" more, a characteristic which he only wants to concede to the novelist. He confesses in a letter on December 26, 1924: "Often I struggle for days with a single word, turn a sentence of three words endlessly in and out and often give up because I can't find a word with the necessary number of syllables. . . ." The last sentence points moreover to a certain musical relationship of Barlach toward language. Especially in *Die Sündflut* there is an impressive example for Barlach's brittle musicality. Awah brings the coming water masses almost onomatopoetically to the ear: *"Schwere schleicht auf leisen Füssen, hört ein Wort und wirft den Schwall der ewig leichten Herrlichkeit ans Herz—es spielen Wort und Welle, heben heilige Gewalten auf und nieder"* (p. 363).

The symbolic field in Barlach's *Die Sündflut* is determined by the "schism between heaven and earth"[126] and by the "struggle for and with God."[127] The main characters of the drama are God, Calan, and Noah. In their meetings and conversations, the theme develops itself: the basic metaphysical question of God. Around this center the parts are grouped. As the minor characters point to the main characters, so the subordinate symbols point to the lead or core symbols. One core symbol stands in the center of the second part of the drama—the hands of the young herder which Calan nails to a post (p. 343). With this deed Calan tries to tempt Noah's God in order to test the degree of Noah's piety, but the symbol means more[128] and it reaches into several spheres of meaning. As a symbol, it can mean raw power, tyrannical cruelty, the brutality of a violent man, or suffering creatures who are denied active compassion by Noah as well as God. The sketch which Barlach put in the first edition justifies the conjecture that this symbol alludes also to the death of Jesus Christ on the cross. The symbol is multivalent. Seen from the narrative, it expresses an absolute ethical negative, a deed which makes all guilty: Calan, Chus, Noah, but also God. In the face of this deed Noah is unable to utter anything but the plea: *"Töte ihn vollends, dass nicht sein Schreien in meinen Eingeweiden schauert"* (p. 343). Noah fears exclusively for his own body. His compassion is basically not greater than that of Calan, only that Calan, as he himself says challengingly to God, has eyes *"die Blut zu sehen nicht blendet, Ohren, in die kein Grausen eingeht, wenn blutende Kinder schreien"* (p. 323). Noah, on the other hand, covers his ears, a defensive gesture which Calan interprets correctly and at the same time uses against Noah's God who, in spite of the herder crying for water, has his feet washed and does not interfere with the gruesome occurrence. He prophesies instead a terrible revenge. Every sigh of the herder would worsen the dilemma. The continuation of this "absurd story" seems almost sarcastic when God in all his revenge has forgotten the sacrifice and lets it drown with the others in the flood. At this juncture we again encounter the question brought up by Calan, why and with what did Noah and his kin deserve to be spared from the flood?, a question which touches upon the question of good and evil.

After the failure of God and Noah, which Calan comments on ironically: *"Dann verliessest du dich auf Gott, und Gott verliess sich vielleicht auf Noah. Und über so viel Vertrauen und Verlass wurde ich zum Totschläger und Schänder"* (p. 344), the actual director of the scene, the most active person in the whole drama, seizes upon a trick: Calan lets Chus catch a *"säbelbeinigen Kobold"* and lets him put it in a sack. *"Er war es, Gott selbst hüpfte über den Weg"* (p. 344), Calan says to Noah and shakes the sack. With this deceiving scene, which does not lack a certain burlesque comedy, Barlach expresses how Noah's God, not only in conception, diminishes to a *"Alterchen, Kobold."* Calan justifiably feels himself the lord and victor: *"Noahs Gott in einem strohernen Sack, welch ein Fang, aber das sage ich dir, wenn er beisst, soll er Schläge haben."* This may have all the characteristics of reality that are in Andersen's fairy tale of the emperor's new garments, but we should not think that it is meant in this toying fashion when Calan says: *"Nun reut es mich, dass dem armen Kerl dahinten die Hände umsonst abgeschlagen sind, viel zu schade um einen solchen Gott!"* (p. 345). This God, whom Calan "symbolically" still keeps prisoner in the sack, subsequently enters upon the scene. Indirectly his entrance is connected with Calan's ironic announcement: *"Gott selbst hüpfte über den Weg."*

He does not *"hüpfen,"* however, but appears *"mit Krücken und steht flehend da"* (p. 345). In his conversation with God (beggar), Calan again points to the sack and says ambiguously: *"Beide, Noah und sein Gott konnten mich nicht hindern"* (p. 346). This ambiguity, which in the conversations creates the impression of two levels of meaning, is often encountered in *Die Sündflut*. Especially the recognition scene between God and Noah, father and son, which takes place with a lot of fuss, has this double basis. It is a recognition which scares those who recognize, since they could miss the right hour. Both parties value the recognition, God because he needs a faithful son; Noah because he wants to stay in the favor of the Lord. Yet as an answer to the sign of recognition *"Ich bin's,"* which Thomas Mann in his Joseph tetralogy has given an almost playful connotation, and which opens to greater depths here, we hear from Noah only in general places, which, however, give the impression of a real plane of everyday life. To this is added that Ahire strengthens this impression: *"Er sieht ihm ähnlich, Noah, hat sein Auge und seinen Bart, auch fast seine Stimme . . ."* (p. 349). But Noah too says to Ham: *"der alte Mann hat dich einst auf den Knien geschaukelt"* (p. 347). Not enough, God (beggar) himself connects to this real plane when he says to Noah: *"Die Kraft des Segens, den ich dir sterbend gab, sei hundertfach vergrössert"* (p. 350). Noah, on his part, seems in spite of the sign of recognition to doubt that God, whom he seemingly never has met, stands before him in the shape of the beggar, because when Awah announces to him the arrival of God, he says: . . . *"Gott sehen: Mit diesen meinen Augen? . . . Zwei Mauselöcher sollen das Bild des Höchsten beherbergen? Sie werden zerbrechen, sie werden verbrennen, sie werden erblinden"* (p. 339). Moreover he cannot decide for the time being to follow God's command to build the ark and give his possessions to Calan. He does this only after Awah's vision, which, with its intuition, seems to grasp more of God than Noah with his piety that is based only on a conception of respect and trust and could almost be called homely. This ambiguous impression cannot easily be dissolved[129] and should not be dissolved since especially this equivocation is a predominant principle in Barlach's drama, a principle that determines also the forms of symbol and language.[130] Barlach, who doubtless aims in his art for the absolute, for *"das Sein des Seins, das Unnennbare,"*[131] makes reality transparent and diffuse, so that a realm is created in which reality and transcendence are simultaneously present and "reality without realization" suddenly appears represented. All this rests on personal experience of which Barlach talks in *Ein selbsterzähltes Leben*:[132]

> *Beim Streifen durchs Fuchsholz aber fiel mir die Binde von den Augen, und ein Wesensteil des Waldes schlüpfte in einem ahnunglos gekommenen Nu durch die Lichtlöcher zu mir herein, die erste von ähnlichen Überwältigungen in dieser Zeit meines neunten bis zwölften Jahres, das Bewusstwerden eines Dinges, eines Wirklichen ohne Darstellbarkeit—oder wenn ich es hätte sagen müssen, wie das Zwinkern eines wohlbekannten Auges durch den Spalt des maigrünen Buchenblätterhimmels.*

This "immanent transcendence" of Barlach, as one could denote the simultaneousness of two opposing principles with a paradox, is also given in the case of *Die Sündflut* by the external frame, the biblical subject-matter of mythical time. Noah, when he says father, means the father period. If we stay within biblical tradition, this could be his grandfather Methuselah, who, at Noah's birth, had only reached half of his life span, or his father Lameck who also reached a "biblical" age, or God-father himself, who might often have been imagined as one of the old patriarchs themselves. Noah alludes definitely to a mythical mode. The word "father" has in this scene a real foreground but a mythical background, whereby foreground and background are, however, imagerially and linguistically overlapping.

"Father" and "son," "servant" and "Lord" in *Die Sündflut* are symbolic conceptions, which also point to the different conceptions of God. When God, in the shape of the traveler complains that mankind is not "what it should be," that it "wants what I do not want," the angels point to Noah "your servant and your child" (p. 322). God takes up this formula of "servant" and "child," which returns in the second part. After that God, nevertheless, calls him "Noah, my son" (p. 346) and before that "God's friend." (p. 325). Noah's relationship is that of an obedient son toward his stern father. Calan does not only feel sorry for Noah, since in his reverence he stands under the yoke of servility, but also for God who needs "praise and service and gratitude and servitude" (p. 323). This conception of God he leads *ad absurdum* in an image: *"Und er melkt mich wie ich die geraubten Kamele, er macht Käse aus meiner Knechtschaft, Labe aus meinem Lob, Butter aus meinem Dank . . ."* (p. 324). With this comparison he thinks to be able to deduce the claim that he may be like God. And that is what he seeks, to prove that he is as powerful as Noah's God, and to show that Noah's piety is not the right one.

He brings back to Noah the possessions believed to be lost and says: *"Noah, für Ansprüche, wie du wohl machst, bin ich so gut wie er"* (p. 331). First Calan tempts Noah with material goods and notions. In Awah's delivery, Noah's weakness, which is expressed in the playful varied "eye-formula," is clearly demonstrated. We already know from an earlier scene that Noah's "eyes remained so young" (p. 327): *"sie verfangen sich gern im frischen Geschlinge von Lieblichkeit und Leichtigkeit und Ergötzlichkeit."* Unfortunately these same eyes must see that Ahire, the married woman, is *"nicht leicht oder frisch oder ergötzlich."* As always, when Noah is concerned, he flees into the gesture of faint: he is then unable to hear and see. In this case he complains: "God, how hard is it to understand you . . ." (p. 332). Ahire, however, sees right away through Noah's thoughts concerning Awah and extorts from him that he give over to her Awah for Japhet. To the formula of the "eyes," which Noah blames for the fact that he likes to see Awah—so again it is basically God's fault and God's will—the resolute Ahire gives a clearcut meaning: *"Es sind wohl nicht nur deine armen Augen, die dieses arme Kind reich machen soll. Gib sie Japhet, Japhets Augen sind bedürftiger als deine . . ."* (p. 334).

Calan's further attempt to show his power and God's weakness is then his bloody deed. Calan says to Noah: "If he is the Lord over life and death, I do not fall short of that." (p. 343). Calan whose attributes are "power, speed, cleverness, endurance, and courage and a magnificent mind" (p. 323) signifies himself toward God as Lord— *"sonst müsste ich glauben, ich wäre das gestohlene Kind eines unbekannten Gottes, schlecht gehalten und seines Vaters unwert"* (p. 324). From Noah and his God, Calan is distinctly different: *". . . ich bin kein Mensch von deiner Sorte, bin das Kind eines grösseren Gottes als deiner—ein Gotteskind, Noah, das abgesetzt, verloren, gestohlen, übelgehalten und verwahrlost ist—aber ein Gott!"* (p. 344). Calan feels himself as a free and fearless son of an unknown God which he later calls the "one" (*"den Einen,"* pp. 366, 376, 382). Even in the downfall, Calan again and again points to the difference: *"Ich bin stärker als er* [Noah's God], *vergiss das nicht, und will sterben wie es dem Sohn ansteht, der kein Knecht seines Vaters ist."* (p. 377). Calan's free *"Sohnesschaft"* is here contrasted with the lower, servile *"Sohnesschaft"* of Noah. Calan cannot recognize an "avenging God," he "shudders at this divinity." (p. 381). Although he lies in the *"Schlamm"* he feels pity for *"seiner geringen Grösse."* Contemptuously Calan calls Noah's God at the end of the drama the *"Gott der Fluten und des Fleisches, das ist der Gott, von dem es heisst, die Welt ist winziger als Nichts, und Gott ist Alles"* (p. 383). Against this formula, which stems from Awah (p. 350) and which Noah takes up, (pp. 351, 358), Calan sets his formula antithetically: about his God should be said, *"die Welt ist gross, und Gott ist winziger als Nichts"* (p. 383). Herbert Meier[133] has seen behind these symbolic formulas the different conceptions of God: "God as pure immanence (Noah), God as the mystical body of this immanence (Awah), God as pure transcendence (Calan). . . ." At the same time they would be the deciding signs of meaning for the antipodes, "immanence and transcendence," for the contradiction "of the incarnate and excarnate God."

Awah, the primordially feeling child of nature, the "treasure out of the distance, where the earth still reaches into heavens," has a direct relationship to the numinous, which can almost be called sensual. She wants to "see," "hear" and "grasp" God: "How beautiful must God feel, perhaps I may fondle him . . ." (p. 354). Her love for God is determined by the senses. When she says God is all, in her first vision, she sees the whole world permeated with God, while Noah uses this formula in the sense that the world may be smaller than nothingness but that God may be all. With Noah the formula is shortened. His conception of God is doubtlessly the most narrow. Although he considers Awah and himself as those who have a fine feel for God (for example, p. 340), it is shown again and again that he possesses only a foolish trust and blind obedience, whereby both can be interpreted as a lack of responsibility at times. His slogan is: "Happiness, freedom, peace" (pp. 340, 344, 365, 367). He considers that a magic formula whose different parts he varies and which are taken over by Japhet when Zebid is at stake (p. 365). Calan rephrases this formula. He calls Awah "sprout of freedom, sprout of happiness" and damns "Noah's freedom and that of his servants" (p. 367). The "peace, happiness, freedom" formula meets here with the contrapuntal setting of the conceptions Lord-servant, father-son. Not only in this passage we see that the symbols stand in a mutual, close relationship. They are, above all, formed dialectically, through the argument Calan-Noah, a dialectic, that can be traced into the different parts of the drama, into the themes, conceptions, and, for that matter too, the symbols.

Already in the beginning Calan poses the age-old problem of the theodicy, which, as God suspects (p. 322), worries even the angels: *"Wenn meine Bosheit nicht aus seiner Bosheit kam, woher keimte also meine Bosheit?"* (p. 323). The leper, too, the embodiment of the suffering creature, asks: "How can a world be good if only a single person is damned in her and rots!" (p. 352). We can continue to question: What kind of God is it who lets innocent men like the herder and the leper die, but who saves especially Noah and his clan, who do not at all prove to be God-fearing. Noah's sons are neither obedient to God nor to their father. They live completely in the external world. Their main problem seems to be that each one gets the right wife. As violently as Noah expresses his opinion about the deeds of others, as loudly as he utters his dread if it concerns Calan, so cunning and double-faced he turns when it concerns the defence of his clan. There, in the face of God, Ham, Sem, and Japhet are described as "good human beings, grateful and pious and obedient," although Ham confesses bluntly: "strictly speaking we have never bothered with obedience and the fear of God" (p. 347). Japhet's passion for Zebid in which "evil" lies dormant, as God the traveler says, is cunningly justified: ". . . is it the fault of Japhet's good heart, that it longs for a godless woman?" (p. 360). His trust in God is proved pragmatic, his religious morality flexible. When things get complicated, Noah gives the responsibility to God. For him all other men cause their own fate. He says clearly: *"Betet zu Gott, so befällt euch kein Aussatz, dient ihm, so behaltet ihr eure Hände, fürchet ihn, so bleibt ihr verschont."* (p. 356). With his sons, however, God has created "an inability to live without women" (p. 360). God rightly fears that he might have little joy in Noah and his children.

But God too refuses responsibility for evil. He does not consider evil people as his work: *"Sie sind aus falschem Samen entquollen, nicht meine Kinder, nicht meine. In überfliessender Liebe ausgeströmt und als frecher Hass geboren, Bastarde, Bastarde, Bastarde!"* (p. 336). An angel explains: *"Erde ist ein schlimmer Stoff für dein Schaffen, es liegt ein Wolfssame in ihr, die Erde durchdringt den Menschen mit ihrem Wesen, sie nährt ihn mit wölfischer Milch"* (p. 335). God has thus nothing to do with evil, he is not the "creator of evil" (p. 361), a thought that Noah cannot understand because it would mean that God had no power over evil, that it transcends him, that he is a powerless God as Calan puts it. It may seem as one possible conclusion to Noah, moreover, that "if God were only good, nothing but good, God's maliciousness would not be evil, and all evil were good." (p. 361). God could not be "all" then, for where as Calan cleverly asks, would be "the evil ones?" (p. 352).

In *Die Sündflut* then we have contrasted heaven and earth, God and world, good and evil besides the old and the new time, distance and proximity. The divine and heavenly, outwardly embodied in the angels and in the human disguises of God ("traveler" and "beggar"), Barlach symbolizes with the attributes *"Licht,"*[134] *"Kraft," "Glut"* (pp. 321, 335). The angels are figures of light, they bathe *"den Erdendunst"* away *"in der Kraft des göttlichen Glühens"* (p. 353). Calan experiences God as *"Glut"* (p. 383), his glowing self, his *"glimmendes Fünkchen"* the divine in man returns to the abyss of God's *"Glut."* For the earthly, Barlach gives the *"Wölfische,"* the *"wölfischen Kinder,"* the *"Wolfsame"* which rests in the earth (p. 335). This symbol remains, however, in an abstract sphere, it shows itself likewise as formula: Noah's sons dig ditches and set traps, since *"die Wölfe und wilden Kinder überhand nehmen"* (p. 337). The beggar is attacked by *"wölfische Kinder"* (p. 345), who with *"Wolfszähnen"* drink the blood of the livestock (p. 347); they have *"tierische Gebärden"* and emit *"Wolfsgeheul"* (p. 352). This *"Zucht des Bösen"* which is in Zebid but also *"bellt"* and *"heult"* in Noah's sons, *"beisst"* against goodness (p. 361). They are obviously beings which stand between man and animal, a stage in which the wolf-seed of evil has even more effect and to which Noah's sons seem to stand closer than Calan, for example, who alludes to this state of affairs: *"Ich habe, wo mir recht ist, deiner Söhne Bastarde unten im Land bei den Wölfen gesehen, sie bellten und bissen mit Mäulern und Zähnen um sich wie alles gottlose Getier . . ."* (p. 376).

Eternal time, mythical time, which has no beginning and end, and terrestrial time whose expression is becoming, the changing state of being, all these are found in *Die Sündflut* in different stages. God is "from eternity to eternity," "all of the beginning without all of the end" comes out of the distance, out of the timely distance, to Noah. He complains: "past time has forgotten me and I have lost her, I am confused and lost" (p. 346). It is time where yet there did not exist the difference of "obligation, thinking, and wanting"[135] between God and man, when man had not yet cut off his hands (p. 346). Through the flood God would like to reinstate the conditions of the "old time," but we know that this is impossible, since the seed of the earth remains potent. The "evil time" may have fallen, the "time is fulfilled" (p. 365), the "time is ripe," as the appropriate formula, which is utilized by both Noah and Calan in order to allude to the "new time." But the return to the "good old days" will be impossible with Noah and his kin.

The elements fire, air, water, and earth which belong to the mythical realm of conception are utilized symbolically by Barlach, as we have shown. While, as a rule, poetical symbolism places the realm of fire over the human life in this world and the realm of water beneath it,[136] with Barlach the element water becomes the symbol of the cycle. Water in *Die Sündflut* comes out of the realm of the earth as well as out of the realm of heaven—it can mean grace as well as damnation. Awah mimics the movements of the waves on water with her hands (p. 363), thus underlining the symbolism of the cycle onomatopoetically with gestures: *"Ich sehe, wie es klingt, ich höre, wie es schwingt, das Ende wiegt den Anfang in den Armen."* This vision is symbolically open; the words can also refer to the new, which is embodied by Calan and also present in Awah—*"du bist zwischen ihnen allen wie ein Samenkorn, vom Wind aus den seligen Bereichen in die verfluchten Bereiche geweht"* (p. 367)—through the earlier intimate relationship with him, as well as to a movement which Calan describes thus: *"Auch ich, auch ich fahre dahin, woraus ich hervorgestürzt, auch an mir wächst Gott und wandelt sich weiter mit mir zu neuem"* (p. 383). The flooding water, approaching death embraced voluntarily, leads Calan to the complete identification with God, to a return into the heavenly sphere of *"Glut."*

Barlach without a doubt has, as Klaus Ziegler noted,[137] deepened the contrast of Noah and Calan to the metaphysically and religiously quite basic question whether the essence of the human, as the worldly existence period, was to be understood "autonomously or heteronomously, anthropocentrically or theocentrically." The theme already yields a dialectical tension which is felt in the different parts of the work. The symbols turn into variable formulas which change, through the different antithetical aspects, their "indicating function" and the direction of their "meaning." Through this change in function an additional growth in the horizon of meaning for these formulas is generated. In the counterpoint of their "meaning" lies the actual import, that which the symbols "mean." Therefore, the meaning of the symbolic formula is to be determined mostly in the appropriate relationship of associations, and that approximately, since they change from instance to instance and move, figuratively speaking, in different gradations from pole to pole. Thereby a cyclical movement is also brought about, which is linguistically articulated by Awah (p. 362) and which conforms to the movement of thought itself. It dissolves "being" into "becoming," the molded

God into a becoming one, a perfect creation into an imperfect one, and the complete and existing into the necessity for new development. Barlach illustrates this movement in the different figures of his drama, figures which are types and never portraits.[138] "He knows appearance and loves the idea, he studies the visible so that the invisible may radiate, he touches the surface in order to reduce all into a single form."[139] Next to the bipolarity of being and becoming, of being and nothingness,[140] there steps in the contrast of reality and idea, immanence and transcendence.

The focal point of *Die Sündflut* is, as in other dramas of Barlach, the metaphysical question, the question about God. Barlach answers this question with possible replies, that is, in the different conceptions of God in Noah and Calan as well as those of Awah, Sem, and the herder.[141] Barlach himself gave the following explanation of Noah and Calan in a letter to Arthur Kracke:[142] "The one gives birth to a high, the other a low interpretation of things. Calan is not a 'nihilist' for me. In the best hours, I seize, no, I am seized by the conception of the loss of individuality, the growing into the higher. I call it the happiness of conquering the self in which the complete consciousness of the I is contained and maintained." In a different passage this mystical process, which takes place in Calan at the end of the drama, is formulated by Barlach in the following manner: "Whosoever would really believe in God would have to die (?), in case he is serious and does not mask a human being in God (idolize)."[143]

Such masking of God Barlach shows in Noah's God, and again and again it is Calan's task to pull on the mask of this God. Calan is the Faustian man who is on the way and strives for understanding. No doubt he has the qualities of the "Quester Hero"[144] who extends from Gilgamesh to Hans Castorp. Calan is the seeker of paths,[145] especially a seeker of God, but also a man in revolt who would like the truth and therefore unmasks the world. In Calan's strife lies Barlach's own thought. In the Güstrow diary (June 12, 1916)[146] he wrote: "The whole longing for the spirit, the purpose of wanting and seeking God has one meaning, namely to become God yourself, to conceive God, to feel like Him, to share His sublimity, to 'view' Him and were it only for the one thing: to learn rightly the meaning of the world and being man." The cyclical movement,[147] which connects the beginning into the end and the end into the beginning, a movement which is not only experienced by Awah but especially by Calan (". . . *Gott, ein glimmendes Fünkchen, und alles entstürzt*

ihm, und alles kehrt in den Abgrund seiner Glut zurück", p. 383),
belongs to Barlach's personal experience. He formulates the process
of repulsion and attraction, of going out and returning: "I cannot
always be pregnant with God, that is God pushes me away from him.
He sprays and spurts me away from him like a cosmic sphere of gas,
flings his drops into space, and yet always attracts them and finally
tears them into himself."[148] All this belongs obviously in the realm
of mystical speculation which comes out of "strife for personal freedom of the meeting in God and the strife for development of individuality out of the experience of God."[149] With Barlach, as with
Hermann Broch, it originates in the consciousness of a religious
gap, that metaphysical remnant which cannot be resolved in reality,
and whose *mysterium* should be made available to experience
through a tremendous process of development. Therein lies an in-
soluble connection, which Max Scheler[150] has already pointed out,
namely the connection of the consciousness of world, self, and God.
The program of all mystics was formulated by Meister Eckhart:
*"Swenne ich predien, sô pflige ich ze sprechende von abegescheiden-
heit und daz der mensche lidig werde sîn selbes und aller dinge."*[151]
This condition of separation and mortification, the cleansing of his
mortal self, is experienced by Calan, when he, in the lowest grade of
his existence, bound to a leper, whose "venom" soils him, is gnawed
on by animals, and becomes a reduced being, only divine self, a small
dot, "only fire and abyss in God" (p. 383). The basic mystical question, *"Wo willst du Gott suchen? In der Tiefe über den Sternen?"* is
answered by Jakob Böhme: *"Da wirst du ihn nicht finden! Suche ihn
in deinem Herzen, im Zentro deiner Lebensgeburt!"*[152] This answer,
reduced to a romantic formula, represents the "way inside," a turn
from the external world and a withdrawal to the inner powers, into
the *"Weltinnenraum,"* into the *"unsägliche Herz,"* and is not rare
in the literature of the 20th century. Next to Ernst Barlach stand
Rainer Maria Rilke, Franz Werfel, Theodor Däubler, Hermann
Hesse, Hermann Broch, and others. Striking is the similarity in *Welt-
anschauung* between Ernst Barlach and Max Scheler, who has expressed the following thoughts in his *Stellung des Menschen im
Kosmos*:[153] "man co-creates, first of all, the 'God' who comes into
being out of the primeval abyss, as the augmenting penetration of
spirit and force." The human heart and the human self is "the only
place where God comes into being." The becoming of man and God
is also for Scheler closely related to one another and that in a way
that reminds us of Angelus Silesius in his *Sinnspruch:*[154]

Ich weiss, dass ohne mich Gott nicht ein Nun kann leben,
Werd ich zunicht, er muss vor Not den Geist aufgeben.

Calan expresses this state of affairs in this way: "*. . . auch an mir wächst Gott und wandelt sich weiter mit mir zu Neuem*" (p. 383). This mutual dependence is also experienced in the act of identification, where the I and the world melt together and become "reconciled," as Barlach says,[155] where the split of object-subject is lifted, where God and world, God and I are bound together so that "He has become I and I have become Him" (p. 383). This identification Barlach calls "*Selbstvergessen*"; the I "*saugt sich in die Wesen, ohne sein Wesen zu verlieren, die Welt in sich, sich in die Welt verwandelt.*"[156] Max Scheler talks about an "incomplete, a becoming God," who only grows with active help of the person.[157] Barlach's God, too, is eternally incomplete and must change again and again. Barlach has cut this transformation in wood as he has shown it in his dramas. In *Die Sündflut* God roams the earth as an elegant traveler, as a beggar, and then again as a traveler, complaining, furious, at odds with himself; he is a suffering incomplete God with human weaknesses. Barlach himself voices the opinion that creation has no end, and finally, creator and creation are one.[158] Calan says that God grew with him and transformed with him into something new (p. 383).

This conception of a God who transforms in the course of man's history stems from the mystic, gnostic, theosophic, and idealistic tradition. Barlach encountered it in the book *Siderische Geburt-Seraphische Wanderung vom Tode der Welt zur Taufe der Tat*[159] by Volker, a pseudonym for Erich Gutkind.[160] This work influenced the artist strongly. He writes to Moeller von den Bruck[161] on March 15, 1913: "I would like to send you a book which I have recently studied intensely, 'Volker, siderische Geburt' . . . to me the work seems in more than one way noteworthy, if not prophetically-grandiose." What Barlach shows in his dramas, Volker attempts to clarify in a theorizing pathetic language, namely: "*wie die Tat der kommenden Zeit nimmermehr darin bestehen kann, das Gehäuse der Welt für uns immer behaglicher zu machen. Nicht behagliches Wohnen, sondern Wanderung und göttliches, grenzenloses Schwingen ist unser Sinn.*"[162] Noah lives in the old realm; he remains in the good old comfortable living, while Calan is in a state of departure and wanders. The divine, boundless swinging is expressed by Awah.

In heiliger Armut werden wir die Enge unserer kleinen Person fortwerfen, um unser höheres seraphisches Selbst zu gewinnen, über dem leiblichen bloss mechanischen noch unlebendigen Ich, das nicht dem Tode unterliegt, teil hat an aller Göttlichkeit, und die stummen Tiefen erlösen wird . . .[163] *Warum ist es schwerer nach oben zu sehen als nach unten? Weil das Untere nur unser eigenes Durchlebtes ist, das wir erblicken, aber das über uns will in seiner göttlichen Fülle erlebt werden, in siderischer Geburt . . . Wir werden noch durchdringend erkennen, wie da die Welt, die uns umwölbte, unter uns liegen wird. Alles Starre schwindet, die Erscheinungen erhalten immer mehr einen fluchtartigen Charakter, alles Feste wird zum 'Schleier der Maya,' zum Schein, Phänomenon, und immer mächtiger erhebt sich die erschütternde Lehre von der Welt als Scheinwelt.*[164]

How this book must have seemed related to Barlach's own thought is made clear by these quotations. In his dramas Barlach constantly unmasks the surface-quality of the external world, the world of illusion behind which lies the essence of things which, through "small cracks . . . glows and reflects," as Sem says to Awah in *Die Sündflut.* Calan, too, wants to see behind the masks. He uncovers the illusional order of Noah's existence, the automatism of this piety, which orients itself according to the simple rule of obedience, servitude, and reward. Noah is a *"wegloser"* man, a man of *"behaglichen Wohnens,"* while Calan embodies the type of the restless *"Wegsucher."* Especially in the fifth part of *Die Sündflut,* the symbolical formula "Way" (*"Weg"*) is demonstrated in its different aspects: the *"Weg"* of the leper, of the herder, and above all the *"Weg"* of Calan. But the search for a path in Calan proves first of all to be without a way out. He asks the herder: *"Welchen Weg ziehst du, wo alle Wege ins Verderben führen?"* (p. 380). Only when Calan no longer searches for being itself, when he sacrifices his I to the world, he comes to the goal of his search, to the identification of I and world, of I and God.[165] Through the diminution of the I to the enlargement of the I; thus Calan's last phase could be summarized. The "seeker" turns into a "becoming one," being in the phase of death transforms into rebirth or becoming. In the *Armen Vetter* Iver says shortly before his death: ". . . God, thank you God that you have cast off everything from me. All surges upward now and beyond, in spite of oneself—beyond oneself." Instead of "beyond oneself," one could also with Volker, in the case of Barlach, speak of the "sidereal birth."

The poetical as well as the plastic work of Ernst Barlach shows a tendency to stylization, to form and formula. In *Die Sündflut* it can, by means of the stratification in the different scenes, easily be depicted that the symbolic formulas undergo a steady transformation and point thus to a cyclical, dialectical movement of thought. The symbolic formula expresses the basic dramatic potential between I and world, I and God, idea and reality, the external and internal world, the world of illusion and being. In the symbol proper the formula points to the image and the image to the abstract idea. The point of reference of the core-symbols is a metaphysical idea which, through the symbol attains concrete form. The *concretum,* on the other hand, refers simultaneously to the metaphysical idea. Through this reciprocal allusion originates a peculiar mixture of abstraction and imagery so typical for Barlach. His style—in language and symbol—is still determined by the act of idealizing, which reduces the reality character of the world in order to lift the essence out of the concrete visible world. The reduction concerns here only the world of chance and accidents, the world of illusion. Reality is made transcendent beyond its limits to a new reality which supercedes the old one and which lifts it at the same time onto a spiritual plane of being. Ernst Barlach knew that his work gives more than philosophical and conceptually bound knowledge. Although he had strong ties to the word, he always preferred silence to the wordy chatter of Noah. On August 18, 1932, he wrote to pastor Zimmermann: "You see, we want to 'know' and long for the word, but the word is inadequate, at the most a crutch for those who are satisfied with limping. And yet the word contains something that penetrates the inner self whence it comes forth from purity itself, from the absolute truth." In the fragment *Dichterglaube,*[166] which also contains his gnostic confession of the "eternally unknown God,"[167] we read: *"Die Wahrheiten vergehen, die Wahrheit selbst bleibt, die wortlose . . ."* ("Truths perish, truth itself remains, the wordless one . . .")

[*Translated from the German by Manfred Keune*]

Notes

1. Friedrich Theodor Vischer, *Kritische Gänge* (2nd ed.; Munich: Meyer and Jesson, 1922), IV, p. 420.
2. Karl Vossler, *Die Romanische Welt* (Munich: R. Piper & Co., 1965), p. 119.
3. *Ibid.,* p. 120.
4. Georg Wilhelm Friedrich Hegel, *Ästhetik* (Frankfurt a.M.: Europäische Verlagsanstalt Gmbh, 1955), I, p. 311.

5. Vischer, *op. cit.*, p. 364.
6. *Ibid.*, p. 421.
7. *Ibid.*, pp. 423-54.
8. *Ibid.*, p. 453.
9. Hegel, *op. cit.*, p. 312 f.
10. Emil Ermatinger, *Das dichterische Kunstwerk—Grundbegriffe der Urteils-bildung in der Literaturgeschichte* (2nd ed.; Leipzig-Berlin: Verlag V.B.G. Teubner, 1923). For our purposes here, see especially the chapter "Das Symbolische," p. 286-311.
11. *Ibid.*, p. 287.
12. *Ibid.*, p. 287.
13. Vischer, *op. cit.*, p. 423.
14. Hegel, *op. cit.*, p. 312.
15. *Ibid.*, p. 299.
16. Elisabeth Frenzel, *Stoff-, Motiv- und Symbolforschung* (Stuttgart: J. B. Metzlersche Verlagsbuchhandlung, 1963), p. 34.
17. Käte Hamburger, *Die Logik der Dichtung* (Stuttgart: Ernst Klett Verlag, 1957).
18. Ernst Cassirer, *Wesen und Wirkung des Symbolbegriffs* (Oxford: Bruno Cassirer, 31 Portland Road; Reprographic reprint Darmstadt, 1956), p. 175.
19. ⸻ *Philosophie der Symbolischen Formen*, 3 vols; (Berlin: Bruno Cassirer, 1923). The triple division is named here, language, mythical thinking and phenomenology of understanding. See also Ernst Cassirer, *"Wesen und Wirkung des Symbolbegriffs," op. cit.*, pp. 24, 151.
20. ⸻ *Wesen und Wirkung des Symbolbegriffs, op. cit.*, p. 48.
21. *Ibid.*, p. 50.
22. *Ibid.*, p. 145.
23. *Ibid.*, p. 147.
24. *Ibid.*, p. 178.
25. *Ibid.*, p. 178ff.
26. This phase touches in many aspects upon the "Symbolik der Einfühlung."
27. Platon, "Politeia," 596 d; compare here also Meyer H. Abrams, *The Mirror and the Lamp: Romantic Theory and the Critical Tradition* (New York: The Norton Library, W. W. Norton and Company, Inc., 1958), p. 30.
28. Cassirer, *op. cit.*, p. 182. Cassirer agrees here with Goethe's differentiation of "simple imitation of nature," "manner" and "style."
29. Susanne Langer, *Feeling and Form: A Theory of Art* (New York, 1953). The theory was developed from the book *Philosophy in a new Key: A Study in the Symbolism of Reason, Rite and Art* (14th ed.; New York and Toronto: The New American Library, 1st ed., 1942), see especially the chapter "The Fabric of Meaning," pp. 224-47.
30. Käte Hamburger, *op. cit.*, p. 245 ff.
31. *Ibid.*, p. 246.
32. *Ibid.*, p. 250.
33. *Ibid.*, p. 246.
34. *Ibid.*, p. 249.
35. For example, Wilhelm Emrich, "Symbolinterpretation und Mythenforschung," *Euphorion 47* (1953), p. 38-67; William York Tindall, *The Literary Symbol* (4th printing; Bloomington: Indiana University Press, 1965); Harry Levin, *Symbolism and Fiction* (Charlottesville, Virginia, 1956).
36. Wilhelm Emrich, *Die Symbolik von Faust II. Sinn und Vorformen* (2nd ed.; Bonn: Athenäum Verlag, 1957).
37. An approach toward such a proof is in my essay "Die 'Todeserkenntnis' in Hermann Brochs *Tod des Vergil*" (Munich: Uni-Druck, 1961), pp. 124-45.
38. F. Th. Vischer, p. 431.

39. Compare the appropriate chapter in Karl Jaspers, *Der philosophische Glaube angesichts der Offenbarung* (Munich: R. Piper & Co. Verlag, 1964).
40. Compare Joachim Seyppel, "Mystik als Grenzphänomen und Existenzial," *Deutsche Vierteljahresschrift für Literaturwissenschaft und Geistesgeschichte*, 35. Jahrgang, part 2 (1961), especially p. 178.
41. Northrop Frye, *Anatomy of Criticism* (New York, 1966), p. 16.
42. *Ibid.*, p. 16.
43. *Ibid.*, pp. 73-132.
44. *Ibid.*, p. 76.
45. Unfortunately Frye does not seem to know Käte Hamburger's book.
46. Frye, *op. cit.*, p. 81.
47. *Ibid.*, p. 79.
48. *Ibid.*
49. *Ibid.*
50. *Ibid.*, p. 82.
51. *Ibid.*, p. 83.
52. Goethe, *Sämtliche Werke, Jubiläumsausgabe*, XXXV, p. 325 f.; compare also Frenzel, *op. cit.*, p. 33 f. Frequently we encounter conceptions which were already mentioned by Hegel (*"Ästhetik,"* p. 386 f.) and Vischer *Kritische Gänge*, p. 453) namely the allegorical image as personification.
53. Gerhard Lietz (*Das Symbolische in der Dichtung Barlachs*, Dissertation, Marburg, 1934), decides on conceptions like "synthetic" and "mythical symbol" which according to him, illustrate an idea and, to the contrary, connect "allegory" and "typification" with the "ideal conception." Joachim Seyppel (*op. cit.*, p. 174) distinguishes between modes of representation of "symbolism," "allegory," "realism," "emblem." We need not emphasize how misleading such distinctions are.
54. Ermatinger, *op. cit.*, p. 290.
55. Johan Huizinga, *Herbst des Mittelalters* (9th ed.; Stuttgart: Alfred Kröner Verlag, 1965), p. 290.
56. Vossler, *op. cit.*, p. 123.
57. Frye, *op. cit.*, p. 59.
58. *Ibid.*, p. 105.
59. *Ibid.*, p. 113.
60. *Ibid.*, p. 116.
61. *Ibid.*, p. 118.
62. *Ibid.*, p. 123.
63. *Ibid.*, p. 119.
64. *Ibid.*, p. 121.
65. Compare Northrop Frye's collection of essays *Fables of Identity. Studies in Poetic Mythology* (New York-Burlingame: Harcourt, Brace and World, Inc., 1963).
66. Frye, *Anatomy of Criticism*, op. cit., p. 71.
67. *Ibid.*, p. 14.
68. *Ibid.*
69. Ludwig Wittgenstein, *Tractatus Logico-philosophicus* (Edition Suhrkamp; Frankfurt, 1963), No. 4.01 (p. 33).
70. *Ibid.*, Nr. 4021 (p. 35).
71. René Wellek, *Concepts of Criticism* (New Haven-London: Yale University Press, 1963), p. 21 f.
72. Works about light, color, and mirror symbolism; see also Elisabeth Frenzel, *op. cit.*, p. 77 f.
73. Werner Kohlschmidt has shown the analogous phenomena, which is of different origin and which is not proven decisively, in Eichendorff, in his essay "Die symbolische Formelhaftigkeit von Eichendorffs Prosastil," in:

W. K., *Form und Innerlichkeit* (Bern: A. Francke Verlag, 1955), pp. 177-209.

74. Hermann Broch, *Die unbekannte Grösse*, ed. Ernst Schönwiese (Zürich, 1961), p. 187.

75. *Ibid.*

76. Compare Broch, *op. cit.*, p. 188.

77. Hermann Broch, "Erkennen und Handeln," *Essays* (Zürich, 1955), II, p. 173.

78. *Ibid.*

79. *Ibid.*, p. 166.

80. Adolf Portmann's distinction between primary and secondary experience of the world would also belong here, especially as he shows it in the volume *Welterleben und Weltwissen* (Munich: R. Piper and Co., 1965).

81. Broch, *Erkennen und Handeln*, p. 172.

82. F. Th. Vischer already pointed to this formation of the symbol (*op. cit.*, p. 448).

83. Compare F. Th. Vischer, *op. cit.*, p. 450 f.

84. Compare N. Frye, *op. cit.*, p. 83.

85. p. 93.

86. Frye, *op. cit.*, p. 88.

87. The manuscript was finished March 28, 1923, and printed in the spring of 1924. The drama in 5 parts appeared in 1924 in the Paul Cassirer Verlag. Barlach's work which is quoted here is the 3 volume edition from the R. Piper and Co. Verlag, Munich, edited by Friedrich Dross: *Die Dramen* (Munich, 1956, 1959); *Die Prosa*, vol. I (Munich, 1958); *Die Prosa* (Munich, 1959), vol. II. The letters of Ernst Barlach, which will shortly appear in their totality in a large edition by Friedrich Dross in the R. Piper and Co. Verlag, I have quoted out of the following editions: Barlach, *Leben und Werk in seinen Briefen*, ed. by Friedrich Dross, (Munich, 1952); Barlach, *Aus seinen Briefen* 1–10. thousand, (Munich, 1947), 33-37. thousand (Munich, 1962). Precise date and name of recipient of letters is marked within the text.

88. An aspect which was unfortunately neglected by Käte Hamburger.

89. Friedrich Schult, *Barlach im Gespräch* (Leipzig, 1948), p. 17.

90. Herbert Meier, *Der verborgene Gott—Studien zu den Dramen Ernst Barlachs* (Nürnberg: Glock and Lutz, 1963), p. 91.

91. Also Walter Muschg, *Die Zerstörung der deutschen Literatur* (3rd ed.; Bern: Francke Verlag, 1958), p. 243, has pointed to that.

92. *Ibid.*

93. *Ibid.*, p. 246.

94. *Ibid.*, p. 240.

95. *Ibid.*, p. 239.

96. Heinz Schweizer, *Ernst Barlachs Roman 'Der gestohlene Mond'* (Bern: Francke Verlag, 1959), (Basler Studien zur Deutschen Sprache und Literatur, Heft 22), p. 126; Willi Flemming, *Ernst Barlach—Wesen und Werk* (Bern: Francke Verlag, 1958), p. 166, however, says: "attention should be paid to the lack of allegory in Barlach . . ."

97. Horst Wagner, "Barlach—*Die Sündflut*," In: *Das Deutsche Drama vom Barock bis zur Gegenwart*, ed. Benno von Wiese (Düsseldorf: August Bagel Verlag, 1958), p. 352 f; compare also J. W. McFarlane "Plasticity in Language: Some Notes on the Prose Style of Ernst Barlach," in: *The Modern Language Review* (October, 1954), XLIV, No. 4, pp. 451-60, who says on p. 457: ". . . Barlach reveals a highly developed sense for pose and gesture as outer signs of inner emotion."

98. Helmut Krapp, "Der allegorische Dialog," in: *Akzente*, 1. Jahrgang (1954), p. 213.

99. *Ibid.*, p. 218.
100. Hans Schwerte ("Über Barlach's Sprache," in: *Akzente*, 1. Jahrgang, 1954) sets the plays on words in the dramatic connection. We read on p. 223: "Barlachs Dramen sind im Grunde nur Handlungsentfaltungen des Wort-Spieles zwischen dessen eigenen doppelten oder gar zwiespaltigen Aussagemöglichkeiten."
101. Barlach's letter to Reinhard Piper on November 5, 1912.
102. Barlach's letter to Reinhard Piper on December 28, 1911.
103. Barlach in a letter to Pastor Schwartzkopff on December 3, 1932. On October 18, 1932 Barlach writes to Pastor Zimmermann: Man "longs for the word, but the word is insufficient, at best a bridge for those who are satisfied limping. And yet, there is something in the word which penetrates the innermost where it comes from the purest of absolute truth."
104. The essay *Johannes Schefflers 'Cherubinischer Wandersmann': Mystik und Dichtung* (Giessen: Wilhelm Schmitz Verlag, 1956), pp. 34-49, by Horst Althaus contains a careful analysis of "Sprachmittel und Sprachwerdung."
105. Compare for the mystic vocabulary especially the basic work of Josef Quint, "Mystik und Sprache," in: *Deutsche Vierteljahresschrift für Literaturwissenschaft und Geistesgeschichte*, 27. Jahrgang, Heft 1 (1953), pp. 48-76.
106. *Ibid.*, p. 75 f.
107. *Ibid.*, p. 72.
108. Compare my essay about Broch's "Todeserkenntnis," *op. cit.*, p. 89.
109. Huizinga, *op. cit.*, p. 383.
110. *Ibid.*, p. 315.
111. *Eckhart, Tauler, Seuse—Ein Textbuch aus der altdeutschen Mystik*, ed. by Hermann Kunisch (Hamburg: Rowohlts Klassiker 31, 1958), p. 17.
112. Karl Jaspers, *Psychologie der Weltanschauungen* (4th ed.; Berlin-Göttingen-Heidelberg: Springer Verlag, 1954), pp. 21, 85.
113. In the last act of *Die Sündflut*.
114. Helmut Krapp, *op. cit.*, p. 212; compare also Walter Muschg, *op. cit.*, pp. 241, 245, 247, and his student Heinz Schweizer, *op. cit.*, p. 124 ff.
115. Concerning "symbols": Willi Fleming, *op. cit.*, p. 166; Gerhard Lietz, *op. cit.*; Horst Wagner, *op. cit.*; Walter Muschg and Heinz Schweizer, *op. cit.*; Otto Mann, "Ernst Barlach", in: *Expressionismus*, ed. Hermann Friedmann and Otto Mann (Heidelberg: Wolfgang Rothe Verlag, 1956).
116. Helmut Krapp (*op. cit.*, p. 217) formulates it this way: "Die Alliteration taktiert die Sätze, und wie sie selbst zur Ausdrucksgebärde wird, darin einzelne Wörter nur um ihretwillen noch gesprochen sind . . . verrät sie etwas von der doktrinären Haltung: als fertig geprägte stabreimende Formeln hämmert sich der Satz ins Gedächtnis."
117. We are talking about the second part, 2nd scene, p. 347 ff.
118. Helmut Krapp, *op. cit.*, p. 214.
119. Helmut Krapp (*op. cit.*, p. 213), speaks too about "style of pure meaning."
120. Ermatinger, *op. cit.*, p. 286.
121. Here quite in the sense of Kenneth Burke, *Dichtung als symbolische Handlung* (Edition Suhrkamp 153; Frankfurt, 1966), pp. 17, 125.
122. There seems to be little sense to speak about "Surrogat—Symbole," as, for example, in Horst Wagner, *op. cit.*, p. 350 ff.
123. Heinz Schweizer, *op. cit.*, p. 121.
124. Güstrow, August 13, 1921.
125. To Karl Barlach, December 26, 1924.
126. Gerhard Lietz, *op. cit.*, p. 42.
127. *Ibid.*
128. It is interesting in this connection, that the first edition by Paul Cassirer in Berlin in 1924, has a page with Barlach's sketch of these hands. This proves

at least that this bloody deed stood for Barlach himself in the focal point of the drama.

129. It is doubtful whether Noah's belief in God is really so "unerschütterlich und grenzenlos" as Helmut Dohle (*Das Problem Barlach—Probleme, Charaktere seiner Dramen*, Köln: Verlag Christoph Czwiklitzer, 1957) seems to think on page 65. In contrast to Willi Fleming (*op. cit.*, p. 222) who thinks that Noah recognizes God in the beggar (p. 66). That this scene is especially determined by this double meaning neither critic seems to have noticed. Werner Hollmann ("Das religiöse Erlebnis bei Ernst Barlach", in: *Monatshefte für deutschen Unterricht, deutsche Sprache und Literatur*, January, 1950, XLII, No. 1, p. 4) thinks that Noah, busy with his hostly duties, does not recognize God.

130. Willi Fleming (*op. cit.*, p. 173) speaks of a seeming "jumping from one 'layer' into the next, from the concrete objectivity, reality, into abstractness."

131. Ernst Barlach, *Die Prosa*, II, *op. cit.*, p. 408.

132. ——— *Ibid.*, I, *op. cit.*, p. 21.

133. Herbert Meier, *op. cit.*, p. 104 f.

134. Compare Northrop Frye, *op. cit.*, p. 145.

135. Herbert Meier, *op. cit.*, p. 92.

136. Northrop Frye, *op. cit.*, p. 145.

137. Klaus Ziegler, "Das Drama des Expressionismus", in: *Der Deutschunterricht*, Jg. 5, Heft 5 (1953), p. 62.

138. Compare Walter Jens, *Zueignungen* (Munich: R. Piper & Co. Verlag, 1962), p. 52.

139. *Ibid.*

140. Here too belong the opposites of "Seins-Ich" and "Schein-Ich" or "Spiegel-Ich," which Franz Werfel uses in his magic trilogy *Spiegelmensch;* see Horst Wagner, *op. cit.*, p. 349.

141. Herbert Meier (*op. cit.*, p. 105) establishes here the following certainly contestable set-up: "Gott als reine Immanenz (Noah), Gott als mystischer Leib dieser Immanenz (Awah), Gott als Diaphanie durch die Immanenz (Sem), Gott als reine Transzendenz (Calan) und Gott als der Unbegreifliche, Verborgene (Hirte). Gott als Immanenz (mystisch und diaphan) ist Inkarnation, Gott als Transzendenz absolute Exkarnation."

142. Of February 4, 1930.

143. Güstrow diary, 28, II (1916) in: *Die Prosa*, II, *op. cit.*, p. 314.

144. Compare Thomas Mann, "Einführung in den 'Zauberberg,'" in: *Gesammelte Werke in zwölf Bänden* (Frankfurt/Main: S. Fischer Verlag, 1960), XI, p. 592 f.

145. Compare Klaus Lazarowicz, "Nachwort," in *Die Dramen, op. cit.*, p. 592.

146. Barlach, *Die Prosa*, II, *op. cit.*, p. 321.

147. Erich Franzen ("Ernst Barlach als dramatischer Dichter", in: *Merkur*, Jahrgang, 1952, VI, Heft 7, p. 625) speaks of a "mystisch kreisenden Bewegung auf 'ein einziges Eins' hin," a movement which returns "durch allen fremden Schein des Lebens an ihren Ursprung."

148. Barlach (Güstrow diary, June 12, 1916), *Die Prosa*, II, *op. cit.*, p. 321 f.

149. Friedrich-Wilhelm Wentzlaff-Eggebert, *Deutsche Mystik zwischen Mittelalter und Neuzeit* [2d ed.; Tübingen: J. C. B. Mohr (Paul Siebeck), 1947], p. 249.

150. Max Scheler, *Die Stellung des Menschen im Kosmos* (Munich: Nymphenburger Verlagshandlung, 1949), p. 88.

151. Franz Pfeiffer, *Deutsche Mystiker des 14. Jahrhunderts*, vol. II (Leipzig, 1857). XXII, sermon, p. 24 f., p. 91.

152. Jakob Boehme, *Glaube und Tat*, ed. by E. H. Pältz (Berlin: Union Verlag, 1947), p. 185.

153. Max Scheler, *op. cit.*, p. 90 f.
154. Or other "Sinnsprüche" as, for example: "In Gott wird nichts erkannt: er ist ein einig Ein/ Was man in ihm erkennt, das muss man selber sein."
155. Letter to Hans Barlach, June, 1921: "The eternal schism of I and world must somehow be lifted or reconciled. We must sacrifice our I to the world without losing ourselves, a great undertaking."
156. Ernst Barlach in a letter of July 31, 1923, to Karl Barlach.
157. Max Scheler, *op. cit.*, p. 91.
158. Letter to Karl Barlach of May 20, 1916.
159. Volker, *Siderische Geburt. Seraphische Wanderung vom Tode der Welt zur Taufe der Tat* (2nd ed.; Berlin: Verlag Karl Schnabel, 1914).
160. This information I owe to the editor of the works of Ernst Barlach, Dr. Friedrich Dross.
161. A copy of this letter was sent to me by Dr. Friedrich Dross.
162. Volker, *op. cit.*, p. 7.
163. *Ibid.*, p. 8.
164. *Ibid.*, p. 14.
165. See also Barlach's letter to Hans Barlach, June, 1921.
166. Barlach, *Die Prosa*, vol. II, *op. cit.*, p. 408.
167. "The gnostic God is the unknown God"; see Gilles Quispel, *Gnosis als Weltreligion* (Zürich: Origo Verlag, 1951), p. 33.

Peter Uwe Hohendahl

THE TEXT AS CIPHER:
ERNST JÜNGER'S NOVEL,
ON THE MARBLE CLIFFS

A book is created to be read. Still, one can imagine books which never find their reader, like the work of a Chinese wise man printed in ideograms standing in a Western library. Such a work persists unredeemed, a state that at the same time bears mysterious, hieroglyphic traits.

Ernst Jünger

SHORTLY BEFORE THE OUTBREAK OF THE SECOND WORLD WAR, ERNST Jünger, one of the few German writers of stature who had not left his homeland after the National Socialist party seized power, completed a novel to which he gave the mysterious title, *On the Marble Cliffs*. Even though there was not a word in this work about the political conditions in Germany, many of its readers formed the opinion that the novel was to be understood in a political way. The world presented in the novel positively cried out for comparison with the contemporary circumstances in Germany. German literary critics could not risk openly exposing this possible interpretation, but it was so interpreted in Switzerland where the National Socialist censors could not interfere. The critics appreciated the novel as a cloaked critique of the fascist regime. Jünger, it was said, had selected the form of a story about the Land of Anywhere in order to describe conditions which could not be called by their true names.[1] Without a doubt, this work fulfilled a political function during the dark years of the war as National Socialist terror became more depraved. By defining his own position, Jünger helped others, especially those of the young German intelligentsia, who had at first hoped for so much from the Third Reich.[2] After the war, when German literature was being searched for some token of intellectual resistance, *On the Marble Cliffs* was introduced to the world as a document of the literary opposition.

The author has not rejected this interpretation entirely, but he has made certain prudent corrections to this widely-held view. Above all, he did not want the novel understood as a piece of tendentious political writing. Jünger intended something more general, for which the contemporary conditions in Germany supplied only the material. The following sentences from his diary (April 2, 1946) provide a first insight into the productive procedure of this writing: "At the outbreak of war, *On the Marble Cliffs* appeared, a book which has one thing in common with the *Arbeiter*: the events in Germany fitted into its frame but the book was not especially shaped to fit them. Thus, I do not like to be considered a tendentious writer. Several could have and can wear the shoe. That it would also happen to us was more than probable, and that I had received stimuli as a witness here, could not be denied" (vol. 3, p. 639).

The readers understood the novel as a *roman à clef*. They looked behind the characters for their originals in empirical reality. Jünger, however, understood his procedure the other way around. He used the topical events as material, transposing them to a higher level in the process of literary composition. He did allow certain parallels between the empirical and the fictitious reality to remain, but he wanted to insure that there would be no translation of the fictitious world back to the everyday world, for this would have cancelled out the artistic condensation and generalization to which he aspired. It is still remarkable that Jünger did not simply reject the allegorical interpretation (allegorein: to set something for something else) but refused only to grant its reductive form which would have committed the plot unambiguously to particular events. Ambiguity is important to him and this is quite reconcilable with the allegorical process, as will be shown.

If one reviews the plot of the novel, the contemporary interpretation will immediately become intelligible. Whoever read the book in Europe in 1940 could not mistake the parallels between the world represented and political reality. Jünger described the slow deterioration and the rapid destruction of the social order in an invented country to which he gave the name Marina. This country, where culture and morality have prevailed for centuries, is invaded by a bar-

baric force. These are led by the Chief Ranger, a figure in whom are combined lust for power, cunning, joviality, and a malicious conviviality. His name fits the dark place from which the character comes. He originally lived in the dim woods of the Marina. The sinister retinue of the Chief Ranger is similarly composed of foresters and hunters. The Marina can be seized by this tyrant, because the inner order of the country has been disrupted for several years, more precisely since the war of Alta Plana. The Chief Ranger has only to encourage the strife of contending parties and then, at the right moment, subjugate the weakened country. The military defense troops offer him no resistance because Biedenhorn, their leader, remains neutral and does not take sides until the inner battle has been decided in favor of the Chief Ranger. In this unsafe arena live two brothers (it remains obscure whether the word "brothers" is to be understood as an expression of family relationship or of membership in an order). They have cut all political and social ties after the war of Alta Plana, in which they took an active part, and have withdrawn to their Rue-Garden hermitage at the edge of the Marina to devote themselves exclusively to their scientific studies. They are botanists and gardeners; their work involves taking an inventory of the flora in the Marina and the adjacent Campagna. Although they regret the decline of the old culture, they remain mere observers of the party struggles, renouncing direct political action. Only once, in order to rescue friends, does one of them come forth to do battle against the Chief Ranger. But this advance also remains a vain effort which does nothing to change the situation. Only flight finally saves the brothers from persecution and death. With the free tribes of Alta Plana, once their enemies, they find succor and protection.

The reader only needed to replace Marina with Germany and the Chief Ranger with Hitler and a recognizable picture of the situation emerged: the inner insecurity of the Weimar Republic after the First World War, the increasing radicalness of political struggle, the undermining of political institutions, the new interpretation of justice. The technique of the Chief Ranger reflects something of the tactics of Hitler and his leaders: strength to resist was crippled by an ostensible legality. Even in detail there was agreement. The brothers belong to a secret political group, the Mauretania, for a time after the defeat. There the members speculate nihilistically on the ruin of the old order and anticipate total reorganization. In these circles the brothers first make the acquaintance of the Chief Ranger, who must be pleased at the radicalness of the Mauretania, although the irrational character of his power instinct distinguishes him in every other respect from the pure intellectual type of Mauretanian. The better-informed readers in Germany knew that in the Twenties Ernst Jünger had been a member of nationalistic, revolutionary circles which had cultivated contact with Hitler and his party. In the history of ideologies they belonged to the same wing. Soon after securing power, Hitler had, nevertheless, persecuted these groups just as relentlessly as the old opponents of Fascism. So it seemed obvious to read the battle between the Mauretanians and the Chief Ranger as a cipher for historical power struggles as well. This interpretation was encouraged even more by the form of the narration. Since Jünger employed one of the two brothers as narrator, the impression is given that the narrating first-person is identical with the author.

If the true contents of the novel were merely identical with its unmistakable political tendency, then On the Marble Cliffs would be regarded today only as an historical document. As a matter of fact, one can foresee that the contemporary background with which today's readers might still be somewhat familiar, will have to be made accessible in the future by a commentary. Even today the critic finds himself in a changed situation. Walter Benjamin described the process of historical clarification in this way: "According to all indications, factual contents and true contents, which are united when the work is new, move apart the longer the work exists, for the latter always takes cover when the former dominates. Hence, it becomes more and more a prerequisite for every later critic that what is conspicuous and consternating, that is, the factual contents, be interpreted."[3] Thus, the first task of the critic is to state that which Benjamin calls the factual contents by means of a commentary. Such a commentary, which measures the various dimensions of the object, has not yet been written in spite of several attempts with this novel. Probably the temptation to treat this novel as a political confession is mainly to blame for that, or else critics had been led astray when they tried to integrate the thoughts couched in the book into the author's general view of the world, without taking cognizance of formal characteristics.

The critics took Jünger's treatment, that is, alienations of the plot, for a technique born of necessity, and concluded that it therefore did not demand a separate investigation. It seemed more important to look behind the phenomena. This was, of course, also the author's view, and it was for this very reason that he attached such great importance to the form of the presentation. It is easy to prove that we are not dealing with a realistic novel in the traditional sense. Place and time of the action remain uncertain. Again and again allusions to familiar reality do betray themselves, but out of all these details there emerges no complete picture. Sometimes the action seems to take place in this century (there are airplanes and cars), again it seems to be during the time of feudalism (the role of the nobility, the kind of weapons, and the type of warfare). Descriptions of landscape remind one of the Lake of Constance or of Switzerland, but also of the Mediterranean basin.[4] Similar difficulties are encountered in placing the persons: the Chief Ranger can stand as a cipher for Hitler, but does this figure not refer just as much to Stalin or to any other power politician? When Jünger amalgamates the disparate and dispersed in this way, he creates an abstract world in which the laws of reality so familiar to us have no force. The reader is never told why the Chief Ranger wants to conquer the Marina. His quality as a tyrant who desires only what is evil is presupposed. The reader with a knowledge of psychology will repeatedly be struck by incidents for which the novelist gives no explanation. To name only a conspicuous example: The narrator has a natural son, Erio, who lives with him in the Rue-Garden Hermitage. When the two brothers flee, they leave Erio and the old cook Lampusa behind, and the author does not say a word about this rather odd fatherly conduct. To accuse Jünger of having suffered an artistic lapse would be judging him according to norms to which he did not want to subject himself. Seeing that a realistic motivation has not been given will only serve as an incentive to search for the design which underlies this novel.

Klaus Mann's novel, *Mephisto*, which appeared a few years before the *Marble Cliffs*, offers itself for comparison. At first glance both the subject and the method appear to be related. Klaus Mann wanted to describe the corruption of the German intelligentsia who had known so well how to accommodate themselves to the altered situation. The characters appearing in this novel represent the old and the new society. Klaus Mann tried to comprehend the times and the milieu by means of character types. In this case, too, the initiated knew that the most important characters were key figures. But here there is incomparably less alienation from empirical reality. Klaus Mann portrayed people known to him. The general meaning of events was supposed to be evident in their particular traits. The general thing, however, which Klaus Mann had in mind was the concrete political changeover of 1933. When Jünger, on the other hand, created the type of the Chief Ranger out of Hitler, Göring, Stalin, and other politicians, his goal lay beyond the concrete historical situation. His abstraction and his stylization were more radical.

The narrative technique confirms this. The novel resembles a Byzantine mosaic. The chronological order remains unclear even after a close reading, whereas the spatial structure is significantly prominent in the divisions of the work. Each of the thirty chapters could be subsumed under a spatial designation, whereas only in the second half of the novel could time be delimited with any degree of precision. There, in telling of the rescue operation, the narrator proceeds chronologically[5] and the limits of the chapters coincide with natural divisions of time. Nevertheless, it cannot be overlooked that even in this part Jünger gives priority to the spatial order. The spatial disposition conceals a strict thematic structure. This peculiarity of composition is even more strikingly prominent in the first part. The structure of a chapter and the composition of chapters is governed not by chronological continuity but by coherence in meaning. Each chapter gives a unit of meaning that is articulated logically by paragraphs. It is expected of the reader that he will find many passages obscure at first.[6] The story pretends to presuppose a reading public which is already familiar with the basic elements of the plot before the events are presented. Hence, the narrator moves, as it were, from the inner to the outer. To begin with, he acquaints the reader with himself and Brother Otho, with their living habits, and particularly with their participation in the great festivals of the country. The first chapter treats the great harvest festival and the second tells of the Carnival in Spring. That is followed by the description of the Hermitage and its inhabitants (third chapter). There the lance-head vipers are introduced to the reader. But Erio and his grandmother, Lampusa, are only touched in passing. Their introduction, that is, the explanation of their origin, their characteristics, and their tasks in the household are reserved for the fifth chapter. The fourth chapter describes the work of the brothers: the gathering, drawing, and classification of those plants which are intended to be included later in the *Flora* which the brothers are preparing. This group of chapters forming the innermost circle closes with the sixth chapter, in which, once again, the scientific work of the brothers is treated. The narrator gives an account of the inner effect of their botanical studies: through a withdrawn, almost ascetic way of life, the surrounding objects become changed, they lose their familiar associations, above all, the relation between things and the words which designate them is severed. The narrator feels that he has entered a new level of life in which there is a higher security. So his fear of the Chief Ranger falls away.

These chapters form a unit which is clearly set off from the following. Its focus is the life of the brothers after the war of Alta Plana. The spatial center of this unit is the Rue-Garden Hermitage. That is the place where the brothers work, where Erio lives, to where the botanists return after their expeditions. Nothing is said explicitly of the outside world, that is, of the political changes in the Marina and in the Campagna. This is reported in chapters 7 through 17, whose thematic center is the social cosmos: the interplay and counterplay of political forces. In this part, too, Jünger waives a chronological unfolding of events. Chronology is only hinted at in incidental remarks. The story proceeds systematically from one aspect of things to the next.[7] Only when the narrator introduces new characters does he deviate from this method by briefly sketching their past history.[9] This abstract and systematic mode of narration is maintained consistently throughout the *Marble Cliffs*. Concrete events and the features of individuals are only described if they have a denoting function.

The narrator employs the preterite tense for his epic statement. He refers, as he says explicitly in the introduction, to events of the past. But the impression of a by-gone past is weakened by the narrative technique. The period of seven years which is accounted for in the first seventeen chapters is not subdivided. Precise designations of time are infrequent; moreover, they do not act as factors of organization. Hence, the fictitious world of the *Marble Cliffs* appears as if time did not exist, particularly in the first chapters. Even when the narrator refers to a concrete situation in time and space, something which took place only once, the chronological element implicit in it is given no weight of its own.[10] Concrete situations are reported only if they fit into the abstract pattern. When that happens it can be observed that the situation depicted is condensed into a visual image and solidifies there. Temporal events are preserved in a timeless image. This presupposes that the situation contains meaning and can serve as a symbol. Thus, it is no accident that the author tarries in situations which resemble a ritual act, for example, Erio feeding the snakes in the third chapter, or the brothers' first encounter with Father Lampros in the fourteenth chapter.[11] In the ritual act, temporal occurrences are merely symbols for non-temporal reoccurrence. The symbol, however, refers to a cosmic order.

The cosmic order has two aspects: the microcosmos, which is represented in the six introductory chapters, and the macrocosmos which the narrator treats in chapters 7 to 17. As long as order prevails, the individual and the world will be in accord. Only a whisper of this harmony is left at the Marina. The festivals connected with the seasons are the last expression of this accord. The broadening fissure between the two parts becomes the subject matter of the novel. While the brothers augment themselves in scientific work which is a form of meditation for them, the social order is in a state of corruption. The very next chapter, the seventh, is devoted to the grave diggers of the old order, the Chief Ranger and the Mauretania League. In the following chapters the novel begins to resemble a treatise. The action—which was never strongly accentuated—stagnates: the narrator tells of the general conditions in the cities and in the Campagna. Unending feuds, increasing lawlessness, decay of cultural institutions, injustice, these symbols of decline are nearly abstract conceptions. Although this change takes place in time, the narrator does not follow the process as an annalist who would record the events successively, but rather as a philosopher who looks for meaning, and who presents the results of his contemplation. He is interested in the pattern and in its conformity to inherent laws. (The concept of conformity cannot, of course, be measured by empirical standards.) This "theoretical" interest is manifested explicitly in the text, inasmuch as Jünger also assigns the task of commentating to the narrator. Through this the author instructs the reader how the book is to be understood. This duality of function is evident grammatically in the change between the preterite tense of epic narration and the present tense of commentary and reflection.[12] Such reflection resembles the aphorism in form: it interrupts the course of action or closes a section of the story by summarizing the intellectual outcome. One example will suffice for illustrating this procedure. In the thirteenth chapter the narrator summarizes the situation once again and then connects the two main themes: the brothers' way of life and the decay of public·life. The brothers have renounced active memberships in the Mauretania and have withdrawn to the Hermitage, even though they realize that the conditions have become worse. This decision, the narrator feels, should be substantiated. He argues that weak people have brought chaos upon themselves, consequently the technicians of power such as the Mauretanians cannot be blamed exclusively. This deliberation is then concluded by an aphorism: "In this respect man-made order is like the universe—from time to time it must plunge into the flames to be born anew" (49 f). Through this analogy, the political establishment is given a metaphysical foundation. The aphorism pronounces distinctly that for which the story is only a symbol. There are two levels. Here a meaning which lies behind the literal meaning of the plot is conveyed to the reader. The aphorism indicates to him that the story must be understood allegorically. This principle was acknowledged immediately upon appearance of the novel, but still, because of the circumstances of that time, a topical political version was favored. Though this coincides with the structure of the book, it does not exhaust the enciphering intended by the author. There are several possibilities of interpretation, arranged hierarchically. The political interpretation is on an inferior level and, according to the intentions of the author, it is legitimized only by the superior levels. The use of the term allegory—used here for Jünger's novel—is still liable to misapprehensions. In particular, the distinction between the symbol and the allegory originating from Goethe and the Romantics has obscured the singularity of the allegorical technique. Allegory was disparaged in order to enhance the literary symbol. It was discredited as being merely rational, as lacking in poetic ambiguity and as artistically illegitimate.[13] Presumably Ernst Jünger would also contest the allegorical nature of his novel under the influence of this prevailing prejudice.[14] Jünger's reservations can be determined more clearly in his conception of myth. Mythological accounts, namely, are distinguished from historical accounts by an ambiguous precision: "Mythical precision is different from historical precision. It is contrary to it in as much as it is based, not on unequivocalness, but on ambiguity" (8, 325). Myth shares this ambiguity with the symbol, thus myth should be understood as a symbolizing process: "Man's myth-forming faculty is mythical power. It has nothing to do with his historical stature or his character, but is something that reoccurs with him and in him. Eternity rises resplendent in him" (8, 325).

The timeless quality also tempts the modern writer to use other myths as symbols in order to overcome the limited validity of the historical situations which he creates. Jünger takes this path on the *Marble Cliffs*. His aversion to allegory should be seen in this connection. Allegory would seem to reduce the desired mythical ambiguity to unambiguous relations. In the following, this question will have to be answered: do myth and allegory exclude each other, that is, does the modern writer necessarily proceed symbolically when he employs mythological elements?

The analysis begins with the characters. Their apsychological quality cannot be doubted. The reader who knows something about psychology will feel that they are shallow and only two-dimensional. They are not like individual people embedded in mimetic reality but are cast in roles and inserted into constructed constellations. They lack the casual, afunctional traits which distinguish mimetic portraits of human beings. All the characteristics alloted to them are necessary to carry out the action. Therefore, they can never shed the role which the author has assigned to them. And so they do not have the capacity to change or to adapt to an altered situation by evolving new abilities.[15] The Chief Ranger as well as Father Lampros remain constant as tyrant and as representative of the spiritual order respectively. The actions and modes of behavior of the characters are pre-established, not, however, because these are psychologically probable, but solely because the characters perform their predetermined parts. Braquemart's attack on the celebrations of the Chief Ranger and Belovar's aid in trying to liberate Sunmyra and Braquemart are just as necessary (according to poetic logic) as Lampusa's indifference to the narrator's desperation when he is pursued by the mastiffs. Jünger's characters resemble chess figures who are only allowed to move according to certain, prescribed rules. For this kind of characterization the term "type" seems to insist itself, but unfortunately, this term has been used in so many different ways in aesthetic discussion that it has become misleading. If one replaces the Greek word *typos* with the Latin *figura,* then Jünger's treatment will be labeled appropriately. For the typicalness of the figures is not that they represent an average complex of characteristics, rather that they refer to something else, something lying behind them.[16] This technique reduces perhaps the unique significance of the figures but it does not cancel it out.

The technique of commentary already described in the treatment of plot corresponds to the method of giving names to the characters. Nearly all the names of people appearing in the *Marble Cliffs* signify something. The author has admittedly disguised the meaning by borrowing words from other languages, from French, from Latin, and above all from Greek. The name alludes to a prominent characteristic or to a quality closely connected with the figure. Thus Belo-

var (arrow-quiver) and Braquemart (short sword) indicate the
warrior-like and military virtues of these figures. A characteristic is
also indicated in the name Sunmyra, which might be translated as
"he who does not speak" and, as a matter of fact, this is just the attitude which the young Prince is shown to have in the twentieth chapter. Whereas Braquemart inquires about the military situation, the
young nobleman seems to be withdrawn, wrapped up in a dream.
Equally suitable names are given to the knight Deodat (he to whom
God gives) and the adventurer Fortunio, a pupil of the mysterious
Nigromontan. In all the cases named so far, the nature of the figure
is conceptualized by means of an expressive name. But the name
adds nothing to the person that could not have been gleaned from
the text by the reader. On the other hand, names like Lampros, Lampusa and, in a certain respect, Erio seem to open a new dimension
in the character named. It might be evident to the reader that the
boy Erio is an exceptional child, but his name, which may be translated "he who is rich in blessings," verifies that this child is more
than simply the natural son of the narrator. His presence in the
house seems to guarantee that the work will prosper and that when
danger threatens there will be salvation. Even though Erio is only a
child, he is just as influential as the adults. It seems, by the way, that
the narrator—though of course not the author—is not completely
aware of the full meaning of the name. He does see the uniqueness
of the child and describes it: "When I felt him sitting quietly at my
side I seemed to be refreshed, as if things had acquired a new light
from the deep bright flame that burned in his little body. And it
seemed to me as if animals were drawn to him; for instance, I noticed every time I met him in the garden how the ladybirds flew
round him, running over his hands and playing around his hair"
(21).

The narrator notices that the presence of the child promotes his
work in a mysterious way. This association, that is, magical causality,
will be treated later.

Less definite is the name of the Father (Lampros=the illuminating
one). The close association of this figure to light is also stressed by
Jünger in the narrative parts of the novel. When the brothers visited
him for the first time, a bright light played upon his cloak. And
again, in chapter twenty-eight Jünger brings out the effect of light
in connection with the monk. The monastery of Maria Lunaris is
in flames. "The high church window on the side of the imaged altar
was already burst, and in the empty space we saw Father Lampros

stand. At his back it glowed like the mouth of a furnace, and in order to hail him we hastened forward up to the cloister graves" (115). Here the meaning of the name is itself also a cipher which hints at the nature of the figure without directly denoting it. The same is true of the matriarch Lampusa, whose name, surprisingly enough, also has to do with light, although in the narrator's description she unmistakably exhibits chthonic traits. The earth is her sphere: she lives with Erio by preference in a cave beneath the Hermitage. It is certainly not accidental that she is said to reap three times as much as the brothers from the same amount of seed. In this case the name seems quite puzzling, for one would sooner expect an allusion to darkness for this half-sinister figure.

The commentator can be satisfied with an explanation of the names, but the critic is obliged to investigate the value of the method. Does not Jünger in so naming his characters, enter the field of personal allegory that he otherwise disavows? The names would appear to strengthen the typifying design of the characters and hence also a conceptual definiteness which he condemns theoretically. In the diaries it is evident that the writer was aware of this danger and tried to dodge it by taking countermeasures.[17] He strove to create certain obscure passages which would elude conceptual penetration. Still more important is the insight that the embodiment of ideas in characters and the irrational, inexplicable presence of the figures do not exclude each other. This possibility can be studied in particular in the figure of the Chief Ranger. According to the thematic construction of the novel, the Chief Ranger represents the ancient autochthonic forces which join with the rationalists "in order, with their help, to revitalize the old power for which nostalgia yearns from the bottom of its heart" (2, 29). Originally this character seems to have been a dream figure, one which concerned Jünger for a long time.[18] Jünger used this dream figure for the first time as a literary image in *Das Abenteuerliche Herz*. There was still no sign there of the political context upon which Jünger reflects in the *Marble Cliffs*. In the course of drawing an analogy between absolute evil and the *figura* of the evil tyrant, and not until then, it would seem, did the figure of the Chief Ranger in the *Marble Cliffs* emerge. A similarly complex origin can be supposed for the other figures as well. Although they all transcend the plane of the plot, they are never quite detached from their base. Erio is both a child and the dispenser of blessings, the Father is both member of an order and a solar being. But in thematic respects the representational function predominates, as will be shown in detail. This is especially apparent if one views them in their relations to one another.

The basic patterns are the pair, which can enlarge easily to a quaternity, and the opposition, which is set up either as an antinomy or as a mirroring. The triad is obviously avoided. It seems for Jünger to be a transitory relationship in need of complementation, thus the relation òf the narrator to Silvia and Lampusa is not stable. The narrator dislikes the mother of his beloved and this clouds his relations to Silvia, too. It remains an episode limited by the war—a chaotic time. It does not become a permanent and fruitful arrangement until Otho steps in. He brings Erio, the child of the liaison and also Lampusa, the matriarch, into the Hermitage. Thus, in a round-about way the grouping of three becomes one of four. More difficult to judge is the constellation between the brothers and the Father. One could perhaps regard it as a triad, but this combination does not behave like one, since the brothers usually form an undifferenti-ated unity in relation to the Father. This is not altered until the twenty-first chapter when the Father turns exclusively to the nar-rator with his command. But at that point the brother Otho disap-pears from the plot until the two brothers flee together. And when they meet the Father in passing by the monastery on their way to the city, they carry with them Sunmyra's head. Once again three are complemented by a fourth. This quaternity is constructed symmetri-cally: on one side the brothers and on the other the Father and the dead, dismembered Sunmyra. An inner connection between Father Lampros and the Prince is intimated in chapter twenty-one: the or-der which the narrator receives from the monastery refers explicitly to Sunmyra, not, however, to the Mauretanian. The parallel is also obvious in other ways. Not only are they both of the nobility in which, according to the value system of the *Marble Cliffs,* the high-est virtues are assembled, but also in their attitude towards life they exhibit the same traits. Both are inclined towards death. It is scarcely possible to imagine that either of them takes part as the brothers do in the celebrations of life. It is said of Sunmyra:

> He cannot have been much more than twenty, yet an air of deep suffering presented a strange contrast to his age. Although tall in stat-ure, he bore himself with curved shoulders as if his height incommoded him . . . I had the impression that great age and extreme youth had met in his person—the age of his race and the youth of his body. Thus his whole being bore the stamp of decadence; one could see two forces at work in him—that of hereditary greatness and the contrary influence which the soil exerts upon all heredity. For heredity is dead men's riches. [80]

Decadence is also the stigma of the father: "As we drew near to him fear laid hold on us, for the face and hands of this monk seemed to us unusual and disturbing. I might almost say that they appeared like those of a corpse, and it was difficult to believe that there was life-blood in them" (54).

In spite of physical weakness, these figures are superior to the others when it is a matter of stepping over the boundary between life and death. Braquemart, who is not lacking in fearlessness, resorts to poison when confronted with torture; for the young Prince, torture is a last ordeal in order to be freed from his body. The narrator understands this as he stands under the impaled head of the tortured man: "On this pale mask from which the scalped flesh hung in ribbons and which looked on the fires from the elevation of the torturer's pike there played the shadow of a smile intensely sweet and joyful, and I knew that on this day the weaknesses had fallen from this noble man with each step of his martyrdom, like the rags of a king disguised in beggar's weeds" (105).

Sunmyra and Lampros do not reveal their nature until death. This is their form of life. In contrast to these heroes—Sunmyra is explicitly called that—the brothers, the pair in the focus of the narrative, seem merely human. Their interest in their own life, as sublimated as it might be, denies them the purity necessary for self-sacrifice. Hence they together stand in contrast to Lampros and the Prince.

The other significant grouping of four is also constructed according to the principle of symmetry—on one side the brothers once more and on the other Lampusa and Erio. Here, too, the distribution of powers is unequal. The brothers, especially the narrator, well realize that their scientific training gives them only intellectual superiority, but that they cannot match the opposite pair in vital powers. Whereas the narrator finds the chthonic attributes of the matriarch sinister, Brother Otho proves to have greater insight into the harmony of the quaternity. He brought not only Erio, but also Lampusa, into the Hermitage. And the narrator has to admit that the enlargement of the household, though not originally planned, has proved beneficial. On other occasions as well, Brother Otho is granted the higher insight and spiritual leadership. He appears to direct the progress of their scientific work. His superiority is also exhibited when the author has him give important and fundamental testimony about the developmental process of both brothers. Even these two figures then, who usually appear as a unit towards the outside, are differentiated within their unity. Brother Otho appears as the older, the one with a stronger spiritual profile; the narrator as the younger, the one more closely bound to life. Significantly, Erio is the child of the latter. But no love affairs are reported for Otho. On the other hand, the difference between Erio and Lampusa is evident. Both have an especially close relation to the snakes which live in the crevices under the hut; but if Lampusa fed them, the lance-head vipers "surrounded the quaich in mixed and glowing braids whereas with Erio they formed a rayed wheel" (21). On the symbolic plane this latter figure is related to the work of the brothers who are especially concerned with the axial arrangement of organic structures. Furthermore, it touches upon the solar disc, which belongs to Father Lampros. This symbol emerges regularly in the *Marble Cliffs* wherever the relation of man to the cosmic order is to be represented. The network with Lampusa indicates the opposite, the lower forces of life, which though not absolutely evil, still do endanger the consciousness in some circumstances. The difference between Erio and Lampusa is heightened to a contrast when the life of the narrator is imperiled by the Chief Ranger's mastiffs. In the moment of danger, Erio utilizes his power over the snakes in order to save his father, whereas Lampusa gazes without compassion at his helplessness. In this instant she stands on the side of the Chief Ranger. She had already had her hand in the affair when she neglected to relay the father's message to the brothers. In this pair, Erio and Lampusa, the influence of the demonic powers, among which the battle is fought, is able to reach into the hermitage.

The contrast in the other pair, namely between Braquemart and Sunmyra, is just as sharply marked. These figures are united only by a common enemy. They do not complement each other; even together they remain only half-beings, and for this reason they are subdued by the Chief Ranger. The one is a "concrete dreamer" who is absorbed in perilous political utopias which lack the legitimacy of life, and the other is wrapped up in a dream of the ancient order. In this case, the narrator comments explicitly on the meaning and doubtfulness of their association. "It seemed that Braquemart had an inkling of his weakness with regard to the Chief Ranger, and for that reason had brought the young Prince with him. Yet to us it seemed that the latter was motivated by quite other interests; in this way there often spring up strange comradeships. Perhaps it was the Prince who was using Braquemart to ferry him to a distant shore" (83).

Braquemart, as a man of direct actions wants to attack the Chief

Ranger in his fortress and destroy him by violence. In this he is like his opponent who also relies upon violence and destruction. In the relationship between this Mauretanian and the Chief Ranger there are consequently two aspects: politically they are opposed, but in their methods they are the same. Thus Braquemart is a mirrored image of the Chief Ranger. It is similar with Belovar who comes forward in the pastoral land of the Campagna as a friend to the brothers. In his predilection for fighting—not as a means to a political end like the rationalist Braquemart, but as an irrational form of life—he is related to the Chief Ranger. Like him, he keeps a pack of mastiffs which is the objectification of his aggressiveness. And like Braquemart, he meets death doing battle against a superior enemy, the Chief Ranger.

By setting up groups of figures all the way through, Jünger accomplishes two things: for one, he compensates for the flatness which is produced when he constructs his character types. The various characteristics expressed in the different figures supplement each other, marking particular units which then come into play with other units. His second gain in forming groups of figures is to facilitate the separations between friend and foe and thus to intensify the dramatic conflict. Every figure is allotted its stable place in a schedule of values, and this implies a certain battle station in case of conflict. The characters either opt for the good old order, as do the brothers and the father, or they work for its overthrow, like the Chief Ranger and, though with a different aim, also the secret society of the Mauretania. The Mauretanians desire the domination of a small elite which would terrorize the population now become a mass. The Chief Ranger, however, wants anarchic power for its own sake. Any differentiated form of political or cultural order is repugnant to him. The antinomy between these two parties is simply assumed. The author gives no reasons for its origin. It seems as though the Chief Ranger has dwelt in the forests of the north with his hunters and rangers since time immemorial and waits only for his chance to rush forth. He represents the principle of evil; hence, the question does not have to be raised why he wants to descend on the Marina. Nor does the narrator give reasons for the decay of order. He does indeed describe it, but he does not explain it, as an historian would do in attempting to comprehend an empirical historical process. The events take their predetermined course with logical consequence. Every attempt to rescue the old order is doomed to failure even before it is begun.

The antinomy of values is finally decided by a battle. In the struggle between Belovar's band and the followers of the Chief Ranger there is more at stake than a military victory. The author heightens the significance of this one combat by having similar fights take place all over the Marina and the Campagna at the same time, all having the same outcome. The forces of good are vanquished—certainly unusual in an allegorical novel. Through the sights of the narrator the catastrophe assumes cosmic features. It is to be seen as a destruction of the world. This expanded meaning is overlooked by Gerhard Loose, when he criticizes the dying birds as unrealistic.[19] Jünger writes: "High above this whirl of sparks, touched with red light, flocks of doves and herons which had risen from the reeds soared in the night. They circled until their plumage was enveloped in flames, then they sank like flames into the blaze" (109). He does not intend an historically exact description, rather a myth-like account of the end of the world. And a part of that are the birds succumbing in the fire.

Battle is a traditional device in the allegorical technique, employed in order to surmount ideological oppositions.[20] According to poetic justice, the victory belongs to the side of the good. *On the Marble Cliffs* does not follow this scheme. The good people are annihilated. Nevertheless, the novel does not end pessimistically. Though the brothers may have sacrificed the hermitage by their flight, still they gain a new home in Alta Plana. If one tries to localize Jünger's allegorical landscape as the area around Lake Constance then it is tempting to understand their escape to Alta Plana as escape by emigrating to Switzerland. This would not agree, however, with Jünger's opinion that emigration was an unauthorized oversimplification of the situation. The meaning of the way to Alta Plana can only be recognized if one pursues its spiritual preliminaries. For their departure and the arrival at Ansgar's farm constitute only the last phase of a long development. It began after the war, as the brothers separated from the Mauretanians and chose the life of scientific activity. They advance then through training and trial until they reach "home." This progress is the most important theme in the novel. Because it ends successfully, the defeat of the good side and the annihilation of the old order are compensated for. Although the old demolished order cannot be saved by the development of the brothers, still their progress seems to be a guarantee for the formation of the new order.

It is necessary to describe the single steps of this progress. From the aspect of development, the "I" or the ego of the narrator must be isolated from the figures surrounding it. Even Brother Otho who stands closest to the narrator will belong then to the Non-I. He is to be regarded as the wise advisor. He warns the narrator against imprudent adventures, but also helps him when he feels unsure of himself. If one asks when he took over the function of advising, there is no answer. The reader is told very little about the origin of the Brother. He seems—just as the other characters, moreover—to be on hand when he is needed. This is first the case in the war of Alta Plana. This war brings the turning point both in major and minor matters. We have already spoken of the macrocosmic change. In the life of the ego, this war and its conclusion signify loss of the old security. When the narrator was called up to fight, there existed between him and the world an undisturbed, hence unconscious harmony. He was a part of the larger order. Therefore he did not need to think about the justice or injustice of the war against the free tribes. During the war, however, his horizon is broadened. He forms obligations whose consequences he at first overlooks, engaged as he still is in fleeting adventure. Silvia becomes his mistress in spite of the Brother's admonition. For the first time, the ego which had been completely absorbed in masculine activities, is confronted with the feminine element. The feminine is differentiated into a benign aspect, that is, the beloved, and into an uncanny-frightening aspect, that is, the girl's mother, who is abhorred as a procuress and a witch by the narrator. For the sake of the girl, he puts up with her mother. His first encounter with the feminine is an encounter with an archetype. The ego meets the anima.[21] It belongs to the characters of these archetypal images, whose description we owe to C. G. Jung, that they are not committed to a certain phenotype. Thus the anima appears to the hero in two forms; as beloved and as dangerous witch. The unity of both of these aspects is intimated in the mother-daughter relation of the figures. Whereas the daughter soon disappears from view and only indirectly is still present in her son Erio, Lampusa will confront the ego again. Lampusa is a comparatively harmless version of the magna mater,[22] who bestows life and kills at the same time. As Earth she bestows nourishment, as the wild beast she demands human sacrifice. We recall that Lampusa lives in a cave beneath the actual structure of the Rue-Garden Hermitage and that she is surrounded by snakes. On the other hand, her fructifying hand is ex-

tolled by the narrator. Which aspect this archetype exposes will depend on the ˏattitude of the one who encounters it. To the naïve,
purely male, combative narrator it at first seemed terrible. But
Brother Otho, in whom one can suspect the archetype of the wise
man,[23] is able to integrate Lampusa into the household which is
being established, for he has the gift of bringing out the best in all
people. Not until the narrator has reached a higher stage of consciousness does he succeed in recognizing Silvia's and Lampusa's
worth: "And since one may recognize the justice of an action from
the fact that through it the past finds its fulfillment, so now my love
for Silvia appeared to me in a new light. I recognized that I had been
prejudiced against both her and her mother, and finding her light,
had dealt with her all too lightly, taking for mere glass a jewel that
sparkled on the open road" (19).

The narrator writes this in looking back at a stage of his development in which his combative masculinity had already been subdued.
With intercession of the wise counselor, the masculine, conscious
side approaches the feminine without, however, merging with it, as
the association with Father Lampros shows. It should be mentioned
here that the rue, which gives the house its name, is a feminine
symbol.

From the narrator's retrospections it can be surmised that his first
encounter with the feminine proved unsuccessful, ultimately because
the ego disdained the other side. Therefore the benign aspect of the
anima disappears at an inopportune time. The unconscious approaches the ego in another form. After the security of the old order
had been lost, the unconscious tries to recreate it in a rational manner. The narrator and his brother join the Mauretanians, that is,
the representatives of pure, abstract intellect. "As soon as we had
become aware of this failure we strove to free ourselves. We felt a
longing for actuality, for reality, and would have plunged into ice
and fire or ether only to rid ourselves of weariness. As always when
despair and maturity combine, we turn to power. . . . So we began
to dream of power and domination, and of the forms that in bold
array advance to combat in the deadly struggle for existence, whether
the outcome be disaster or triumphant victory" (25 f).

It is not accidental that during this crisis the brothers meet the
Chief Ranger, the embodiment of instinctual aggressiveness. When
the narrator says about him "Then we took pleasure in his company" (25), we are being told that the brothers had not yet differentiated themselves from this potentiality. The brothers overcome

this stage. They learn that the spirit of the Mauretania is unfruitful (symbolically speaking, it is purely masculine and hence sterile) and that the forces lying behind the Chief Ranger are pernicious. Expressed in psychological terms, this means that the ego experiences the insufficiency of pure intellect and the danger of the repressed unconscious.[24]

The process of transformation enters a new phase when the brothers decide to devote themselves to botanical studies. It is not simply a matter of a change of objects, but more like the reverse: plants replace politics because the brothers' way of life has changed. "We had arrived with the plan of studying plant life intensively, and had therefore begun in accordance with old and well-tried methodology with their breathing and nourishment. Like all things of this earth, plants too attempt to speak to us, but one requires sharp senses to understand their speech" (21 f).

The brothers feel that the two of them are not sufficient for founding a household in which the new life is to unfold. They broaden the base by taking in Lampusa and Erio. This move proves to be beneficial because the new co-inhabitants supplement the masculine-determined world of the brothers. In psychoanalysis this would mean that the inferior function, that is, the anima for a man, becomes conscious.[25] The terrible aspect of Lampusa is mitigated since she is taken into the house along with Erio, that is, the third, the unconscious auxiliary function. Connected with Erio, Lampusa seems more amiable. Erio and Otho, the two auxiliary functions of the ego, are the given mediators between the ego and the unconscious. Otho, as the conscious auxiliary function, is closer to the ego, whereas Erio is closer to the unconscious. "Since the conflict between the two auxiliary functions is not nearly so great as that between the differentiated and the inferior function, it is possible for the third function —that is, the unconscious auxiliary one—to be raised to consciousness and thus made masculine,"[26] says Jung. Expressed in poetic terms: out of Silvia has issued Erio. Hence, Silvia is not able to appear again; her symbolic function is taken over by Erio. The narrating ego finds himself by this time in a better position, for three conscious functions are opposed to only a single unconscious one. Lampusa, however, is still sinister to the narrator: "It was seldom that I entered this part of the Hermitage, for the presence of Lampusa awoke in me a feeling of constraint that I preferred to avoid. But Erio knew every nook and corner" (18).

One recognizes that Erio is closer to the unconscious than Otho also from the observations that he can control the snakes just as well as Lampusa can. One difference has already been noted: when he feeds the snakes they form the pattern of a rayed wheel. Under his influence the snakes pass over to a masculine sign. A gem from late antiquity, described by Jung, depicts how the snake as a symbolic animal can be classified on both the feminine and the masculine side at the same time: "In the middle stands an androgynous deity. On the masculine side there is a snake with a sun halo round its head; on the feminine side another snake with a sickle moon above it." The figure of the radiating disc symbolizes a positive value, namely the psychic life force.[27]

It is well known that Ernst Jünger was especially interested in snakes. His diaries recall that he returned again and again to these mysterious and sometimes offensive animals in different phases of his life.[28] Quite often he describes dreams about snakes. Jünger's literary utilization of the snake-motif in *Das Abenteuerliche Herz, On the Marble Cliffs, Heliopolis,* and *Besuch auf Godenhohm* indicate clearly that his interest in this animal was not only, not even primarily, a zoological concern, but rather a fascination with its symbolic aspect. Jünger's growing familiarity with Asiatic and ancient European mythology and with the history of religion furthered and clarified the symbolic use of the snake. When Jünger was working on the *Marble Cliffs* he was already completely conscious of the mythological background, as one can infer from an ironic remark about the gnostic sect of the Ophites. Snakes were such a major consideration with Jünger that he at first wanted to mention them in the title of the novel.[29]

Just as the snake is not limited to one meaning either in mythological accounts or in dream visions but possesses a series of aspects of meaning, each of which excludes the others logically, so the snake images in Jünger's writing cannot be fixed to one meaning. Henri Plard has demonstrated that their symbolic function changed with Jünger's psychic and spiritual development.[30] But even within the *Marble Cliffs* several perspectives are revealed. So far as the snakes belong to Lampusa, they are classed in the lower regions and are equivalent to the dragon or to dogs.[31] Psychologically they stand for the unconscious, just as Lampusa does. Braquemart, the rationalist, who has no contact with the unconscious, shuns them, whereas Sunmyra disdains them. Where regression is feared, the snakes assume a terrible aspect. At the same time these snakes are symbols for the life-force and for the possibility of renewal, for the vipers kill the

Chief Ranger's dogs, these being in this context more probably the symbols of death. It is noteworthy that in this battle the snakes are under the command of Erio. Both positive and negative value have been preserved in the symbol of the snake since ancient times. It could be associated with Christ but also with the Devil. The Ophitics mentioned above worshipped the snake as an agathodaemon. In ancient gnostic pictures this agathodaemon is shown wearing a crown of seven or twelve rays.[32] In a similar manner the narrator describes the Griffon, the most splendid animal among the snakes, which Erio loves especially. "The body of the lance-head viper is metallic red, patterned with scales like burnished brass. But this griffon was cast in pure and faultless golden brilliance, changing, at the head to jewel-like green and gaining in lustre. When she was aroused, too, she could swell her neck till it was a shield that sparkled like a golden mirror in the attack" (15).

Not without intention does Jünger allude to the mythic age of these snakes: they have lived in the crevices of the Rue-Garden since time immemorial. And it is not surprising that Erio, to whom the intermediating quality of Mercury has been given, is especially devoted to these animals, for the snake appertains to Hermes/Mercury and he is to some extent identified with that.[33]

The apsychological construction of characters discussed at the beginning does not exclude an enrichment and deepening of their meaning. On the contrary, this disdain for psychological differentiation is the prerequisite to deepening the meaning for Jünger—in this he differs from Thomas Mann. By type stylization, parallels to mythical figures are maintained. For example, behind Erio there stands the divine child, a type often attested in mythology. The mythological accounts about Apollo, Hermes, or Dionysus say that this child was both helpless and powerful. Frequently his mother dies at his birth, the child is exposed and is threatened by destruction. On the other hand the child demonstrates superhuman strength even at a tender age. "The richness of life and meaning in the wonder-working child is no whit smaller than in the bearded god."[34] We find the same traits in Erio. Although he can scarcely toddle, he is already the master over dangerous snakes that allow him to treat them in a way that would bring a deadly bite to any ordinary mortal. His great power over them is shown best in chapter twenty-seven, where he commands the snakes to kill the Chief Ranger's dogs. These divine children have a dark aspect, too. They, namely Hermes and

Dionysus, are also guides of dead souls. This does not seem to harmonize with Erio's poetic function in the *Marble Cliffs,* for there the appearance of the child alludes unmistakably to a new phase of life. Though it is certainly a new phase, nevertheless it is not the final one. And it is precisely this situation of suspension between life and death that the child expresses. C. G. Jung has attempted to determine the psychic relevance of this archetype: The divine child stands for surmounting a conflict first seen as insuperable.[35] The ego, torn back and forth by two alternatives, is presented with a new wholeness which lies beyond the conflict. Hence the child appeared to the primitive man as a bringer of salvation. In a similar way, the narrating ego feels himself altered by the very presence of the child, though his consciousness can give no cause for the change. It is consistent with this function that Erio disappears as fast as he appeared, as soon as the developmental process has been brought to a close. Erio does not accompany the brothers in their flight to Alta Plana. The possible significance of this extraordinary feature will be discussed later.

Among the various and diverse source material used by the author, his student years in Leipzig are used as a "model," as it were, for the scientific studies of the brothers. Still this biographical background alone would not be sufficient reason for its inclusion in the novel. It is possible that the student Jünger was looking for more than positivistic knowledge in Leipzig, but certainly the figures of the two brothers are not merely ordinary modern scientists. They are admittedly empiricists, as much as they gather their material from the country-side, but they are not positivists who rely on an inductive chain of reasoning. When they strive for knowledge of the whole order which is to be found ultimately in every object, they have in mind a mystical insight. Since Jünger does not tolerate anything incidental in his work, it is to be expected that the brothers' research goal, namely the axial arrangement of organisms, will refer to something. The axial arrangement alludes to the ancient mandala symbol.[36] The mandala (magic circle) is a concentrically arranged figure; it develops from the center and refers back to the center. If it is a religious mandala, a divinity is frequently observed in this center. Jung draws attention to the fact that a mere external likeness is not significant for the eastern Lamas. They demand the construction of the mandala in meditation. Comparable to that, the brothers do not come across the mandala until after the right preparation. Then the meaning of phenomena is suddenly disclosed to them. In the sixth chapter the narrator tells of the first vision: "One morning as I looked out on to the Marina from the terrace, her waters appeared to me deeper and more translucent, as if I were seeing them for the first time with unclouded vision. . . . I had seen a fragment of the iridescent veil of this world, and from that hour my tongue failed me" (22).

Before, when the first step was taken by leaving the Mauretania, new forces presented themselves, and here again, with inner necessity, there appears a helper who raises the ego and its conscious auxiliary function to a new level: Father Lampros. The brothers make his acquaintance after coming upon the writings of Phyllobius in their studies. Phyllobius is the name used by the Father. In the middle of the fourteenth chapter which is devoted to the Father an initiation is described. Without words the Father draws the brothers' attentions to a mysterium: he shows them an unusually large and very regularly formed plantain flower: "Its circumference was a green circle divided off by the oval leaves which patterned the fringe with their points; in the centre rose in its brilliance the focal point of growth. It formed something as fresh and tender in its living tissues as it was indestructible in the genius of its symmetry" (57).

The brothers see an ordinary flower that grew among weeds and ought probably to be pulled up. At the same time they see more: "Then a shudder ran over us; we felt how closely united in us were the life wish and the death wish. When we raised ourselves up we looked into Father Lampros's smiling face. He had allowed us to partake of a mystery" (15).

The last sentence seems almost a superfluous explanation. After the moment described, it could not be anything but an initiation. The botanical studies of the brothers climax in a mystical experience in which the object becomes a symbol. In this passage the interpreter is confronted with the difficult task of going one step beyond what the author writes in order to grasp it conceptually. Mystical experience, however, is by nature not capable of being adequately expressed in concepts. Still the interpreter has no other choice; he holds an obligation to conceptual thinking. Even Jung, who stressed so insistently the irrational, ambiguous character of the symbol over against the presumed shallowness of the allegoric, when he interprets cannot abstain from a fixed definition.[37] After numerous studies of dreams he came to the conclusion that the mandala symbolism was an essential image for the process of becoming a self.[38] The mandala represents the wholeness for which the ego, though often un-

consciously, seeks. For Jung, the ego is at first not at all identical
with the self. Of the four functions that comprise wholeness, two
are usually unconscious, the inferior one and its auxiliary function.
The purpose of the process is to integrate these unconscious parts.
Thus the mandala symbol touches upon the fundamental problems
of individuation, and the brothers feel themselves affected in their
innermost being as they look at the plantain flower.

Beholding the flower makes the problem clear but does not provide its solution. Lampusa as unconscious anima still remains sinister for the ego. Trials will be necessary before this part, too, will be
recognized. The brothers repeatedly have hours and days of depres-
sion in their Hermitage. Not until the last great ordeal, in doing
battle with the Chief Ranger and being hunted by the dogs, does
the narrator cast off his fear. In the language of the text: the paraly-
sis resulting from his wound is healed. It is possible, though it cannot be proved, that the text illustrates this process by the arrangement of its chapters (not the chronological one). The initiation by
the Father mentioned above falls in the fourteenth chapter. In the
twenty-eighth chapter the mandala symbol is once again at the center. Between these two, following the rhythm of seven, is the twenty-
first chapter in which the Father dispatches his order to help Sunmyra. This is the introduction for the last and decisive ordeal. In
retrospect, the seventh chapter, too, proves to be a turning point.
In contents the negative certainly predominates, for this chapter is
concerned with the Chief Ranger and with the Mauretania. But
out of this negation, understood as the condition in which everything is limited by intellect alone, there emerges the decision which
leads to further development. In accordance with this thematic-
systematic arrangement, it is shown in the fifteenth chapter, just
after the initiation, how the narrating ego and its advisor are confronted with an important alternative. They have to repeat the
decision of the seventh chapter, where they turned their backs on
the Mauretania, but this time at a higher level: "When the tide of
destruction raged more furiously round the Marble Cliffs memories
awoke in us of our Mauretanian times, and we weighed up the possibility of a solution through force" (59). "But when we discussed
the situation more thoroughly in the herbarium or library our decision was strengthened to resist with spiritual forces alone" (59).

The path on which they find themselves demands renunciation of
violence, even if it were to be employed in the name of justice. When
violence occurs as the legitimate use of power the temptation is

greater. But the use of violence would nevertheless be a regression. It is not accidental that Belovar, a clearer mirror image of the Chief Ranger, is on the spot immediately. The brothers restrict themselves to reconnaissance trips in the forests. Translated into the language of psychology, the ego attempts to draw closer to the unconscious as an observer. The eighteenth and nineteenth chapters show that the ego has underestimated the perils which accompany such an attempt. In seeking the red woodland orchid, a rare species, in the forest domains of the Chief Ranger, the narrator and his companion come across the flayer's yard at Köppelsbleek. They are confronted with death. At the very moment when they have the sought-after treasure before them, their eyes fall on the Chief Ranger's torture place. The ego threatens to despair at this experience, which is the opposite pole, as it were, to the vision of mandala. The brothers flee, until Otho—characteristically it is the wise counselor—exhorts the others to return to recover their find. With thoughts of their scientific work they master their fears of danger, for contemplation of order fills them with new strength: "Therefore we felt that even the tender flower in its imperishable pattern and living form strengthened us to withstand the breath of corruption" (76).

Obviously the red woodland orchid is no more an ordinary flower than the plantain flower in the monastery garden. Form, color, and location seem significant. In this connection, the crimson color of the petals stands for the life-force. As early as the second chapter, Jünger uses the color red as a sign for intensified life-force. In *Das Abenteuerliche Herz* he says of this color: "It makes the breath of life grow faster but simultaneously more anxiously." A person is especially close to himself in this color and the same thing is signified by the structure of the flower which is to be interpreted as another form of the mandala. And finally, the place where it is found is meaningful. When the narrator invades the forest for the second time, after the battle, he will stand at exactly the place where he found the flower, and from there he will see Sunmyra's impaled head. Anticipating the analogy between Sunmyra and Christ, to be discussed later, the red woodland orchid could be understood as a prefiguration of the Prince's death.

At their first encounter with the power of the Chief Ranger, the brothers get off with no more than a severe fright, so to speak. Still this ordeal shows that they have ventured too far forward. Greater legitimacy is required to take up arms against the Chief Ranger. A second, far graver trial is in store for the narrating ego. This time he does not go to find a flower, rather to rescue a human being. His stake is increased. Instead of his brother, the narrator has brought Belovar with his servants and dogs along. Furthermore, the Chief Ranger himself appears for the first time, in order to destroy the invaders. This second expedition reminds one—though certainly with one very important discrepancy—of the night sea journey (*nekyia*) of the mythical hero. He sets out to kill the snake or the dragon, or to vanquish a wicked magician who guards a treasure. He finds his adversary either in the forest or in a cave. Both of these are female symbols that express the unconscious. Similarly, the narrator of the *Marble Cliffs* must return once again to the region of the unconscious. But he does not succeed in overcoming the wicked one, and in this the novel deviates from the archetypal plot. The narrating ego is the hero only in a technical sense; in his nature he is primarily human. Nevertheless, the task is accomplished, although in a manner different from what the reader expects. Through Sunmyra's death the power of the Chief Ranger is somehow subdued in a mysterious way. Sunmyra, with Braquemart, had set out to defeat the Chief Ranger and had met death in the forest. His body was maimed and his head impaled. The narrator comes too late to help him. But it seems to be his own predetermined task to rescue the head of the hero and to deliver it to the Christians. The author leaves no doubt that Sunmyra is to be regarded as a hero. "Then a shudder ran through my inmost heart, for I realized that he had been worthy of his forefathers, the tamers of monsters; he had slain the dragon fear in his own breast" (105).

But there is more to be said: the death of the Prince is to be seen as a substitute sacrificial death. This perspective is also intimated by Jünger. When the Christians rebuild the great cathedral in the Marina, they place the dead man's head in the cornerstone. By the symbolism of the cornerstone an analogy to Christ is drawn. For by uniting the head with the cathedral, the union of the sacrificed lamb with the Church is symbolized. Tradition has conceived of the Church as the virgin mother-consort of Christ.[39] And this union is, in its turn, a symbolic representation of rebirth.

But we have anticipated. Rebirth follows the night sea journey and death. We must call to mind again the constellation that determines this dramatic action. Six important persons are involved in the expedition and the battle: the pair Braquemart/Sunmyra who suffer death. They are followed by the narrator with Belovar. The latter, who bears traits of the enemy, will also remain dead on the battlefield. And then the two figures, in which the antinomy is most sharply etched: the Chief Ranger and Lampros. They are both evidently father figures. Lampros is explicitly labeled as Father, but to the Chief Ranger is also attributed an advanced age. The Father is characterized by a spiritual quality that is almost inimical to life. His body has nearly withered away. The opposite pole to this sublimation is taken by the Chief Ranger. He seems mighty in his corporeality which gives the impression of inexhaustible strength. He loves the hunt and celebrations at which the instinctual side of life is exalted. Whereas leaves and flowers belong to the Father, rapacious mastiffs are the proper attendants for the Chief Ranger. In the poetic process Jünger separates here two aspects of the father image. Just as there was a nourishing and a devouring mother, the archetype of the father is also comprised of opposing components. On one side the father, or in myth, the father-God, as an agent of law and order. From this aspect, he is equivalent to the sun: "The sun, as Renan has observed, is the only 'rational' image of God, whether we adopt the standpoint of the primitive savage or of modern science. In either case the sun is the father-God from whom all living things draw life; he is the fructifier and creator, the source of energy for our world."[40] Lampros reflects some of this solar quality. His connection to light is mentioned a number of times but there is no trace in him of the power to create life; he rather seems to point to death. Nevertheless the mythical parallel is in keeping with him. For the sun god grows old in the fall and destroys himself in order to be reborn. So Lampros also presses toward death. His death has a cosmic function.

How can the double aspect of the father image in the *Marble Cliffs* be explained? The psychological answer would be: the oneness and wholeness of the self, for which the ego is searching, has not yet been produced. The inferior function has not yet been raised to consciousness. Not until he stands beneath the impaled head of Sunmyra does the narrator feel clearly what the meaning of the last ordeal is: Sunmyra subdued the dragon in himself. Hence, the narrator must also penetrate through the dark regions of the unconscious once more before he can free himself completely. Jünger relies on mythical models in describing the advance. Before the men reach the Alpine forest, they have to traverse a swamp. "And out of the high broom, the reedy thickets and the bushy willows the loud refrain echoed back. In this confusion we saw wild-fires dance on the stagnant waters, and waterfowl skimmed past on startled wings" (96).

Mythologically, this band crosses the waters of death and enters then into the regions of the netherworld proper. They cut a gap in the hedge in order to penetrate the high-lying forest. In this passage a comparison brings out the symbolic character of this act. "Soon the breach was as wide as a barn door. We kindled torches and entered the *high* forest through the dark *jaws*" (97). The stomach of a dragon or whale or, as here, the interior of a forest, all symbolize the unconscious. The narrator does not, however, encounter the Mother there, she who is the goal of regression, but instead he meets her masculine representative,[41] the terrible Chief Ranger, whom he must overcome in battle. Unlike the mythical hero, however, he does not overcome the Chief Ranger. Belovar and his mastiffs, the aggressive portion of his personality, as it were, succumb to the superior strength of the Chief Ranger. The narrator has to flee. The second trial thus seems to end negatively. As a matter of fact, the narrator would have been defenseless and at the mercy of the Chief Ranger's mastiffs had it not been for Erio's intervention. Indeed, what is not possible for Belovar's dogs, Erio's snakes manage with no effort: they destroy the pursuing dogs in a twinkling. After that the spell is removed from the narrator forever. "Then I felt my blood flow more freely, in my veins, and sensed that the spell which had seized me was broken" (113).

The menace from the side of the terrible Father is overcome with the help of the Mother's side. It is precisely Erio who is empowered to save the narrating-ego; that means, he is authorized to reconcile the conflict between the consciousness and the unconscious side. The Child is the acknowledged intercessor.

The description of the battle is the culmination of the psychic drama—the conflict between consciousness and unconsciousness—as well as of the cosmic drama—the struggle for order which is at an end with the destruction of the Marina. Following the principles of poetic justice, the loss of macrocosmic order is compensated for by the gain of a new microcosmic order. The twenty-eighth chapter correlates both of these aspects once more. The death of Father Lampros relates to both themes. With regard to the macrocosmos he represents the decline of the old order; with regard to the narrator's development he is the guarantor of a renewal. The larger correlation illuminates the brothers as they view the death of the Father: "—we saw the still undamaged circle of the rose window fill with green light, and its pattern was strangely familiar. It seemed to us as if the image had gleamed for us once before in the plantain Father Lampros had shown us in the cloister garden; so the secret symbolism of the spectacle was revealed" (116).

The rose window or rosette is a Christian version of the mandala. Seeing it reminds the brothers of the first vision in which they experienced the relation between life and death. So now they dare to hope that they will find a new life beyond the present ruin. The guarantee of a new order is Sunmyra's head which the brothers carry with them and which has undergone a remarkable change in the amphora. It seemed "lit with dark purple splendor" (116). Once again we find the color red that was anticipated in the red woodland orchid. The symbolic meaning of the color cannot be determined conclusively, but it is possible that Jünger wanted to allude to the *rubedo* of the alchemists. We know that he was familiar with the ideas of alchemy. In the opus *alchymicum,* the *rubedo* is the highest level attainable, after going through the *nigredo* and the *albedo.*[42] The goal of this process is to extract the *lapis,* but this is sometimes replaced by Mercury or *filius macrocosmi.* These alchemistic parallels are not precluded because of the fact that Lampros is a Christian monk. Then, for one thing, it is emphasized in the novel that the dogmatic severity of belief recedes in his person and, furthermore, medieval alchemy was fully aware of the analogy between its opus and Christ's work of redemption.[43] Christ, as the *filius microcosmi,* that is, the redeemer of man, is complemented by the alchemistic *filius macrocosmi,* in whom the world is redeemed by the *opus alchymicum.* In spite of the striking difference in basic attitude—the Christian feels that he is the one to be redeemed whereas the alchemist wants to redeem nature actively—the two conceptions do intersect. This is the sacrifice of the mass. And it seems to be precisely the Eucharist to which Jünger refers when he describes the death of the Father in the following way: "As I stretched the head towards him, the Father turned his eyes on us, and slowly raised his hand as at the consecration of the Host, half in greeting, and half pointing; on it the great cornelian glowed in the fire. As if with this gesture he had given a sign of terrifying power, we saw the rose window disintegrate in golden sparks, and, with the arch, tower and horn of plenty collapsed upon him in mountainous ruin" (116). When this happens it is striking that the sign given is the *causa efficiens* of destruction. In a similar way, the sacramental words in the Eucharist are to be understood as the efficient cause. In the transubstantiation, Christ's sacrifice is renewed. Simultaneously, however—and this is the aspect that interested the alchemists—the substance of bread and wine is transformed. "For the alchemist, the one primarily in need of redemption is not man, but the deity who is lost and slumbering in matter."[43a] In the alchemistic conception, a purified material, the *lapis,* emerges from the Eucharist, and the *lapis* can be equated with the *filius macrocosmi.* Under these circumstances it is possible that Jünger wanted to create an embodiment of the *filius macrocosmi* in Sunmyra, whose death opens the way for general rebirth after the ruin of the world.[44]

In addition to the theme of cosmic renewal, we should not lose sight of the development of the hero. At the beginning, the narrating-ego stands alone, if one disregards the chronological uncertainty in Otho's case. During the process of development new figures appear. Some of them, like Brother Otho, Erio, Father Lampros, and also Belovar, prove to be helpers along the way. Others bring a trial along with them, like Silvia, Lampusa, and the Chief Ranger. The gradual enrichment of figures from the beginning to the climax is matched by a diminution at the end: Erio and Lampusa disappear in the cave; Belovar is killed in combat; the Father dies in his monastery. Only Otho accompanies the narrator on his flight and together with him reaches Ansgar's house in Alta Plana. This diminution is not a loss. After the narrator has passed through the big trial, that is, after the ego has surmounted the dangerous regression, he no longer needs helpers outside of himself. In other words, the division of personality into different figures can be withdrawn after the hero has gained his own self, which was the goal of his peregrination. In Ansgar's house the brothers find a new home. This house is quite evidently a *temenos,*[45] a hallowed place. The grounds are surrounded by a grove of oaks. In the house, which is obviously built like those in Lower Saxony, the old order still prevails, founded on symbols that remind the narrator of his northern homeland. The end flows into the beginning again. When the brothers enter the *temenos,* it signifies that wholeness has been reached: the various psychic functions, which had been detached as benign or pernicious figures, are integrated again. It is upon this integration that the confidence at the end, which at first glance seems astonishing, is based. The end of the novel must have seemed fantastic in 1939 when war was breaking out. For what cause had the emigrant at that time for hope? But for Jünger the center of gravity was not on the aspect of flight, rather on that of returning home.

A factual commentary creates the prerequisites for criticism, which is interested in the artistic integration of the elements. This goal justifies the broad scope of the material involved—description of mythological, religious, psychoanalytical, and historical components. If the author rejects an interpretation along the lines of contemporary history, he is not required to explain his reasons in detail, but the text must prove his claims. The commentary pointed to the factual foundations. In the novel, historical, mythological, philosophical, and psychic motives are combined to form a unity which cannot be interpreted reductively. Reductive interpretation would tend to undo the interconnection, because it passes off one single aspect of the novel as the most important. The task of the critic, however, is to question the integration as such, that is, to examine the legitimacy of the artistic process. Every one of the elements involved changes in character in the process of integration. This process does not show up clearly in the factual commentary, because it is brought to a standstill by abstraction. The most conspicuous change is in the treatment of history. The historical events to which Jünger referred, above all the emergence of a fascist dictatorship in Central Europe, lose their specifically historical character when they are joined with mythological and philosophic-hermetic elements. They are detached from time and thus stylized to expressions of typical, reoccurring constellations. The fall of the Weimar Republic assumes the proportions of a cosmic catastrophe. This modification is the more remarkable as Ernst Jünger did not feel at all committed to the Weimar Republic as a citizen. Other elements are also modified. In his conscious use of mythological figures and situations—and there can be no doubt that it was conscious—he does not simply rehabilitate myth. Likewise there is something new added when the author refers to the hermetic teachings of the alchemists and gnostics in order to intensify the meaning of his story. These traditional elements are translated and in the process their substance and meaning are redefined. The question is, then, what the nature of a work of art is that is composed of these elements. The author would likely answer using traditional definitions: for example, that by this translation a symbolic work of art has arisen. Probably he would not agree if one called *On the Marble Cliffs* an allegorical work.

A conceptual distinction between the symbol and the allegory is of a comparatively recent date. In the eighteenth century the two terms were used synonymously. Not until Goethe and the Romantics does one notice the intention to set up these two concepts in opposition to each other. Goethe expressed this opposition in a well-known formula, which, however, tends to obscure the problem rather than clarify it: the allegory proceeds from the general to the particular whereas the symbol begins with the particular and contains the general without having to refer to it expressly. "The symbolic way of thinking around eighteen hundred was so alienated from the original allegorical form of expression that the very isolated attempts in theoretical analysis are worthless for fathoming the allegory—but the more symptomatic for the depth of the antagonism." So writes Walter Benjamin with regard to Goethe's definition.[46] Indeed, little can be expected of the definitions at that time because as a rule the allegory was employed solely as a residual category. The Romantics, on the other hand, are more promising in their attempts to indicate various possibilities within the symbolic process. These attempts served, to a large degree, also the need to set themselves off from the Classicism of Weimar. They separated the mystical symbol from the aesthetically-defined artistic symbol of the Classicists.[47] Whereas the visual symbol stressed the organic connection between appearance and idea and also the agreement between form and meaning, the mystical symbol is marked by a tension between its expression and its meaning: Goethe and his circle referred to Greek art and mythology, but the Romantics had recourse to the Orient, whose myth and whose symbols seemed to them to be more pregnant with meaning. In the case of mystical symbols, as Creuzer was the first to show, there is a necessary disparity between appearance and idea which cannot be abrogated. "It belongs to the nature of the mystical experience that no form of expression is adequate to it, so that the mystically inspired poet often circles around and paraphrases the ineffable in his experience by constant amassing of images."[48] As much as the symbol intimates the infinite—the concept around which romantic speculation revolved—it can be accepted only as a cipher for the "other," that which cannot be uttered. The notion that nature is an enciphered book awaiting exegesis and that mythology and poetry are to be understood as hieroglyphic expressions of nature, recurs again and again among the Romantics. The Romantic conception of the symbol places the emphasis less on organic compactness than on the potential of many-sided references.

If one would wish to undertake a classification, then Jünger would stand closer to the Romantic understanding of symbols than the Classical. He is more interested in the referential features than in a well-rounded visual structure. For him, too, there is a primary relation of tension between expression and meaning. There is perhaps a connection between the world of appearances and the transcendental world, but this connection can only be hinted at by the artist: "We depict the worlds above according to human, that means temporal, blueprints. Upon this is based the corollary of absurdity that is attached to our religions and often predominates there. These are descriptions by the blind who have a presentiment of a world of light, since its warmth touches them. Still, because they cannot divine what is entirely different, they imagine sublime forms of darkness" (8, 321).

These sentences, written many years after the *Marble Cliffs,* mark with all clarity the delineation between this world and the other to which the symbol has the task of referring. Thus Jünger too loves the cipher-formula. He uses it in regard to nature as well as in regard to the work of art. Jünger's studies of nature, his passion for flowers and insects, are concerned in the last instance with explicating a higher law, one which has very little in common with the laws of modern science, but which is so much the more associated with the emblematic thinking of the old humanists and theologians. In 1958, on the occasion of Adolf Horion's birthday, Jünger wrote: "The plants and animals are not only objects of scientific measurement and observation, but are incomparably more. They are also beautiful, mysterious and manifold in a manner that can never be completely fathomed. They are not sections of nature, they are no specialities, but rather keys to nature in its entirety" (8, 513).

In precisely this sense the botanical studies of the brothers in the *Marble Cliffs* are attempts to find the key to nature and to mankind. The time-honored comparison between the artist and a creative nature that reveals its order in all living forms is revived. The phenomena of nature are to be read like hieroglyphics in a book, and the artist is another, though only secondary, creator, who with the help of the mediating imagination creates a new but analogous ordering.[49]

If one presupposes a division between the visible and the invisible world for the time when the *Marble Cliffs* was written, then Jünger was faced with the problem of so alienating empirical reality that it would be discernible as a cipher. He would be forced to let the reader in on the secret at crucial passages. Enciphering led to the allegorical structure of the story, revelation led to the mystical symbol. Each mode of expression implies the other. Creuzer writes about symbolic experience: "It is like a spirit suddenly appearing or like a bolt of lightning that illuminates the dark night but once. It is a moment that claims our whole being, a glimpse into a boundless distance, from which the spirit returns enriched."[50] Such moments are given in the *Marble Cliffs,* in beholding the plantain flower in the monastery, in finding the red woodland orchid and in the glimpse of the rose window. But this mystical experience is compressed into an instant. Thus the mystical symbol is short and concise, whereas the allegory can be expanded once its principle has been selected. It is for this reason that Creuzer finds mythology an allegorical manner of presentation.

The crucial question is the relation of symbol, allegory, and mythology to each other in Jünger's work. It is worth bearing in mind that Creuzer brings mythology into association with allegory. His interpretation would be questionable if Goethe's classification were followed, as it was to a great extent in the nineteenth century, for mythology does not proceed from conceptually determined ideas. Now, however, more recent criticism has shown that Goethe's concept of allegory describes only its late and decadent form; indeed, that the opposition between allegory and symbol is quite relative and depends on the point of view of the observer. Gadamer says: "The fixed availability of the conceptual contrast: the 'organically' developed symbol—the cold, intellectual allegory—loses its binding force if one recognizes its tie to the aesthetics of creative spontaneity [*Genieästhetik*] and the aesthetics of subjective experience [*Erlebnisästhetik*]."[51] Mysticism in nature, a current in recent German literature in which Jünger should also be included, reaches back to poets and thinkers of the sixteenth and seventeenth centuries, who were still completely under the sway of the allegorical, emblematic tradition. As soon as one moves either forwards or backwards away from the realm of *personal poetry,* the categories which emerged in that time also lose their value. In particular, the traditional classification is in error when it accuses allegory of being only abstract and rational and having only one meaning. This would fit only the narrow type, the conceptual allegory, and does not at all take the dimensions of the whole field of allegorical method. On the contrary, the possibility of many meanings, the multitude of potential references, these are the real characteristics of allegory in a wider sense, and even more of the emblems which in certain respects can be regarded as a forerunner of the symbol. The emblematist starts with a concrete object which has explicitly to be taken from nature and then he assigns it a meaning. He starts then with the particular, not from the general:

"the emblem puts the *pictura* which is to be explicated ahead of the interpretation through description [*subscriptio*] and compels the observer and reader to accept the *priority of the image*."[52] The emblematist is allowed to extract a meaning out of this image from nature, because in the theological and natural mystical tradition nature is regarded as a divine, meaningful book. A differential power dwells then in natural things, and although this remains hidden to ordinary mortals, it can be perceived by the philosopher. This process threatens to become a meaningless game whenever the credibility of the correspondence is questioned. When that happens, the emblem yields to an equivalent of the *concetto,* a game of wits.[53] Allegorical ambiguity can lead both to devaluation of the object, in as much as "every relation [can] mean any other one at random" as well as to consecration, in as much as "those requisites of meaning, each pointing to something else, acquire a power which makes them seem incommensurable to profane things and raises them to a higher elevation."[54] The danger of conventionalizing which has made allegory so suspect is eluded by the skillful allegorist by means of intensified hermeticism. He fights against vulgarization through complicated enciphering, as can be demonstrated also in Jünger.

As soon as the critic has freed himself from the bias that prejudiced the allegory for more than 150 years, he will be struck by the allegorical features in the *Marble Cliffs*. The construction of the story, the shaping of characters, the realization of the theme—all are allegorical. But that is not to claim that the novel is exclusively allegorical. The relation between the central mystical symbolism and the allegorical elements of the narration is one of subordination in which the allegorical method is the vehicle of symbolism. Since the mystical symbol is by nature momentary and concise it is prohibited from any broad extension. From the symbol alone no action can be developed. At this point the novelist has recourse to allegorical method. His decision is encouraged by the fact that the mystical symbol and the allegory both have a representing function and even the tension between sign and signification is similar. Because Jünger chose such typical allegorical schemes of action as the battle and progress, because he made his characters demonic agents the way allegory does, and finally because he gave them names which firmly circumscribe their traits and their functions, he achieved a structure that could serve as a support for symbolism.[55]

The procedure can be illustrated with two examples. The countryside described by Jünger is allegorical in spite of certain similarities to real landscapes. The position of the forests, the pasture lands, the vineyards, and the lakes with their islands is not geographical but ethical. The map of the *Marble Cliffs* is determined by social and cultural factors. Each type of landscape corresponds to a certain level of culture and to a particular moral refinement. The Campagna is the place of a wild but also just life of nature. The primitiveness of this area is distinct from the dark brutality of the forest on one hand, and the cultural refinement of the Marina on the other. According to allegorical logic, the Campagna thus is situated between the Marina and the forests of the Chief Ranger. In the process of allegorizing, however, Jünger is careful to digress from allegorical consistency: there are passages written in such detail that they resemble a mimetic description. In this way a state of suspension is attained, in which allegorical reference and the autonomy of things themselves do not exclude each other. Through this the concrete detail can unfold into symbol. The red woodland orchid that the brothers find at the Fillerhorn is a concrete, momentary symbol within an allegorical frame of reference. The same is true of the moment when Belovar's men lay bare a breach in the hedge. The opening becomes the jaws of a beast. The second example is given by the snakes. In the framework of constructive allegorical strategy they play their role on the side of the forces of good. The Chief Ranger's dogs are their opponents on the side of evil. Still, at the same time, the novel creates symbolic situation, as, for example, when the snakes place themselves in the form of a rayed wheel when they are fed. The description of the Griffon also proves to be a traditional symbol when examined more closely. Deciphering presupposes in this case some familiarity with contexts in religious history. The author who uses this form of hermetic ciphering finds himself in the position of an emblematist. He relies upon a nexus of meaning which has been handed down to him—although, of course, within a hermetic tradition. His creative accomplishment consists of reactivating the neglected relationships. This example proves the relativity of definitions fitted to a certain situation. An advocate of the organic art-symbol might very possibly be annoyed by the predetermined context. The study of symbols owes to C. G. Jung the insight that man's symbolizing faculty is not original in the sense that original is used in affective poetry (*Erlebnis-dichtung*). Agreement between mythical tradition and the reports of his patients' dreams induced Jung to assume the existence of a collective stock of symbols. This realm supplied Jünger's snake symbols, as his diaries indicate. If the poet had recourse to gnostic ideas, then this probably happened because he found his own experience mirrored there. The forgotten image whose *pictura* has been preserved in museums and books has received new powers of life.

[*Translated from the German by Alice Kennington*]

Notes

Quotations from the *Marble Cliffs* are taken from the English translation by Stuart Hood (London: New Directions, 1947).

Other quotations from Ernst Jünger's writings are translated from the *Gesamtausgabe*, 10 vols. (Stuttgart: Ernst Klett Verlag, n.d.). This edition of his complete writings was authorized by Jünger. References are given by volume and page number.

1. The *Neuer Züricher Zeitung* wrote "It (this form) has inviolable right if it arises not from mere aesthetic artfulness, but from a vital necessity, when a thing cannot be said at all except so disguised and in ciphers." Quoted from Hans-Peter Schwarz, *Der Konservative Anarchist. Ernst Jünger, Politik und Zeitkritik* (Freiburg/Breisgau, 1962), 139.

2. Jünger's enciphered analysis of tyranny probably offered no new insights to the liberal and the Marxist opponents of National Socialism, and they presumably could not be satisfied with the assertion of the novel. Jünger was reputed to have assisted the National Socialists ideologically in their seizure of power. He was regarded as a nationalistic writer and his books were promoted even after 1933. Only a few confidantes were in a position to know that this author of heroic war books had distanced himself from the new rulers shortly after they had come to power.

3. Walter Benjamin, *Schriften,* eds. Th. W. Adorno and Gretel Adorno (Frankfurt/Main 1955), I, 55.

4. Jünger's diary, April 10, 1939: "Models for the Marble Cliffs: the rocky slope near the lighthouse in Mandello, where I climbed with the Magister. Then the way from Corfu to Canoni, the Rodino Valley on Rhodes, the view from the monastery Suttomonte over to Corcula, the way through the fields from the Glacier Mill to Sipplingen on Lake Constance" (2, 34).

5. Meanwhile the reader has become aware that according to the chronology of the novel, it is the seventh year after the war of Alta Plana. The decay of order is already far advanced. Now for the first time, in the eighteenth chapter, a definite, concrete event is described in its chronological context, namely the excursion to the Flayer's Copse. This movement forward which leads to the first real encounter with the Chief Ranger is treated in Chapters 18 and 19. In the evening of the same day, Braquemart's and Sunmyra's portentous visit takes place (Chapter 20). The chronological gap before the following chapter is not stressed. the narrator gives an account of the few

hours after the visitors had gone until he receives the Father's message which calls for his help. The tempo in which the action is driven forward accelerates in the next chapter. In Chapter 22 there is a description of the departure with Belovar's men, in Chapter 23 their advance and the pursuit by the enemy vanguard. The twenty-fourth chapter is reserved for a description of the battle whereas the twenty-fifth is concerned with rescuing the impaled head of the Lord Sunmyra. In the following chapters, too, the narrator limits himself nearly exclusively to reporting events, for example, the retreat, pursuit by the mastiffs, rescue by the snakes, and finally, in the twenty-eighth chapter, parting from the Rue-Garden Hermitage and the death of the Father in the rubble of his monastery. The last two chapters which present the brothers' arrival in the ruined city, their departure from the Marina and their arrival in Alta Plana, have the effect of a coda.

6. "In those times, I will confess, it seemed to me that many cares and troubles darkened our days, and, above all, we were on our guard against the Chief Ranger" (7).

7. The arrangement can be given approximately in the following way. Chapter 7, the Chief Ranger and the Mauretania; Chapter 8, the decadence of social order; Chapter 9, the conditions in the Campagna; Chapter 10, the decay of cultural institutions; Chapter 11, the military sphere of influence in the Marina; Chapter 12, the realm of the Chief Ranger; Chapter 13, Belovar; Chapter 14, Father Lampros; Chapter 15, the decision of the brother; Chapter 16, Nigromontanus' mirror; Chapter 17, the excursions.

9. Thus the reader learns, for example, of Belovar, that he has remained loyal to the brothers ever since Otho aided him in a court case, or of Father Lampros, who is portrayed in Chapter 14, that he "sprang from an ancient Burgundian house" (56).

10. A good example for this way of "making a vacuum" in time is the description of the encounter between the narrator and Lauretta in the second chapter. A description of the annual Spring celebration provides the framework. "Everywhere in these nights the shrill bird song rang out until the dawn—in the dark lanes and along the great Marina, in the chestnut groves and vineyards, from the lantern-decked gondolas on the dark expanse of the lake, and even among the high cypresses of the burial grounds. And always, like its echo, one heard the startled, fleeting cry that answered it" (11). The preterite tense here does not express so much the temporal past as it does constancy in recurrence of the past. The concrete, solitary event is also related to this level: "So this play of voices lies deep in my ear, and above all the suppressed cry with which Lauretta met me on the wall" (11 f). It is not said in which year the event happened, for its value consists primarily in conforming to the pattern.

11. "The first time that we stepped through its doors we saw the Father, who had just come in from the garden, standing in the quiet room with a spray of gladiolus in his hand. He still wore his wide-brimmed hat, and on his white cloak played the bright light which fell through the clerestory windows" (54).

12. In the seventh chapter, for example, "Anyone acquainted with the history of the secret Orders knows that their ramifications are difficult to assess. Similarly it is common knowledge with what fertility they form branches and colonies, so that attempts to trace them down end in a maze" (26). With this commentary the narrator introduces a description of the internal condition of the Mauretanians. Following that he then says: "For the Mauretanians too this held good" (26). The logical transition from the particular to the general or vice versa is especially transparent in this narrative technique. When the Swiss critic Nef attacked Jünger for too frequent use of the

conjunction "so," Jünger defended himself with the argument that the logical structure had to be clearly worked out. This argument was sound within the framework of the method selected. Both Jünger and his critics overlooked the factual reason, for Jünger's demand is unreasonable as a general stylistic norm. This peculiarity is justified within the scope of allegorical method. Cf. Gerhard Loose, *Ernst Jünger, Gestalt und Werk* (Frankfurt/Main, 1957), 173.

13. Cf. Edwin Honig, *Dark Conceit, the Making of Allegory* (Oxford University Press, 1966), 3. "If we were asked why allegory is so conscientiously mistrusted while speculations about symbolism abound as never before, one might say that in a scientific age allegory suggests something obvious and old-fashioned, like Sunday-school religion, but symbolism is something esoteric and up-to-date, like higher mathematics. It is a glib answer but not too far from the sources of the modern prejudice." This prejudice has contributed to the fact that neither writers nor critics have reached unanimous agreement about the allegory as a literary form. In Germany, Walter Benjamin was the first to turn against the prevailing opinion *(Ursprung des deutschen Trauerspiels*, Berlin, 1928). Among more recent American studies, we should mention in addition to Honig, Angus Fletcher, *Allegory, The Theory of a Symbolic Mode* (Ithaca, New York: Cornell University Press, 1964).

14. In the *Sanduhrenbuch* he calls the allegory a sunken form of the symbol. "The symbol sank in the course of the Baroque to an allegory, and now in our time it has settled into a cliché. That which is transitory becomes a symbol for us when it is illuminated by being." This rather lazy definition owes much to Goethe. Jünger's negative value-judgment arises from a narrow conception of allegory which is moreover questionable from an historical view. Allegory is evidently regarded as a purely rational sign, available at random.

15. The change in the two brothers lies on a level different from the psychological and cannot be regarded as a counter argument.

16. To that extent the *figura* is a variation of the allegory. Erich Auerbach, however, draws a distinction: "But it differs from most of the allegorical forms known to us by the historicity both of the sign and what it signifies." Erich Auerbach, "Figura," in *Scenes from the Drama of European Literature* (New York, 1959), 54. In this sense it was customary to understand persons in the Old Testament as prefigurations of Christ. Jünger relies less on history than on myth although the former serves as a model.

17. Jünger's diary, April 5, 1939: "It is to be avoided, however, that the tale assume a purely allegorical character. It must live out of itself, complete without reference to time, and it is even good if obscure passages remain which the author himself is not able to explain" (2, 29). It is noteworthy that when Jünger comments on his work he does precisely what he wanted to avoid: he interprets his characters as embodiments of ideas. For the figure of the Chief Ranger, cf. especially the diary entries from 5 April 1939 and *Das Abenteuerliche Herz* (7, 214 ff).

18. *Das Abenteuerliche Herz* (2d. ed.). This is a reference to the Chief Ranger. (7, 214, also 2, 29).

19. Loose, p. 172.

20. Cf. Fletcher, p. 147 ff.

21. For the concept of the anima, see C. G. Jung, *Psychological Types*, trans. by H. Godwin Baynes (New York, 1923), 588 ff. The anima is an image of the soul, representing the inner attitude of human consciousness that is turned toward the unconscious. The image is feminine in the case of a man, but masculine for a woman. The ego is frequently not conscious of its identity

with the anima. In such a case, it projects the unconscious part of the psyche (anima) into a real person. Jung's discovery is relevant for literature to the extent that Jung assigns this archetypal soul-image to a collective unconscious. Myths are also nourished from this realm and Jung often uses them for comparison. Likewise, Jung regards literature as articulation of the collective unconscious. "We cannot, therefore, afford to be indifferent to the poets, since in their principal works and deepest inspirations they create from the very depths of the unconscious, voicing aloud what others only dream" *Psychological Types*, p. 237. Jung's psychoanalytical beginning is distinguished from the similarly-directed one of Freud and his school by the conviction that neither mythology nor literature can be interpreted reductively: "When the Freudian school maintains that every artist possesses an auto-erotically limited personality, then this might be true for him as a personality, but it does not hold for the creator in him," C. G. Jung, *Welt der Psyche, Eine Auswahl zur Einführning* (Zurich, 1954), 55. Jung is interested primarily in the psychic analogy whereas the literary critic is more concerned with the collective cultural accumulation as such.

22. See especially, C. G. Jung, *Symbols of Transformation. An Analysis of the Prelude to a Case of Schizophrenia, Collected Works,* Vol. V (London, 1956). As nourishing earth-mother, p. 159 f.; dual nature, p. 431.

23. C. G. Jung, *Symbols of Transformation,* p. 332, cf. also "zur Psychologie des Geistes," *Symbolik des Geistes* (1948), p. 3 ff.

24. If one reads the hero's progress as the process of individuation, then the figures surrounding the narrating-ego will be regarded as projected archetypes. For the problem of individuation see Jung, *Symbols of Transformation* and Jung, *Psychology and Alchemy* (London, 1956 & 1953, respectively).

25. For the psychological concept of function vide Jung, *Psychological Types,* p. 513 f. Jung distinguishes four functions (547) of which two are rational and two irrational. Out of these one primary function emerges and is joined. by one conscious auxiliary function (p. 514 f), while two functions remain unconscious. The fourth one, the so-called inferior function is the anima in the case of a man. "The anima also stands for the 'inferior' function and for that reason frequently has a shady character; in fact she sometimes stands for evil itself," C. G. Jung, *Psychology and Alchemy,* p. 143 f.

26. C. G. Jung, *Psychology and Alchemy,* p. 144.

27. "The psychic life-force, the libido, symbolizes itself in the sun or personifies itself in figures of heroes with solar attributes," C. G. Jung, *Symbols of Transformation,* p. 202.

28. *Vide* Henri Plard, "Ex ordine Shandytorum. Das Schlangensymbol in Ernst Jünger's Werk," *Freundschaftliche Begegnungen. Festschrift für Ernst Jünger zum 60. Geburtstag,* ed. Armin Mohler (Frankfurt/Main, 1955).

29. Jünger's diary, April 3, 1939. (2, 27)

30. Cf. 28.

31. Jung, *Symbols of Transformation,* p. 372.

32. Jung, *Psychology and Alchemy,* p. 364, and *Symbols of Transformation,* p. 383.

33. Cf. Jung, *Psychology and Alchemy,* pp. 109, 241.

34. C. G. Jung & K. Kerenyi, *Introduction to a Science of Mythology* (London, 1951), p. 37.

35. "It is a personification of vital forces quite outside the limited range of our conscious mind; of possible ways and means of which our one-sided conscious mind knows nothing; a wholeness which embraces the very depths of nature. It represents the strongest, most ineluctable urge in every being, namely the urge to realize itself." Jung/Kerenyi, p. 123 f.

36. Concerning the origin and currency of the mandala, Jung says, "It seems to

me beyond question that these Eastern symbols originated in dreams and visions, and were not invented by some Mahayana church father. On the contrary, they are among the oldest religious symbols of humanity and may even have existed in paleolithic times." *Psychology and Alchemy*, p. 92 f.

37. For Jung's concept of symbol which wants above all to set itself apart from the rational sign, see Jung, *Psychological Types*, p. 601 ff. "It (the symbol) certainly has one side that accords with reason, but it has also another side that is inaccessible to reason; for not only the data of reason, but also the irrational data of pure inner and outer perception, have entered its nature" (p. 607).

38. *Vide* Jung, "The Symbolism of the Mandala," *Psychology and Alchemy*, part II, chap. 3, p. 91 ff.

39. Cf. Jung, *Symbols of Transformation*, p. 217.

40. *Ibid.*, p. 121.

41. Mythological parallels in Jung, *Symbols of Transformation*, p. 351ff.

42. Jung, *Psychology and Alchemy*, p. 218 ff.

43. *Ibid.*, p. 332 ff.

43a. *Ibid.*, p. 299.

44. The relation between Lampros and Sunmyra calls to mind the alchemistic allegory of the king and the king's son. In the "Visio Arislei," there is an account of the *rex marinus* in whose kingdom there is no procreation. The king is advised to mate his son Thabritius with his daughter Beya. "The brother-sister pair stands allegorically for the whole conception of opposites." Jung, *Psychology and Alchemy*, p. 317. Thus their union involves a *conjunctio oppositorum* which is admittedly punished at first because of its incestuous character. The son suffers death, that is *mortificatio*, so necessary to the alchemistic process. Later he is returned to life by his friends. Alchemistic allegory likewise provides the basic pattern of death and rebirth. For this complex cf. Jung, *Psychology and Alchemy*, p. 313 ff.

45. *Vide:* Figures in Jung, *Psychology and Alchemy*, p. 79, fig. 31, and p. 187, fig. 93.

46. Benjamin, *Schriften* volume I, p. 284.

47. *Vide* Bengt Algot Sørensen. *Symbol und Symbolismus in den ästhetischen Theorien des 18. Jahrhunderts und der deutschen Romantik* (Copenhagen, 1963), especially Chapters 8-10.

48. Sørensen, p. 197.

49. Cf. Jünger, vol. VIII, p. 327.

50. Fr. Creuzer, *Symbolik und Mythologie der alten Völker*, vol. I (1810), p. 69. Cf. also Sørensen, p. 267.

51. Hans-Georg Gadamer, *Wahrheit und Methode, Grundzüge einer philosophischen Hermeneutik.* (2d. ed.; Tübingen, 1965), p. 76.

52. Albrecht Schöne, *Emblematik und Drama im Zeitalter des Barock* (Munich, 1964), p. 25.

53. Nevertheless, the possibility of corruption does not prejudice the principle of the emblem. In attempting to distinguish the emblem from the allegory in a narrow sense, Schöne writes: "It is true of the really crucial ideal type of emblem, one which is true to type, that it represents that which exists, as that which has meaning" (Schöne, p. 32).

54. Benjamin, *Schriften*, vol. I, p. 298.

55. For the allegorical process cf. Fletcher, *Allegory, The Theory of a Symbolic Mode*. The present essay is indebted to this copious work in some points.

Robert John

THE LADY AS SYMBOLICAL FIGURE IN MEDIEVAL ITALIAN LITERATURE

THE RICH LITERARY PRODUCTION OF SOUTHERN FRANCE FOLLOWED THE
Latin poetry of Late Antiquity as the first European literature composed in a national tongue. Long before Julius Caesar had annexed
northern and central Gaul to the Roman Empire, southern France,
or *Gallia Narbonenis,* was a cultural territory, which was regarded in
Rome as a comparable area to the Italian fatherland.

Here in the *Provincia* the *Langue d'oc* arose which was a clearly
different language from the *Langue d'oïl* which developed further
north. It happened, therefore, that the Provençal of the south had a
definite advantage over the French of the north and it conferred
powerful impulses to the budding European literatures. The Provençal poetry was primarily love poetry. Throughout two centuries it
impressed its unmistakable stamp upon the art of the Provençal
bards, the troubadours, and other lyrical motifs remained largely in
the background.

This love poetry was of a strictly courtly-aristocratic nature. It
presupposed an exclusive society of nobility and limited itself directly to this society. The "Lady" deified by the troubadour was
almost always a lady of a castle, who, however, produced the effect
of an other-worldly being towards whom the troubadour hardly
dared lift his glance, even though he himself commanded highest
social and political positions. It is striking that still shortly before

the year 1100 the Provençal poets could be counted on one hand, whereas at the beginning of the 12th century they traversed the country in large numbers. Their number increased, sometimes more quickly and sometimes slower, until about the year 1290. Today we know the names of approximately 700 of these lyric poets of southern France, though often not a single line of their songs has been preserved. The long succession of troubadours was inaugurated by William IX, the Duke of Aquitaine. Born in 1071, he is also known as Guilhem VII, Count of Poitiers. It was concluded by Guiraut Riquier (1230–94), the last significant representative of this poetry which once had cast its rays over all of Europe.

Its swan song was the funeral dirge for King Robert of Naples (died in 1343), who, during his time, was the most learned monarch. As a sign of his admiration for Petrarch, the bard of Laura, King Robert bequeathed his own coronation robe to the Roman capitol for the poet laureate ceremony. King Robert was also the Count of Provence and as such the vassal of Emperor Henry VII.

Troubadours of high rank did not travel in person to those citadels and castles where their lady-loves resided. They were represented by their *jongleurs* who, with their stringed instrument (the *vielle*) in hand, offered the artful songs of their lord to the high-born lady. Troubadours of lower rank naturally were their own *jongleurs* and as bards often were designated also by this term.

This courtly love was a kind of science as well, such as the famous "gay saber" *(gaye sience)* illustrates, which had definite gradations: from *fegneire* (aspirant), to *pregneire* (postulant), to *entendeire* (auditor), and finally to *drutz* (lover), who could expect a kiss as a token of distinction.

The sudden increase in the number of troubadours after the year 1100 brought with it an equally noteworthy counterpart, namely the over-flowing wealth of metrical forms (with the exception of the sonnet!) and the accompanying dearth of motifs. Spring, battle, war, reprimand, and the joy of attack personally and politically are the constantly recurring themes, which, however, stand in the background when compared to the cult of the Lady.

It is small wonder that the glorifications intended for the high-born ladies lapse into a tiring monotony, or that frequently the feelings expressed are surprisingly insipid and the comparisons drawn even by troubadours of great poetic talent become grotesque and ridiculous. Peire Vidal's Lady, for instance, is more precious than a hundred camels ladened with gold.

The factor which especially characterized this poetry and which caused it to remain unique despite its universal influence throughout two centuries was that, without exception, the Lady deified had to be a married woman. A maiden of nobility, such as the unmarried daughter of the Lord of a castle, could never be the center of attention of the "gay saber"; rather, the focus could only be continual adultery in a spiritual sense. At the court of King Arthur, at least so goes the saga, this type of love formed an indispensable norm. Marriage, plainly spoken, could be no excuse to eliminate love. We see that those versed in the "gay saber" were very concerned with investing their strangely conceived ethics, which centered around extramarital love, with as respectable an age as possible.

For two hundred years, however, could every castle lord of Provence really have ignored, overlooked, in fact even tolerated and supported the arrival of a troubadour or *jongleur* at his citadel? If we were told even once that a troubadour was soundly thrashed by the husband of his lady-love, it would only mean that the husbands of the noble ladies very seldom allowed themselves fits of anger; in fact, it seems that an amazing lack of jealousy was one of their chief characteristics. Seriously, however, such a strange frame of mind can hardly be assumed for the citadel masters of that time. The story about the delicately prepared heart of a troubadour (Guillem de Cabestanh), which a lady was forced by her husband to eat, only to discover afterwards the true nature of her repast and then to commit suicide, points rather in a different direction.

On the other hand it seems obvious that a love poetry, whose subject matter was exclusively the married woman, could not thrive for six or seven generations if the entire social stratum for which it was fashionable had not been basically in accord with this continual "mental" adultery. These lyricists, in contrast to those schools of poets in the rest of Europe who learned from them, must have detected, in principle, something inferior and repugnant in marriage as an institution.

This frame of mind of the Provençal nobility, which appears so strange to us today, did in fact exist. It was the interpretation of marriage held by the Albigenses. Since we are still often of the opinion that the Albigenses were the Huguenots of the Middle Ages, we are prone to commit an error which is accompanied with weighty consequences even for literary history; namely, we overlook the true core of their teaching. The Albigenses—not the Waldenses—were true Manichaeans in their avowal of a good and an evil Original

Principle. As logically consistent dualists, therefore, they were no longer monotheists and despite their nomenclature, naturally they were also not Christians in the consequential sense of this term. For the Albigenses the good divinity was the creator of the entire world of the spiritual and psychic, whereas the evil divinity brought the material world into being. Thereby the physical nature of the human being was condemned because it too was a creation of the evil Original Principle. Hence marriage, which serves to propagate physical life, could only stem from evil. Every sexual misdemeanor was more excusable than was marriage as a bourgeois and religious institution. We should consider the entire love poetry of Provence in the light of this dogma.

We know that the great pillars and bases of the Albigenses were the Provençal castles and citadels which stood on the numerous mountain peaks and hilltops of this richly blessed land. The earliest center of this movement, the city of Albi, from which the Albigenses took their name, soon became less significant than Toulouse. The Counts of Toulouse stretched out their protective hand over this broadly diffused sect, even though they themselves probably did not belong formally to the Albigenses. Indeed, the question of actual membership in the Albigensian sect very often defies the possibility of historical proof because the members of this sect were masters in the art of camouflage. Furthermore, the Albigensian baptism, the *Consolamentum*, frequently was received only at the hour of death, in order not to again endanger the purity of soul which could only be obtained through effort. Even disregarding the Albigensian academy of theology, the capitol city in the earldom of Toulouse represented a center of southern French anti-Curial trends. Moreover, it undoubtedly was also a fortress of the radical Franciscans, of ecclesiastically critical Joachimism, and of the so-called "Latin Avveroism," which can be, mutatis mutandis, easily compared to the Russian intelligentsia in the era of the czardom. Those who were connected with these deep movements which extended throughout wide areas of Europe were drawn, it seemed, irresistibly to Toulouse.

Hence Dante's friend, Guido Cavalcanti, who was ostensibly on a pilgrimage to Santiago de Compostela, lingered in Toulouse and fell in love with a lady there only because she so deceivingly resembled his lady-love in Florence. An equally beautiful and gifted lady as Cavalcanti's Donna Mandetta from Toulouse was the Donna NaLombarda of the Gascon troubadour Bernart-Arnaut d'Armagnac, who knew her only from hearsay. He made a lightning-like visit to her, sent her a poem from his lodging, and disappeared on horseback as quickly as he had come.

Jaufré Rudel, "Prince" of Blaye, heard a great deal from returning pilgrims about the beauty and kindness of Countess Melisende of Tripoli. This was reason enough for him immediately to fall in love with her and to undertake the difficult sea voyage to Tripoli in Syria. As he was not equal to the exertion of this trip, he was carried ashore in the harbor of Tripoli so weakened that he died in the arms of Melisende, who quickly had been summoned. The countess, deeply affected by this service of love, entered a cloister on the very same day. First, however, she had Rudel's body interred in the Knights Templar cemetery of her city.

In actuality, the Prince of Blaye died at home, a countess of Tripoli never entered a cloister, and Melisende was a little countess eight years old when her troubadour died. Historically viewed then, it is all absurd. But at the same time the matter has another mien, when we learn that the Counts of Tripoli were identical with the Counts of Toulouse. To die in the arms of the Countess of Toulouse was an expression in the secret language of the Albigenses for the reception of the *Consolamentum* on their death-bed. We have an analogous report, but in a much more concise form, from the troubadour Peire Raimon, who was also active as a poet for a long time in Aragon: after his return he fell in love with a Lady from Toulouse. This report sounds quite similar to the one about Guido Cavalcanti.

Since the popes in the Middle Ages were almost always political personalities as well, naturally those opponents of the Curia policies who conformed with the Bishop of Rome in matters of religion and dogma also formed a significant group. However, when voices were raised in these circles against the Curia of Rome, this circumstance as such was not a proof that the source of dissent was Albigensian; on the contrary, there were speeches and writings from canonized saints who had disputed with the Curia more sharply than is customary today, such as Hildegard of Bingen, Bernhard of Clairvaux, and Catherine of Siena, just to mention the most famous ones.

Attacks on the Roman church in connection with the Provençal cult of the Lady, however, indicate without doubt a genuine Albigensian source. Furthermore, as previously suggested, this applies only to the circumference of Provence. The numerous European affiliations of the troubadour art do not necessarily bear the stamp of the Albigenses. In Palermo at the court of Frederick II the celebrated

Lady is no longer synonymous with a married woman and this is the case to an even lesser degree in the two Tuscan schools of poetry.

What we generally do not consider is that for centuries in the Near East there had been an unorthodox spirituality pitted against the orthodox Islamic faith. This unorthodox spiritual stream used a poetic secret language, a poetic cult of the Lady, to express their ideas of opposition. This was the lyrical poetry of the Persian-Arabic Sufi, which existed for centuries and whose leading lights were Mewlana Dschelal-eddin Rumi (died in 1262) and Ferid-eddin Attar (died in 1330). Their love poems, which are of great beauty, are never to be taken literally but always symbolically in a mystical sense as the expression of a pantheistically conceived love of God. The same applies to the Sufi poems which extol the "friend," who is always called Jussuf. For a long time these poems were basically misunderstood in the Occident, but at last we know that also this glowing love of the friend means exactly the same thing as the other Sufi lyrics.

Accordingly, we are concerned here with a highly perfected poetry which was at home along the Eastern basin of the Mediterranean and in which the allegorical Lady played a very decisive role. This allegory of purely spiritual matters and conditions, which stood in complete opposition to the governing orthodox Islamic mentality, had its European analogy in the Provençal cult of the Lady. Furthermore, just as the poet-dervishes travelled around in the Orient and sang their songs, so did the troubadours and *jongleurs* travel about with the similar intention of spreading new ideas through poetic song or at least preparing the soil for them.

The task was made essentially easier for them in that they did not have to become familiar with the Persian-Arabic poetry from a far distance, but found it, so to speak, right at their own doorstep, namely in Spain. There were also Sufi poets of great significance there. An investigation, which was published in Switzerland, about the connections between Arabic, Provençal, and German love poetry, brought into the open astonishing evidence of countless parallel phenomena within these three literary worlds; evidence which remained unfortunately almost entirely disregarded.

The much earlier investigations about the close literary connection between Dante's friend, Cavalcanti, with the Spanish Sufi Ibn Bağğa (died in 1138), or between Dante himself and the Spanish Sufi poet Abenarabi (died in 1258), were also disregarded. The question of how Provençal or even Italian poets, who hardly understood Arabic, could acquire a knowledge of literary models from the Arabic world, is easily answered: the connection could be established without difficulty through a circle of spiritually interested people who had perfectly mastered the Arabic. This group, upon whom the searchlight of investigation rests, were the adepts of the Knights Templar of Jerusalem. From 1135 A.D. onward these circles of adepts formed an international ring of the most highly cultured artists and writers. These individuals could find knights or chaplains in each of the most important temples or religious houses who had mastered Arabic through lengthy visits to the Near East. Generally, we imagine the two hundred year epoch of the crusades as all too filled with war and fighting. Actually the pauses in fighting lasted much longer than the fighting, and during these quiet periods the Knights Templar came into contact with the spiritual "upper stratum" of the Near Eastern countries. A significant number of members of the Knights Templar Order were from Provence, hence they undoubtedly were capable in many respects of acting as conveyors of Arabic ideas in philosophy and poetry. From the literary point of view, the chief figure seems to have been the troubadour Arnaut Daniel, who as *Gran Maestro d'Amore* enjoyed the highest respect of Dante and Petrarch.

Thus in Dante's *Vita Nuova* (XXIX) it reads that the Nobilissima Donna Beatrice died according to Arabic chronology in the first hour of the ninth day of the month, according to Syrian chronology in the ninth month of the year, and according to the Christian calendar in the ninth decade of the century of her birth (1290). Dante could have learned these Oriental calendar dates without difficulty in the house of the Knights Templar Order in Florence.

Beatrice mentions her name to Dante only once, namely in Paradiso Terrestre, where she appears to him in the full glory of her triumph. The verse, *Purgatorio* XXX,73, is noteworthy. The Beatrice of the *Vita Nuova* is always in some manner accompanied by the number nine. Here also the sum of the 72 preceding verses constitutes a nine as well as the 72 verses which follow. The 30th Canto of the *Purgatorio* is the 64th of the entire *Divina Commedia,* so that the sum of the numbers of the preceding 63 cantos produces the number nine, but also those of the 36 following cantos. This is a truly amazing architectonic structure, a crowning of the thesis of the *Vita Nuova* XXIX,3: that Beatrice herself was the number nine, hence exactly that number which has always been considered the sign of initiation and adepthood.

The *Dolce Stil Nuovo,* as the second Tuscan school of poetry was called since Dante, betrays its Provençal origin very quickly to everyone well acquainted with the facts; nevertheless, it is not identical with the cult of the Provençal Lady. The cult of the Tuscan Donna became bourgeois and above all lost its original tendency of depreciating the institution of marriage.

Yet despite the fact that the *Dolce Stil Nuovo* obviously was not Albigensian, it was surrounded by a cloud of mystery and esotericism.

On the occasion of his coronation as poet, Petrarch in his famous speech discussed questions of style and commented that a style is so much the sweeter the harder the shell is which first must be cracked open. This passage was especially intended for the second Tuscan school of poetry. Thereby we have corroboration that we should not regard the cult of the Tuscan Donna, who likewise always seems like a being from a Higher World, in a literal sense but rather symbolically.

Whereas the Lady of Provence was always without a name, or was occasionally fictitiously named, the Donna of the *Dolce Stil Nuovo* was always provided with a specific name. Among them were Francesco da Barberino's "Donna Costanza," Guido Cavalcanti's "Donna Giovanna," Lapo Gianni's "Donna Lagia," Cino de Pistoria's "Donna Selvaggia," and many others. They were all radiant beings of light who brought peace and good breeding to the entire world. Furthermore, their admirers were made so happy by venerating them that for each Donna they wished as many admirers as possible. Actually, however, all these Ladies were only one being, whom Luigi Valli always designated as *Santa Sapienza,* but whose undefined spirituality in its actual philosophical-religious content is, in reality, a templar-gnostic Sophia, similar to C. G. Jung's archetype of the *Anima.*

The most famous Donna of all is Beatrice, who made Dante blissful. Indeed, there was a certain Beatrice Portinari, whom Boccaccio first mentions as an historical personality. Today on a sarcophagus in the small Florentine church of S. Margherita we can still see a bas-relief depiction of her nurse, Monna Tessa, who inspired Beatrice's father to found a hospital in Florence. There are so many and such weighty reasons which speak against an identification of the Beatrice of the *Vita Nuova* or the *Divina Commedia* with Bea-

trice Portinari, after marriage Beatrice de Bardi, that no one famil-
iar with this highly subtle material can believe that the Lady de
Bardi was Dante's Beatrice. Even a section of the *Vita Nuova*
(XXXII,1) suffices to destroy conclusively the Beatrice fable which
Boccaccio fabricated. This report states that shortly after her death,
Dante's second best friend, Lapo Gianni, asked Dante for an elegy
to a deceased Lady. Lapo does not mention her name, but Dante,
nevertheless, immediately recognized her as the Nobilissima Donna
Beatrice. Moreover, although Lapo was connected with her through
closest blood ties, this same Lapo, nevertheless, accepts two poems
by Dante as a posthumous homage for the Lady of his love.

The fact that the topography of the Dantesque Paradiso Terrestre
exactly corresponds to the medieval map of Jerusalem and, in addition, that the place of Beatrice's triumphal coach was precisely the
antipodal point to the mother church of the Knights Templar, certainly provides food for thought. Whom else could such a deliberate
placing of this point have interested if not an adept of the Templar
Order? Let us consider, leaving aside everything else, just the colors
of Beatrice's clothing at this solemn hour: the cloak green, the dress
red, the veil covering her eyes white. These are the colors of the
ancient initiations, as we repeatedly encounter them, for instance
with Virgil, who was himself a mystic of Eleusis. Such an instance is
the famous fourth eclogue where the white lambs upon the green
pasture offer their wool which has become red of itself.

We meet this color triad again and again from the period of high
medieval literature until well into the literature and painting of the
Renaissance. Dino Compagni's *Donna Intelligenza* is garbed in the
same colors as the triumphant Beatrice; Raphael follows these models in the Vatican stanzas with his *Theology;* Michelangelo's Father
God, in the fresco of the *Creation of Adam* on the ceiling of the
Sistine Chapel, appears with the forceful gestures of His omnipotence in a white tunic (chiton), with a red cloak puffed out by the
tempest and a green scarf fluttering behind.

Hence, we see that the adepthood of the Knights Templar can
be recognized easily by this tricolor scheme. Moreover, this cursory
survey shows us that despite Clemens V's liquidation of the Order
in the year 1312 (during the Council of Vienne), it secretly continued to exist for a long time to come.

Dante damned Clemens V to Hell more often than any other sin-
ner, six times altogether. The last word of all which Beatrice directs
to her loyal companion, her final word in the *Divina Commedia,* as

it were, deals with nothing other than just this condemnation of Clemens V, who summoned the Council of Vienne.

I believe that with these few indications about Beatrice as the symbolical Lady par excellence, the meaning of this unique figure has also been disclosed. She is the great representative of the temple wisdom, whose task it is to clearly announce to the world that the third Joachimistic world-epoch, the *Ecclesia Spiritualis,* is imminent. Moreover, during this epoch the *Patrimonium Petri,* or church state, which destroys peace, will no longer exist and the new World-Guide will be also the Re-establisher of the Order of the Knights Templar, that is, a new Zorobabel, who in 515 B.C. reconstructed the old temple which had been destroyed by the Babylonians. For this reason Dante named him the "Five Hundred and Fifteen" (DXV). It was precisely this enigma of Beatrice which led to catastrophe during Mussolini's era through a misconstruction of *DUX.*

The Nobilissima Donna is, as was stated, only one of the many Ladies of the *Dolce Stil Nuovo.* If she, however, once is recognized in her intrinsic being as the most significant of them, by like token so are all the others. They enjoy a similar stereotype glorification like the great Ladies of Provence and, all things considered, like them must acquiesce to the same irksome monotonous homage. Whereas the troubadours, who followed in the footsteps of the Sufi poetry, were the notorious pace-makers of the Albigenses, the Tuscan poets, also strongly influenced by Sufism, were the torch-bearers for the knowledge of a new epoch for church and empire. That they could only do this symbolically through the flower of poetry, belonged to the heart of the matter. This flower was a special kind of love poetry in which the vocabulary continually repeated itself in an obvious manner. Certainly this too was an emanation from Provence.

The Arabic philosophy, which attained its peak with Averroës (being primarily indebted to Plotinus and Aristotle), influenced the Tuscan poetry to a far greater extent than the Persian-Arabic poetry affected the Provençal. The power of knowledge and the doctrine of wisdom which the Tuscan Lady imparted to her disciple is actually the Occidental reflection of the blessing which in the Orient was attributed to the *intellectus activus,* to the Greek Νους ποιητικος. The Islamic philosophy of that time thought of it as a kind of spiritual stratosphere out of which all higher knowledge radiated into the human soul. This same blessing was also bestowed by the Lady whom the poets of the *Dolce Stil Nuovo* deified. Today we would call her

"Lady Enlightenment." In the final analysis her treasure house of blessing also is Neoplatonism, in particular, the *Enneads* of Plotinus, but in addition to this, the prophetic-reformatory spirit, Joachim of Fiore, who appears to us again and again precisely in the *Divina Commedia*.

With these considerations naturally it is not to be concluded that there was no realistic love poetry in Provence and Tuscany. Undoubtedly, however, we would completely fail to recognize much of the most significant poetry of that time if we did not understand that the worshipping of the Lady of the castle in southern France and of the Lady of the spirit in central Italy is not to be taken historically and literally in a superficially realistic sense. Rather, this worshipping should be regarded in a symbolical way which then corresponds to the style and thinking of the authors of that time.

[Translated from the German by Virginia Sease]

Alice Raphael

ALCHEMISTIC SYMBOLS IN GOETHE'S "WALPURGIS NIGHT'S DREAM"

TO CONJURE THE SPIRIT OF A THING MEANS TO SEEK AFTER THE TRUTH which that thing represents. To see the spirit of a thing means to recognize the character of that thing, with all its qualities and attributes. To make the spirit of a thing subservient to one's power is to know how to use the powers that are hidden in a thing for our own purpose.[1]

The alchemists were well aware of the danger involved in awakening psychic powers of an unpredictable character. They sought to define such powers, as if in so doing they could delimit them. Serious attempts were made during the Middle Ages to define sorcery. De Givry in his compendium, *Witchcraft, Magic and Alchemy*, gives an excellent interpretation in a chapter entitled "The Sorcerer as Priest of the Demoniacal Church." He makes it clear that not all sorcerers attended the Sabbath, the notorious gatherings of sorcerers and witches belonging to a specific area at which the Devil supposedly presided. Many sorcerers practiced their arts in less evil gatherings.

They told fortunes, read the future by the tarot cards . . . and devoted themselves to divination by any of the innumerable methods. . . . This kind of sorcery especially seems to have been practised by the people known as Bohemians or Gypsies, and it is a point worth noting that these were wanderers, while the Satanizing sorcerers in distinction were attached to their villages.

Finally, there were sorcerers whom we should now class as "intellectuals." They were called sorcerers because an exact notion of what we mean by a "learned man" did not then exist. . . . But the man who

made up his mind to manipulate matter and wrest its secrets from it
in the shadow of a laboratory, . . . was still regarded as a variety of
sorcerer.[2]

Faust is thus regarded by two simple old people at the opening of
the Fifth Act, Part II.

Often the Wanderers seen upon the highways during the Middle
Ages were neophytes seeking work in one of the many alchemical
laboratories. Or a Wanderer may perhaps have been one of the Albigenses, since innumerable preachers of this sect, variously disguised,
crisscrossed Europe in the hope of making converts to their mystical
heretical Church.

Goethe has stressed, in the Eighth Book of his memoirs, the impact
made upon him when he first read Gottfried Arnold's *History of the
Church and of Heretics*. In so doing he came to have an entirely different attitude to men who had been represented to him either as
mad or impious.[3] Thus he was on familiar historical territory when
he presented Mephistopheles as a wandering scholar upon his first
appearance to Faust. Still another factor contributed to this disguise
—and perhaps even to the lordly appearance of Mephistopheles in
the third Study Scene. Many noblemen—in Provence especially—
were members of the Manichean sect, an influence which runs
through *Faust,* Parts I and II. Manicheism first entered Europe in
the third century, again in the seventh, and the sect accompanied
the Catholic Church until the fourteenth century when it disappeared into Calvinism. When the historical Faustus styled himself
Faustus *Junior,* one title among many others, he may have intended
to communicate to those in the know that he was a Manichean, perhaps even a disciple of the renowned Doctor Faustus, the eminent
Manichean teacher with whom Augustine engaged in a celebrated
theological argument.[4]

The manner in which the young student of Secret Doctrines participated in his own dialectical arguments is actually told in a long
passage in the memoirs, the full meaning of which the reader may
not notice unless he is familiar with the alchemical art of the *meditatio*. Of a sudden, in the Thirteenth Book, Goethe begins to speak
of himself in the third person, as he does on rare occasions in his
autobiography. He says that

> . . . he had the habit, when he was alone, of calling before his mind
> any person of his acquaintance. This person he entreated to sit down,
> walked up and down by him, remained standing before him, and dis-
> coursed with him on the subject he had in his mind. To this the per-

son answered as occasion required, or by the ordinary gestures signified his assent or dissent. . . . The oddest part of the affair was that he never selected persons of his intimate acquaintance, but those whom he saw but seldom, nay, several who lived at a distance in the world, and with whom he had a transient connection. . . . He often summoned contradicting spirits to these dialectic exercises.

Now mental dialogues often accompanied the visions which the alchemists produced during their labors. They gave a particular meaning to the word *meditari* which did not mean to contemplate. According to Jung, citing Ruland's *Lexicon alchemiae,* " 'The word *meditatio* is used when a man has an inner dialogue with someone unseen. It may be with God when He is invoked, or with himself or with his good angel.' "[5]

The long conversations between Faust and Mephistopheles in the Study Scenes of Part I can be regarded as a sustained *meditatio.* The opening scene in Forest and Cavern is Faust's *meditatio* with himself, and the dialogue in the Prologue in Heaven (written in the same year) can also be regarded as "an inner dialogue and hence a living relationship to the answering voice of the 'other' in ourselves, i.e., of the unconscious."[6]

In 1795 Goethe had been brooding over the question of a religious *meditatio.* Speaking of the Sixth Book of *Wilhelm Meister,* Schiller commented favorably (August 17, 1795) upon the manner in which Goethe dealt with the subject of "the silent communion between the person and the Divine within him," a subject which Goethe had treated earlier that summer in *The Parable.* Goethe returned to the subject of a silent communion in a Prologue to *Faust,* probably written in June of 1797.

The "Prologue in Heaven" is a *meditatio* between one aspect of Goethe's nature, projected forth as an ironical realist, perhaps even somewhat of an amusing rogue (an aspect Goethe is seeking to dispose of or cast off, somewhat in the manner of a cabalist), and a deeper aspect of his being, a divine element projected forth as The Almighty. Goethe is asking himself whether he had made any perceptible advance upon the philosophic path, and with ironical realism comes to the conclusion that he is "still as odd as on Creation's day."

The Almighty, neither denying Goethe's accusations nor questioning his motives, merely affirms a faith—a faith that "the Good Gardener of Life"—as the Logos was called in the cult of Thrice Greatest Hermes—will bring to maturity the blossom and the fruit of a

new life;[7] and here the very words Goethe introduces into the Prologue are taken from a passage from Schiller's letter of January 17,
1797:

> You must have passed through a certain, and not very short period
> which I shall call your analytic period, where your endeavors were
> toward completeness . . . where your nature, so to speak, was at vari-
> ance with itself, and sought to reinstate itself, through Art and Science.
>   It seems to me that now, when fully developed and mature, you are
> returning to your youth, and will unite the fruit with the blossom.
> This second period of youth is the youth of the gods, and immortals
> like them.

Together with its poetic sweep which carried Goethe to a new
eminence two years later, "Walpurgis Night's Dream" contains a
number of interpolated stanzas which interrupt the action of the
scene. These stanzas are perhaps the "bits of paper" which Goethe
dropped into what he called his "Walpurgis Sack," and when he
explained the term to Falk he said that it was

> . . . a sort of infernal pocket . . . originally destined for the reception
> of certain poems which had a near connection with the witch scenes in
> Faust, if not with the Blocksberg itself. . . . Every bit of paper that
> falls into my Walpurgis Sack falls into Hell; and out of Hell, as you
> know, is no deliverance. . . . In it burns an unquenchable purifying
> fire, which, when it seizes its prey, spares neither friend nor foe. I, at
> least, would not advise anybody to go very near it. I am afraid of it
> myself.[8]

As we follow Goethe toward this purifying fire, we enter the
region of Schierke and Elend, where granite masses tower far above
primeval forests and the peak of the Brocken rises beyond three
thousand feet.

"Walpurgis Night's Dream" opens in a gentle key and, at the
beginning of Faust's steep ascent to the Brocken, Mephistopheles
might be none other than a middle-aged nature philosopher taking
a walking trip with a favorite pupil. Suddenly the beauty of a night
in early spring changes rapidly into a night of uncanny terror as the
world begins to shift backwards, dissolving into the cabalistic World
of Emanations, which always preceded Creation proper.

Mephistopheles reveals himself again to be a conditioned being,
as indeed all sorcerers are, since they are dependent for the successful
outcome of their magical practices upon certain rigid conditions.
Just as Mephistopheles was dependent upon the good will of a rat
in order to be released from the study, so, too, he cannot enter the
Brocken without the aid of a Will-o'-the-Wisp.

This flickering light was essential since Mephistopheles intends to use knowledge for sorcerial purposes by creating an alchemical *tria prima* in the reversed sense. The possibility of disturbing the harmony of the universe was an established doctrine in antiquity. Plotinus believed, and other thinkers too, that by means of the Black Art, a lower form of theurgy, the wicked magician could disturb the parts of the universe, held together by harmonious sympathetic relationships. Songs, invocations, numbers, and incantations were devices taught to students of the Black Art. These could be harmlessly employed, as in the second Study Scene of Part I, when Mephistopheles summons his minions of "dream-senders," a term attributed to Simon Magus by the Church Fathers.

But now we are to witness an incantation fraught with diabolical power, and the song, chanted in unison by Faust, Mephistopheles, and the Will-o'-the-Wisp, upsets the balance of the universe. The laws of nature governed by Sublime Reason yield to irrational forces; the tranquil night in early spring gives way to a tempest.

Like the woods of Dunsinane, the trees begin to move forward, the cliffs to bend and bow, while the flowing brooks run ever faster, and forest-creatures are rushing onwards. They know not why, they know not whither! Violent winds hiss above the cliffs, the stars and moon are withdrawn from sight—indicating that the forces of the universe have been successfully disturbed.

Faust and Mephistopheles have now entered a primordial world of pure matter, ruled by Lord Mammon, as villagers from adjacent districts begin to stumble up the Brocken where they are joined by witches and wizards flying to its craggy heights. No separation exists between real and purely symbolical creatures as, for example, when Dame Baubo, a stock-in-trade character out of the Eleusinian rites, enters upon a farrow sow—a reference to the pig of purification in this Mystery. The Orphic Mysteries are hinted at in a character named Proktophantasmist who is compelled to sit forever in mud.[9]

"Walpurgis Night's Dream" poses the question of evil from the standpoint of choice. Since Faust does not surrender to the young witch, and his will for the first time runs counter to the will of Mephistopheles, does not the outcome of the scene place Faust on the side of the angels?

Goethe has deleted from the final arrangement of the text several scenes which refer to the Black Mass. As the scene now stands, it can be read without knowledge of the sacrilegious rites which arose in France during the thirteenth century. The Black Mass sustained a tradition of the Sabbath, originally a pagan religious celebration.

But since Goethe did write the episode in questionable taste (now deposited in paralipomena to "Walpurgis Night's Dream") our reconstruction according to Goethe's original text affords the reader a new perspective.

From his Strasburg studies Goethe knew the thirteenth century to have been the darkest period in Church history, and that social conditions then prevailing had given an impetus to the Albigensian movement. In this era a counter-movement began which aimed in aristocratic circles at the restoration of the Feminine Principle. The Black Mass, according to Professor Jules Michelet, signified the "redemption of Eve from the curse Christianity had laid upon her. At the Witches' Sabbath woman fulfills every office. She is priest, and altar, and consecrated host. . . ."[10]

The Black Mass, enacted upon a heath and in certain parts of a forest, began with an *Introit* patterned upon a pre-Christian processional. Soon after the celebrants had assembled on the Brocken, an analogous procession was formed. The Wizards chanted that they were creeping along as slowly as snails—a reference to the *Homagium,* an indecent ceremony which followed the *Introit.* Men and women took part in homage to Satan and the chant of Goethe's Wizards implies that the women, who are marching ahead of them in the procession, are eager to reach the Devil's house, that is, where the *Homagium* will take place.

The deleted scene, "The Summit of the Brocken," is an adaptation of the medieval *Homagium.* Goethe's scene is neither witty nor provocative in an era when literature seems to have reached the nadir of sensationalism. Certain engravers with a taste for the macabre have represented the *Homagium* in its spectral as well as its pornographic character in a far more convincing manner than did Goethe.

The Black Mass was always interrupted at the close of the *Homagium* by a banquet, and Goethe creates a parallel to the original banquet scene when Mephistopheles calls Faust's attention to

> A hundred fires in a row; they drink,
> They cook, they chatter, they dance, they kiss;
> Tell me, where can you find anything better than this?

The banquet was invariably followed by the notorious "Witches' Round" in which partners danced alone, back to back. "Little by little each man lost all knowledge of self and of the person beside him. Old age and ugliness were abolished by a veritable satanic miracle; she was still a woman, still lovable and confusedly loved."[11] Glossing over with good taste the abolition on this night of the social and religious taboos against incest, Michelet points out that, since it was extremely difficult for a serf to marry, the sacrilegious license of this night indicated a defiance of church and state. The daring young woman who played the role of the Devil's Bride in the Black Mass, upon whose naked body the Credo was recited, often paid with her life for this sacrilege.

Goethe departs from the order of historical events which followed the Witches' Round when the central ceremony of the Mass performed in reverse took place. This scene Goethe could not write. However, he consigned to paralipomena a scene which hints at the above sacrilegious ceremony as if it had actually taken place and as if Faust had witnessed it. In the scene entitled "On the Brocken," Faust, standing in a crowd of people, watches a naked young woman (called in the text an Idol) whose arms are bound behind her back. Preparations are being made for an *auto da fé*. By suggestion we assume that this young woman has played the role of Devil's Bride and later, in the second part of the rite, that her body had served as an altar upon which a demon celebrated Mass.

As the young woman is being consumed by flames Goethe says that she makes a "familiar sign," easily interpreted as the sign of the cross in reverse, the defiant gesture which an unrepentant witch would indubitably make. Possibly the two groups of men on either side of the burning pyre are spies who have caught and immediately punished the Devil's Bride. At the close of this scene, with which "Walpurgis Night's Dream" ended in the original draft, Goethe had written: "Thereby Faust learns."

But what precisely does Faust learn? That heresy does come to no good end? The conclusion is lame, the play within a play does not really ring true, and for the very reason which Mephistopheles gives to the Peddler Witch in refusing her wares:

> Gossip, you are out of date!
> What's done is past, what's past is done.
> Get in a stock of novelties,
> By novelties only are we won.

Goethe offers his readers a far more interesting and up-to-date novelty. A certain mysterious something, a something sacred, an epiphany even, makes its appearance in this realm of chaos—and yet precisely here, for the first created Light appeared in the World of Emanations, preceding creation. Mephistopheles points to a curious luminosity within a clump of bushes, which is luring him toward it, hinting perhaps at the epiphany of the Burning Bush. And taking Faust by the hand, Mephistopheles leaps with him to a higher level of the Blocksberg, leaving the rabble to their revels.

Goethe is calling attention to the Monad, the germ of individuality which radiates by means of its own light, even in the general Witch Mass where individuality becomes lost. Indeed, from our viewpoint, the "knotty riddle" which will be either "tied" or "untied" on the Brocken refers to the Work of Philosophy, the kernel of the present situation. Will Faust follow the light of the Monad, and in so doing perform the work of Mind as Spirit, which the ancients called the work of "Creation"; or will he succumb to sensuality, and give himself over to the work of "Generation?"[12] The latter is hinted at in the lines which immediately follow, as Mephistopheles takes upon himself the role of a go-between and assigns to Faust the role of a suitor. They pass from fire to fire and come at last upon two witches, separated from the crowd, who are sitting alone as if very fatigued.

We are free to believe that Faust has come upon the girl who played the part of the Devil's Bride, with whom he dances, while Mephistopheles takes the old witch as his partner. Soon Faust breaks away because a little red mouse sprang from the girl's mouth. The importance of this incident cannot be understood without an insight into the finale of the Black Mass.

After the *Agnus Dei* had been celebrated in ribald mockery, a skinned toad was brought to the Devil's Bride which she tore to pieces with her teeth, uttering these peculiar words: "Ah, Philip, if only I had you between my hands I would treat you the same."[13] By this defiant gesture Jesus was supposedly vanquished. Then villagers who had played the roles of nimble demons ran upon the scene, leaping over blazing fires, biting and destroying toads which were considered to be poisonous, partly to amuse the onlookers, yet at the same time to make them laugh at the supposed dangers of Hell.

Now a skinned toad is not dissimilar to a red mouse, and it would seem as if Goethe were veiling, and yet revealing, the character of the witch with whom Faust has been dancing, since at this significant moment a soul-figure appears to Faust in the likeness of Gretchen, and she recalls Faust to his better self. An image has now come between Faust and his lust. The image of Gretchen has the power to hold Faust to the work of "Creation" despite the sophistries of Mephistopheles who tells Faust that the image is a negative phantasy, that is, nothing but an *eidolon,* nothing but Lilith, nothing but a Medusa head.

A clash of wills is taking place. An unconscious opposition is being set up between Faust and Mephistopheles. As long as Faust had acquiesced in every plan, even though he had called Mephistopheles a sophist and a liar to boot, there was no hope of escaping his domination. But with the appearance of Gretchen's image, a *tertium quid* enters the situation, namely, the power of the image in opposition to the power of Mephistopheles to underestimate or demean this image.

A well defined Pair of Opposites—Sacred and Profane Love—are creating an *enantiodromia,* a term which C. G. Jung has used to good advantage when describing the emergence of the unconscious opposite in a critical situation.[14] The term means literally "a running counter to," and according to Heraclitus everything must go over into its opposite at a given moment of time as, for example, youth to age, night into day, and so on.

Once Faust's will runs counter to the will of Mephistopheles (and only in so doing could Faust become conscious that he had a will), once Faust refuses to believe that the image was a mere phantasy, then Mephistopheles loses the lead, the scene crumples up and comes to an abrupt end.

The original draft of "Walpurgis Night's Dream" had a far more dramatic ending. It closed with the *auto da fé,* and there was, therefore, a logical transition to the scene entitled "Open Field" which now seems to hang in mid-air. How much more dramatic this scene becomes once the sequence of events, as Goethe first conceived them, is reconstructed! The spectral horses of Mephistopheles are waiting impatiently at the edge of the woods; Faust dashes away from the *auto da fé,* conscious that he has participated in a Black Mass. The black horses are carrying Faust and Mephistopheles away in the mad gallop typical of an anxiety dream and, as they pass the gibbet where the witches are performing their libations, the words, "On, on!" have an intensity lost now that Open Field follows the "Dream."

"Walpurgis Night's Dream" affords an insight into that very moment when a so-called Mystery above Nature assumed a form because of the will of Faust to behold this form. It prepares the way for the closing stanza, which hints at illumination, the end goal of a Mystery Religion. This again is an intimation of the Platonic awakening out of darkness and error to Truth, the gist of the opening scene of the second part of the drama.

Goethe had found great difficulty in making a proper transition from "Walpurgis Night's Dream" to "Intermezzo," and a number of attempts were made before he found the incident in which Mephistopheles guides Faust to the little theater in which a seventh play in a series of seven is about to be performed. This seventh play introduces the planetary system of Astralism, a cult to which, during the long era of the Graeco-Roman world, many scholars and cultivated men had belonged.[15]

According to Astral theology the soul, upon its arrival at each of the seven spheres above the earth, was compelled to present correct passwords and credentials to the planetary Ruler, both in its descent into the passions of humanity and upon its Return Journey to the source of life and light, or Mind as Spirit. Upon its Return Journey to the Light the soul gave back to each of the Rulers or Powers the qualities the soul had originally acquired in its domain; and to Saturn, the Seventh and last Ruling Power, the soul surrendered its slothfulness: then only could the soul rise above its limitations to the Eighth Sphere where the soul "hymned the gods."[16]

An analogy between seven planes of consciousness, seven astrological spheres, seven elements, and seven virtues had been popularized by Numenius, a neo-Pythagorean who connected an earlier theology concerning the ascent of the soul with neo-Platonism. In the Persian cult of Mithra the seven elements also played an important role, symbolizing the labors of the soul in its ascent to Mithra the Victorious, identified with the sun.

The "Intermezzo," from the standpoint of an ascent of consciousness, is a unity in diversity. We shall interpret this unity—its concealed content—bypassing its manifest contents, that is to say the identities of diverse persons, referred to as "spirits," whom Goethe has characterized according to their physical traits.[17]

Oberon, Titania, Puck, and Ariel are obviously not intended to lead the reader's thoughts to Shakespeare, far from it. These names merely set in motion a work of *imaginatio*, for

> The poet's eye, in a fine frenzy rolling,
> Doth glance from heaven to earth, from earth to heaven;

And, as imagination bodies forth
The form of things unknown, the poet's pen
Turns them to shapes, and gives to airy nothing
A local habitation and a name.[18]

The opening lines are spoken by The Manager, and The Stage Manager appears in "The Prologue in the Theatre," also written in 1797, but apparently as a Prologue for a second part to Mozart's *Magic Flute,* a project Goethe abandoned. Next the Herald enters, and seems to anticipate the august Herald in "Masquerade,"[19] behind whose mask Goethe interprets a series of allegories as they present themselves. The Herald performs a somewhat similar function, stating the theme of Goethe's enigma as follows:

> *The Herald*
> To have a golden wedding,
> Let fifty years fly by;
> Yet it would seem more golden
> Were quarreling to die.

He is referring to the strife engendered by the Pair of Opposites,[20] for even the bodily plasm is said to be composed of warring elements.[21] In alchemy "an equalization of principles, a putting in order of contrariety, is symbolized by a representation of a marriage ceremony between the king and queen . . ."[22] The warring elements of body and spirit must be reconciled by the sacred gold or wisdom of soul, more important than a marriage anniversary. The meaning of gold as sacred occurs in *The Golden Verses, The Golden Ass, The Golden Tripod,* and these titles allude to the Wisdom-Teachings contained in all Secret Doctrines. Throughout the first part of *Faust,* gold is identified with magic and with human love; but in the second part the treasure guarded by the Griffins is the *aurum potabile,* the drinkable gold of wisdom, which according to the adepts, was not of this world *(non vulgaris).*

Oberon's first stanza to which a reply is made by Titania follows verses spoken by Ariel and Puck, and Oberon:

> *Oberon*
> Couples, if you would agree,
> This we clearly state:
> If you want to stay in love,
> Quickly separate!

Titania
If he scolds or she be cross,
Seize the pair, be bold!
Take her to a sunny clime,
Take him where winds blow cold.

These stanzas refer to a process during transmutation in the Vase of Hermes which was called "Separation." to which Goethe returns at the close of the first court scene of Part II. According to the definition of Basilius Valentius: Separation, i.e., purification by distillation, implied the draining of water out of matter, comparable to the mist which forms when water rises out of the earth.

The symbolism of mist was used in Astralism to designate the ascent of consciousness out of error, and many Latin authors, Cicero among others, adopted the idiom of the initiated. Certain Mystery Religions dramatized the plane of mist through which the soul must pass upon its Return Journey to the Clear Light of Reason. Via initiation, salvation could be stepped up, so that the initiate did not need to wait for after-death purifications in order to attain salvation. Allegorical ceremonies were devised which recapitulated the Return Journey to the Light. Passing out of a darkened, mist-like state of consciousness, the postulant achieved illumination, the end goal of a Mystery. A state of cosmic illumination is hinted at in the closing lines of "Intermezzo":

The Orchestra
Veils of mist and drifting clouds
Aloft are shining bright;
Breeze in leaves and wind in reeds
Banish all from sight.

Ariel, a character new to the drama, had a long Gnostic history behind him ere he "flamed amazement" to Prospero. From his high position as a planetary Ruler of Fire (in the Coptic Codex, *Pistis Sophia*), Ariel descended into a proscribed manual of magic, the *Constitution of Honorious,* which found its way into Germany.[23] The German *Honorious* opens with an invocation to Ariel; and Ariel in a priestly role opens the second part of *Faust.* In the following lines Ariel's role is that of the "heavenly Hermes" of the Astralists[24] or the leader who guides the souls upon their ascent:

Ariel
If loving nature, or the soul
To you a wing discloses,
Then follow fast my airy trail
To the Hill of Roses.

Ariel is inviting Faust to the metaphorical Hill of Roses, associated with the exoteric ceremonies in The Mysteries of Isis and Osiris. These ceremonies are described by Apuleius at the close of his auto-biographic novel, *The Golden Ass*:[25] as an initiate, Apuleius was placed upon a pedestal, representing his ascent; and he was crowned with roses, the flowers sacred to Isis, symbolizing a love freed from carnality. At the close of the second part of *Faust,* Mephistopheles will be defeated by means of a shower of rose-petals, suggesting the above meaning.

Since every alchemist created his own structure, based more or less upon his own analogies,[26] it was quite permissible for Goethe to construct a poetic *tria prima* (representing Body, Soul, and Spirit) from parts of animal forms which were in general use in alchemical illustrations. With this in mind we read the following lines:

Spirit in Embryo
Belly of toad, the spider's feet,
A tiny creature's wings
Do not make a little animal,
Yet a little poem sings.

The toad, one of the most familiar alchemical animals, invariably represents earthy matters. In an epigram of Avicenna, cited by Read, the student is counselled as follows: "Join the toad of earth to the flying eagle and you will see in our art, the Magisterium: i.e., the Philosopher's Stone."[27]

Although minute wings are a far cry from wings of a flying eagle, yet emphasis is upon *elevation,* also represented in alchemical pictures by winged animals, such as dragons, lions, serpents. In general, birds signified elevation or sublimations, and sometimes their wings are placed downwards, sometimes upwards, denoting different stages of the Work. To these analogies Goethe adds the image of a spider, whose web well represents the concept of an alchemical center.[28] Goethe makes the following point in this enigmatic quatrain; namely, that a *tria prima* does not make a little animal, for this is

the work of "Generation"; but it makes a work of "Creation" or
Mind, that is to say, a little poem.

The Spirit in Embryo throws light upon Goethe's conscious and
symbolical efforts at this period of life to recreate himself as a metaphysical poet. Just as the author of *Werther* had been sacrified to
the Counsellor, and later the Counsellor to the Scientist, the time
had come when it was essential to sacrifice the empirical scientist for
the sake of Wholeness. Goethe knew that "the essence of neo-
Platonic mysticism is the belief that the Soul, which lives here in
self-contradiction, must break in succession every form in which it
tends to crystallize."[29] How important this was to Goethe in 1797
can be gathered from the concluding passage in his undated letter to
Schiller from Frankfurt during August of 1797:

> The matter is an important one, for it annuls the contradiction which
> lies between my nature and direct experience, and which in former
> years I was never able to solve immediately and happily. For I confess
> that I would rather have turned straight home again, in order to work
> out of my inmost being phantoms of every kind, than to have again, as
> hitherto, to buffet with the million-faced Hydra of Empiricism; for he
> who does not seek pleasure or advantage from it had better draw back
> in good time.

Goethe never lost interest in empirical science—far from it—but
he did not complete the vast outline which he made upon his return
from Italy, intending to coordinate all branches of knowledge. It was
more important to him to reconcile his Pair of Opposites, to press
forward to his self-appointed goal. Schiller had written to him with
this in mind on October 20, 1797, following a reading of the "Golden
Wedding of Oberon and Titania":

> As you are in a position where you have to demand the highest of
> yourself, and where the objective and the subjective have absolutely to
> become one, it is positively necessary to take heed that that which your
> genius can place in one work, should always grasp the purest form, and
> that nothing concerning it should be lost in an impure medium.

Thinking back upon the experiences which went into the making
of "Walpurgis Night's Dream" Goethe remarked to Eckermann, February 16, 1826: "I made devils and witches once; I was glad when I
had consumed my northern inheritance, and turned to the tables of
the Greeks."

Notes

1. Franz Hartmann, M.D., *The Life of Paracelsus* (London: Kegan, Paul, Trench, Trubner and Co., Ltd., n.d.), pp. 150-51.
2. Grillot de Givry, *Witchcraft, Magic and Alchemy* (Boston: Houghton, Mifflin Company, 1931), p. 52.
3. In Paralipomena to his memoirs Goethe placed the reading of Gottfried Arnold in the year 1769, hence prior to Strasburg. The book is not mentioned in Ephemerides.
4. The following is condensed from: C. W. King, *The Gnostics* (New York: G. P. Putnam's Sons, 1887); George Foot Moore, *History of Religions*, II (New York: Charles Scribner's Sons, 1920); and Carl H. Kraeling, *Anthropos and Son of Man* (New York: Columbia University Press, 1927).

    Manes, originally an initiate into the Persian sect of the Magi, unfortunately altered the Zoroastrian doctrines in his efforts to reconcile Zoroastrianism with Christianity. He claimed that the Two Principles had been immutably opposed throughout time and all eternity and would so remain. Although his Principle of the Good was identical with that of Zoroaster, his principle of Evil became a satanic matter from which man could only free himself with the greatest difficulty and strictest asceticism. The forces of Good and Evil were represented by a definite number of Light and Dark elements; in the first round of the cosmic struggle a certain number of Light-elements were captured and imprisoned in the realm of satanic matter. It was man's paramount duty to redeem and release his own particles of imprisoned Light; in setting them free, Primal Man (who, in the Manichean system, was often interpreted as analogous to Christ) received back his own missing elements of spiritual power. Thus Primal Man, by becoming once more Whole, achieved salvation from the piety of the faithful individuals in whom Primal Man had his being. Here, as in Kabbalah, the danger lay in the fact that Primal Man was dependent upon mortal man for his salvation.

5. C. G. Jung, *Psychology and Alchemy* (New York: Pantheon Books, 1953), Bollingen Series XX, p. 262.
6. *Ibid.,* p. 262.
7. G. R. S. Mead, *Thrice Greatest Hermes* (London and Benares: The Theosophical Publishing Society, 1901), vol. II, p. 133, "On Thought and Sense": "i. The single sense-and-thought of Cosmos is to make all things, . . . and (then) dissolving them, make them all new again; and thus, like a Good Gardener of Life, things that have been dissolved it taketh to itself, and giveth them renewal again."
8. Cited by Sarah Austin in *Characteristics of Goethe* (London: Effingham Wilson, 1833), vol. I, p. 115.
9. This refers to an Orphic rite in which a candidate was compelled to bedaub himself with a species of white clay, symbolical of spiritual cleansing. This peculiar rite implied that if an impious man had neglected initiation dur-

196 ALICE RAPHAEL

ing his lifetime, he was compelled to thus purify himself in the after-death condition. Goethe may likely have dropped this satiric stanza into his Walpurgis Sack in order to rid himself of his antagonism to Nicolai, a minor literary enemy whom he thus ridiculed and inadvertently immortalized.

10. Jules Michelet, *Satanism and Witchcraft* (New York: The Citadel Press, 1946), p. 102.
11. *Ibid.*, p. 106.
12. Mead, *Simon Magus* (London: The Theosophical Publishing Society, 1892), p. 84:

What Magic, the 'Great Art' of the ancients, was in reality is now difficult to discover. . . . It was an art, a practice, the Great and Supreme Art of the Most Sacred Science of God, the Universe and Man. . . . its method was what is now called 'creation.' . . . But 'creation' is not generation, it is a work of the 'mind,' in the highest sense of the word. By purification and aspiration, by prayer and fasting, man had to make his mind harmonious with the Great Mind of the Universe. Such spiritual operations required the greatest purity and piety, real purity and true piety, without disguise or subterfuge, for man had to face himself and his God, before whom no disguise was possible.

13. Michelet, *op. cit.*, p. 108, note 7: "Can it be she says *Philip* here, from the odious name of the King who gave France a hundred years of English wars, who inaugurated at Crécy the series of national defeats and cost the country the first invasion of her soil? . . . Philippe de Valois, author of this interminable war, was held accursed and perhaps left behind him in the popular ritual a never-forgotten word of malediction."
14. C. G. Jung, *Psychological Types* (New York: Harcourt, Brace & Company, Inc., 1923), pp. 541-42:

I use the term *enantiodromia* to describe the emergence of the unconscious opposite, with particular relation to its chronological sequence. This characteristic phenomenon occurs almost universally whenever an extreme, one-sided tendency dominates the conscious life: for this involves the gradual development of an equally strong, unconscious counterposition, which first becomes manifest in an inhibition of conscious activities, and subsequently leads to an interruption of conscious direction. A good example of *enantiodromia* is seen in the psychology of Saul of Tarsus and his conversion to Christianity; . . . in the Christ-identification of the sick Nietzsche with his deification and the subsequent hatred of Wagner. . . .

15. S. Angus, *The Religious Quests of the Graeco-Roman World* (London: John Murray, 1929), p. 258:

Wide, therefore, was the appeal of this religion, despite the fact that it was essentially a learned religion and a cult for the elect. . . . Because of its scientific interest and speculative acumen it appealed to the intellect. Because of its Nature-mysticism it awakened exalted sentiments. Because of its cosmic unity it promoted that pantheism which drew the Greek mind like a magnet and fostered the cosmic emotion to which the ancients were so susceptible. Because of its evident centre in the shining Sun it promoted monotheism. Because of its demonstrated harmony and mathematical regularity it confirmed faith in a Providence and adumbrated order within man as without, in the microcosm as in the macrocosm. Because of its silent contemplation it proved congenial to the mystic tendencies of the age. Because it required special knowledge or instruction it appealed to the ancient spirit that considered that there must be something secret in a true religion to be divulged only to the esoterics.

16. Mead, *Thrice Greatest Hermes, op. cit.*, Commentary upon Poemandres, The Shepherd of Men, p. 42: "The Eighth Sphere, 26. The soul of the initiate strips itself naked of the 'garment of shame,' the selfish energizings, and stands 'clothed in its own power.' This refers probably to the stripping off of the 'carapace of selfhood,' the garments woven by its vices, and the putting on of the 'wedding garment' of its virtues."

17. Goethe to Eckermann, February 17, 1829: "Lavater was a truly good man, but subject to strong delusions; the whole sole truth was not to his mind; he deceived himself and others. . . . He walked like a crane, and therefore figures as a crane in the Blocksberg."

18. *Midsummer Night's Dream*, Act V, sc. 1.

19. *Faust* II, Act I, sc. iii.

20. The Sanskrit term for the pair of opposites in the psychological sense is *Dvandva.* Besides the meaning of pair (particularly man and woman) it denotes strife, quarrel, combat, doubt, etc. . . . Not to allow oneself to be influenced by the pair of opposites (nirdvandva-free, untouched by the opposites), but to raise oneself above them, is then an essentially ethical task, since freedom from the opposites leads to redemption.

21. Mead, *op. cit.*, vol. I, p. 171; John Read, *Prelude to Chemistry* (New York: Macmillan Co., 1917), p. 263.

22. Angus, *op. cit.*, p. 302: "In the *Tusculan Disputations* Cicero tells how the soul, the most 'swift of all things, escaping from the air,'" must enter and pass through all this region in which clouds, storms, and winds gather, and which is damp and misty by the exhalations from the earth. When the soul has risen above this region and attained to a nature resembling its own and recognizes it, it takes its place with the fires composed of the most rarefied air and of the tempered heat of the sun; the soul then ceases to ascend.

23. E. M. Butler, *Ritual Magic* (Cambridge: University Press, 1949), pp. 154-55.

24. Angus, *op. cit.*, p. 311. Corresponding to the increasing sensibility to a doctrine of divine grace, we find that the soul, though endowed with the upward-tending nature and purified, welcomes for the ascent the personal assistance of a divine escort. In a passage of Plutarch "the heavenly Hermes" is the patron . . . at "the second death" of the purified one whereby he attains to the unity of spiritual existence (Nous). As a psychopomp, notably Hermes, had formerly conducted souls on the downward journey to Hades, so now he performed like functions on the upward transit. In a like manner Hermes guides Helena and her attendants in Act III, as they proceed out of the dark mists to the Sacred Marriage with Faust.

25. In the *Golden Ass* or *Metamorphosis*, Apuleius, under the character of Lucius, describes the ritual ordeal in which he was transformed into an ass, one of the primitive forms of Typhon. The ass symbolized the carnal or lowest form of sensuality. The candidate was compelled to realize it in all its worthless aspects until he was ready to sacrifice this side of his unredeemed nature. Then Isis appeared to him saying, "Behold, Lucius, moved by the supplication, I am present: I, who am *Nature*, the parent of things, mistress of all the elements."

26. Jung, *Psychology and Alchemy, op. cit.*, pp. 277-78:

Every original alchemist, as it were, builds himself a more or less individual edifice of ideas consisting of the dicta of the philosophers and of composite analogies to the fundamental concepts of alchemy. Generally these analogies are taken from all over the place. Treatises were even written for the purpose of supplying the artist with analogy-making material. The method of alchemy, psychologically speaking, is one of boundless amplification. The *amplificatio* is always appropriate when dealing with some dark experience which is so vaguely adumbrated that it must be enlarged and explained by being set in a psychological context in order to be understood at all. . . . This *amplification* forms the second part of the *opus*, and is understood by the alchemist as *theoria*.

27. Read, *Prelude to Chemistry, op. cit.*, p. 258: This seems to mean that the seeker after the Philosopher's Stone should combine the fixed and volatile principles—sophic sulphur and mercury. "The vulture flying in the ayre, and the Toade going upon the Earth, is our Maistry," writes Artephius in similar vein.

28. Jung, *Psychology and Alchemy, op. cit.*, p. 207: ". . . For this reason the center is—in other cases—often pictured as a spider in its web, especially when the conscious attitude is still dominated by fear of unconscious processes."

29. William Ralph Inge, *The Philosophy of Plotinus* (London: Longmans, Green and Co., 1918), vol. II, p. 239.

Eugene F. Timpe

ULYSSES AND THE
ARCHETYPAL FEMININE

SINCE 1922, WHEN ULYSSES FIRST APPEARED, IT HAS BEEN SUBJECTED TO processing and interpreting by commentators with all sorts of convictions. Such explanations have probably been not only more useful but actually more necessary for *Ulysses* than for any other work of literature except *Finnegans Wake*. Its macrocosm built upon a microcosm seems to invite supposition and conjecture *ad infinitum,* and the non-specialist lacking guidance through this maze is likely to become discouraged and irritated. Even Carl Jung, hardly a non-specialist, called it "seven hundred and thirty-five unendurable pages,"[1] and the general reader must, in his despair, have often been tempted to mutter something like Carlyle's remark when he translated *Wilhelm Meister:* "Bushels of dust and straws and feathers with here and there a diamond of the purest water."

It is distressingly likely that *Ulysses* has become, in the eyes of the public at large, one of those books which is too forbidding to be read in its entirety. Yet there seems to be little doubt that it is one of the prime works of genius, and this being so, it is doubly important, in spite of the obstacles which stand between it and us, to come to terms with it. The obstacles, of course, are nearly overwhelming. For just the most obvious level of understanding, we need to know Homer better, especially in relation to myth and culture; and we should have Joyce's knowledge of languages, songs, the history of Ireland, the Catholic religion, the geography of Dublin, and so forth. For some of these bodies of knowledge we have aids: Weldon Thornton, for example, has helped greatly with his list of Joycean allusions (*James Joyce Quarterly*), and others, too many to detail, have left us deeply indebted to them for justifying the ways of Joyce to man.

But still, as we read *Ulysses,* we sometimes pause in wonder at the depth of Joyce's subtlety. Buried here and there are clues which lead us to suspect that Joyce dealt in the esoteric. Among careful readers of Joyce there is now considerably more than a suspicion that in order to follow him through his intellectual mazes it is necessary to know what he knew of Hermes Trismegistos, Paracelsus, Swedenborg, Böhme, Buddhism, Theosophy, Gnosticism, Egyptology, Cabalism, and one or two other "isms" not commonly subjects for required courses in the public schools.

Knowledge of Joyce's use of each of these subjects could light our way in following his tracks through the labyrinth. Each could offer some explanation of one or more of his turnings and help to disclose those tracks which he so carefully obliterated. But to illuminate the whole labyrinth, to show us the direction in which he was moving, his progress, we need more than a candle—we need at least a flare. We have been given something of the sort with the assurance that Joyce was following Homer. Even though this only equates one unknown to another, it helps. At least we understand that certain basic questions about *Ulysses* should first of all have been asked about *The Odyssey,* and that even though the warp and the woof may have been altered, *Ulysses* was at one time stretched on the same loom that held *The Odyssey.* William York Tindall, in his *James Joyce: His Way of Interpreting the Modern World* (New York, 1950) quite rightly stated:

> Joyce considered Homer's myth the complete expression of man. In the departure of a family man from his home and in his return Joyce saw everybody's pattern. By adapting this general pattern to his own purposes, Joyce provided support for himself. Lonely and eccentric, he could feel one with mankind. His exile seemed only a departure to be followed by return. Away from home, he could feel at home. In the hunt of Telemachus for his father, Joyce found sanction for himself as artist. Telemachus can represent not only man's search for social support but the artist's search for humanity. Finding his father, Telemachus fulfills the wish of every man and every artist. Exile, home, humanity, and art, Joyce's concerns, found expression in Homer's *Odyssey.* [p. 102]

Further, in the same work, Tindall noted of Molly Bloom, "Her concern with metempsychosis supports the Homeric parallel by suggesting that Joyce's characters are the reincarnation of Homer's" (p. 97). Joyce, of course, made it quite clear that his *Ulysses* at least partially paralleled *The Odyssey* when he circulated among his friends a chart showing the relationship between the eighteen chapters of *Ulysses* and eighteen of the books of *The Odyssey*. Each chapter in *Ulysses,* furthermore, was identified by location of scene, hour, organ, art represented, color, symbol, technique, and correspondences with any of a variety of things, a large number of which were derived from *The Odyssey*. Stuart Gilbert, among others, published this chart later.[2]

All of this, at any rate, makes it appear that one of the most logical approaches to *Ulysses* is through *The Odyssey,* and it implies, too, that our knowledge of the latter is something less than perfect. Neither of these ideas is new. More than half a century ago Samuel Butler, famous for his pronouncement that *The Odyssey* had been written by a young Sicilian woman (and more lately seconded in this assertion by Robert Graves), made some canny observations and posed some provoking questions.[3] Even if we ignore his conclusion or replace it with one of our own devising, we still have to reckon with his preliminary points, some of which seem now to have central importance. Why, for example, did Penelope not do *anything* to discourage the suitors? She did not nag them or send them on useless errands or praise them to their competitors or even simply order them away. And why is there no credible male-female relationship? As Butler remarks, "The infatuation of man, with its corollary, the superior excellence of woman, is the leading theme" (p. 77). Even Minerva is a sort of fairy godmother. "There is," continues Butler, "no love-business in the *Odyssey* except the return of a bald elderly married man to his elderly wife and grown-up son after an absence of twenty years, and furious at having been robbed of so much money in the meantime" (p. 77). Further,

> Throughout the *Odyssey* the men do not really care for women, nor the women for the men; they have to pretend to do so now and again, but it is a got-up thing, and the general attitude of the sexes towards one another is very much that of Helen, who says that her husband Menelaus is really not deficient in person or understanding: or again of Penelope herself, who, on being asked by Ulysses on his return what she thought of him, said that she did not think very much of him nor very little of him; in fact, she did not think much about him one way or the other. True, later on she relents and becomes more effusive; in fact, when she and Ulysses sat up talking in bed and Ulysses told her the story of his adventures, she never went to sleep once. [pp. 78-79]

Butler explains the matter by suggesting that the Sicilian girl who wrote *The Odyssey* was determined to revenge herself and her sex on men as they had been shown in *The Iliad,* wherein women were "always to be treated as a toy or as a beast of burden, or at any rate as an incubus" (p. 80). The result was plain to see: multiform characterization of women; uniform characterization of men.

Now if Butler has led us in passing to tentative agreement with his supposition about a revenge-seeking authoress of *The Odyssey*, he has also led us beyond, to the idea that *The Odyssey* is both more and less than a story: it is a cultural extrusion containing mythology and narrative convenient for its purposes and expressing a great deal more than the genius of some blind bard at one unique period of time. It must have at its source some totally pervasive concepts which reconcile its ambiguities; therefore, it must also be reducible to terms which have not been applied to it as yet. For a clue as to just what these new terms might be, we turn to Tindall's *A Reader's Guide to James Joyce* for the statement that "However complex the setting, and whatever our consequent expectations, the action of *Ulysses* is not only simple but archetypal. The journey or quest is one of the oldest and most familiar in the world."[4] Step by step we approach the formulation of an hypothesis derived from a hitherto ordinarily unrelated discipline—depth psychology. The hypothesis, introduced severally by Butler and Tindall, is simply that *The Odyssey*, and *Ulysses* for that matter, since Joyce addressed himself to the application rather than the creation of an existing myth, embody archetypal forms and symbols. This would help to explain why Penelope seems to be not so much a person as a type, and not so much a type as an archetype, and not so much an archetype as a manifestation of several forms of one totally encompassing archetypal pattern.

The most natural source to which one might turn for support of such an hypothesis is Carl Jung, the curator of the collective unconscious. Unfortunately, Jung proves a disappointment for seekers of archetypal patterns in *Ulysses*. In " 'Ulysses': A Monologue" Jung regarded *Ulysses* as a drastic purgative, created to undermine values that were already disintegrating (p. 119), a book

> written in the full light of consciousness; it is not a dream and not a revelation of the unconscious. . . . Ulysses does not bear the features of a symbolic work. Of course, one senses the archetypal background. Behind Dedalus and Bloom there stand the eternal figures of spiritual and carnal man; Mrs. Bloom perhaps conceals an anima entangled in worldliness, and Ulysses himself might be the hero. But the book does not focus upon this background; . . . It is obviously not symbolic and has no intention of being so. Were it none the less symbolic in certain parts, then the unconscious, in spite of every precaution, would have played the author a trick or two. [p. 123]

Jung's judgment notwithstanding, some Joyceans—Damon,[5] Gilbert, Tindall, and Kenner,[6] principally—touched upon the subject, but without the proper tools to give the necessary leverage.

Then new impetus for the application of psychology to literary studies was provided when Erich Neumann brought out his *The Origins and History of Consciousness*[7] and *The Great Mother*.[8] Creatively synthesized studies inspired partly by Jung, these two books have given us the concepts and characteristics of archetypal forms, in particular that of the Feminine. This has been provided so conveniently that we are now in a position to erect interpretations of Homer and his successor to our heart's content; and such interpretations will be as valid as our reasoning and Neumann's findings, the latter of which at least hardly seems subject to question. Rather than attempt to correlate several archetypal forms—for example, water, sun, wind, creation, hero, rebirth, the quest—with *Ulysses,* I will limit myself to that one which was described most exhaustively by Neumann and which appears to have great application to *Ulysses*—the Archetypal Feminine. This form seems related to the purpose of *The Odyssey,* if we accept Butler's thesis, and by association, to *Ulysses* also; in addition, the phenomenology of the workings of archetypal forms, this one included, is relevant to one common denominator shared by the two works—mythology. As Neumann asserts, "The archetypes of the collective unconscious are manifested, as Jung discovered many years ago (*Wandlungen und Symbole der Libido,* 1911-12), in the 'mythological motifs' that appear among all peoples of all times in identical or analogous manner and can arise just as spontaneously—i.e., without any conscious knowledge—from the unconscious of modern man."[9] The *modus operandi,* then, is obvious: using Jung's concept of archetypal symbolism as a basis, we take one particular form of the archetype, the Feminine, for which we accept Neumann's impressive characterization, and trace its manifestations within certain apparent limits in Joyce's *Ulysses.*

The question of whether or not Joyce intentionally based his work on archetypes will have to be ignored. Joyce was familiar with the new psychology[10] and was altogether capable of constructing his book around an intricate plan which included archetypal symbolism among the maze of themes, allusions, techniques, and designs. But he might also have done about the same thing unconsciously. Or the archetypal symbolism might have derived from Homer's symbolism (or from the Sicilian maiden's). Possibly a combination of reasons explains its existence. So, since this line of inquiry poses unanswerable questions, and since one logical order of reasoning is to assert the "truth" of a matter prior to explaining the reasons which lead to the conclusion—our inductive leap having been made long ago while perusing Butler, Jung, and Tindall—it will profit us most if we turn at this point to the examination of the hypothesis.

As we proceed, we must keep in mind that our hypothesis is not exclusive. No doubt, as has often been asserted, *The Odyssey* and *Ulysses* symbolically represent the return pattern, the related search for a father image,[11] and a progression towards and search for consciousness. The Archetypal Feminine, as Neumann describes it, conflicts with none of these as a source or cause of creativity.

Since a complete discussion of the archetype is the subject of Neumann's classic work, and since the majority of non-specialized readers are unlikely to be familiar with this volume, a summary of as much of it as is necessary to relate it to *Ulysses* might be helpful. Neumann's work is basically a structural analysis of one fundamental archetype, the Feminine or Great Mother. His avowed purpose is to make a contribution to the solution of those problems of our present culture which arise from the "one-sidedly patriarchal development of the male intellectual consciousness which is no longer kept in balance by the matriarchal world of the psyche" (xlii). His aim is a synthesis including the Feminine, which results in cultural wholeness, described by him as "the consciousness of every individual . . . creatively allied with the contents of the unconscious . . ." (xlii).

The archetype itself is an "inward image at work in the human psyche" (p. 3) which is expressed symbolically, and which has its effects in rites, myths, dreams, and creative works of man. It controls human behavior unconsciously, in accordance with its own laws, independent of the individual and his unique environment. It operates in the unconscious and it acts as a liaison between the unconscious and the conscious, at which time it manifests itself symbolically. Its material or sense content is that which is perceived by the consciousness, and its structure consists of the total complex of dynamism, symbolism, and sense content, at the center of which is the essence of the archetype itself. The symbols are the manifest visibility of the archetype, and the accretion of symbols—stone, tree, pool, fruit, animal, and so on—no one of which completely represents the central archetype, comprises the total manifestation of the archetypal pattern. Its characteristics are static and dynamic, consistent and contradictory.

The basic feature of the Great Mother, the one which is least often contradicted, is containment. Its symbol is the vessel. Visually, this relates to the belly, the lowest region of which is the underworld or womb of the earth. Associated with this are hell, night, chasm, cave, tomb, abyss, and others. Containment also invokes associations with nest, bed, ship, wagon, and coffin. The elements of the vessel, linked to the womb of life, are earth and water. But water is linked also to the breast and to rain, and for this reason it is not exclusively feminine but more basically it relates to both male and female elements and produces a total image of fructification. Blood, too, is thematically connected with the Great Mother, because after childbirth the mystery of blood changing to milk occurs, a mystery, incidentally, which Jung claimed to be the foundation of the primordial mysteries of food transformation. Like other archetypes, the Feminine contains apparent inconsistencies. Just as it can be joined to the masculine to produce a completed image, it can also combine within itself contradictory symbols such as earth and heaven, death and life, or night and day.

In addition to symbolizing containment, the Great Mother stands for protection and nourishment. The latter comes from the symbol group of the breast and has to do with bowl, goblet, chalice, or grail. In relation to all three functions, the Earth Mother is the bringer of life and the source of vegetation. At the center of the vegetation symbolism is the tree, since it nourishes, protects, contains, and on occasion represents the earth phallus or death.

Graphically, the Feminine archetype may be thought of as a circle with two diameters crossing at right angles. One diameter represents the static or elementary characteristics; the other represents the dynamic or transformative. The elementary diameter extends from the absolute negative to the absolute positive, from the Terrible Mother, typified by the mysteries of death, to the Good Mother, related to the mysteries of vegetation, birth, rebirth, and immortality. Transformatively, the diameter passes from the positive, the inspiration mysteries, to the negative, the mysteries of drunkenness, ecstasy, madness, impotence, and stupor. On the periphery of the circle, between the Good Mother and the most positive degree of the transformative character, is the Virgin Mother; between the Terrible Mother and the most negative transformative character are the witches.

Between the main features of the Great Mother, considered thematically and graphically, and the theme and structure of *Ulysses*, taken chronologically for the sake of order and simplicity, there exist many conjecture-provoking parallels. One of the first of these to be noticed was the nativity theme. E. R. Curtius observed that it was symbolized by the tower, generally conceded, in spite of the contrary opinion that the towers were suggested to Joyce by the towers of death found in Irish myth, to be manifestations of the Omphalos complex.[12] Gilbert himself saw a relationship between the navel motif and Eastern religious beliefs, and he associated the tower-navel-Omphalos with birth, reincarnation, metempsychosis, and even Bloom's musings ("One born every second . . .").[13] The text of *Ulysses,* of course, offers ample support, not only for this interpretation, but also for the entire Great Mother analysis through the extremely frequent and pointed use of certain words—ball (37 times), birth (31), cow (9), metempsychosis (10), mother (122), navel (7), omphalos (4), tree (46), womb (14), and water.[14] To Kenner, "The tower and the sea are primordial male and female symbols. The sea, Mulligan's 'great sweet mother' and for Stephen the remainder of his mother's corruption, U 7, signifies Joy and Destiny in the *Portrait,* the feminine, material, and corrupting in *Ulysses,* father and home in *Finnegans Wake"* (p. 246). Navel, omphalos, tower, mother, cow, and water appear to be the key words to the Great Mother theme as introduced in the "Telemachus" chapter, and in relationship to Neumann's schema for the Great Mother, they seem to focus on the Good Mother, Demeter, Isis, birth, rebirth, immortality, and the subsidiary symbolism of Joyce's milkwoman.

Since Joyce's use of archetypal form followed a dramatic rather than an ordered progression, themes and motifs were introduced and developed with due consideration for the important matters of movement, suspense, and climax. Thus it is that the motifs introduced in the first chapter were only echoed in the second, and the only theme extended was that of the cow and by remote association, the milkwoman, done through Mr. Deasy's tractate on foot and mouth disease which was offered to Stephen, the "bullock-befriending bard," for placement. The last chapter of the Telemachia, however, that known as the "Proteus" chapter, significantly furthered the development of the archetypal pattern. Along with a gradual deemphasis on rebirth, the concept of the Good Mother gradually dissolved as the pattern of the Terrible Mother evolved. Devouring, dismemberment, death, water, and death by drowning ran through Stephen's thoughts as he walked on the beach, his meditations reflected in the upswelling tide. Curtius as quoted by Gilbert (p. 128) remarked, "That primordial element, giver and taker of life, beats about the Ulyssean world of life-experience. As in Mr. T. S. Elliot's *Waste Land,* so through the work of Joyce runs the *motif* of the Drowned Man." And in the Proteus chapter, well-named, incidentally, when it is remembered that the holding fast and ensnaring characteristic of the Terrible Mother is most likely not unrelated to the traditional process for extracting truth from Proteus, the metempsychosis theme is reintroduced: "God becomes fish becomes barnacle goose becomes featherbed mountain" (p. 51). Death, however—"Bag of corpsegas sopping in foul brine. . . . Dead breaths I living breathe, tread dead dust, devour a urinous offal from all dead" (p. 51)—emerges as a central theme in association with the sea. This is all bound together with the Terrible Mother type—" old hag with the yellow teeth" (p. 51), the single tooth being a phallic characteristic connected with Hecate or the Gorgon[15]—and that lofty symbol of containment, the ship: "He turned his face over a shoulder, rere regardant. Moving through the air high spars of a threemaster, her sails brailed up on the crosstrees, homing, upstream, silently moving, a silent ship" (p. 51).[16]

The middle section of *Ulysses,* the countertheme in a different key devoted to the adventures of "Ulysses" himself, follows Leopold Bloom, alias Henry Flower, through twelve chapters of his adventures—Calypso, Lotus-Eaters, Hades, Aeolus, Lestrygonians, Scylla and Charybdis, Wandering Rocks, Sirens, Cyclops, Nausicaa, Oxen of the Sun, and Circe—as he wanders through the maze of Dublin. The Eternal Feminine is dominant in the initial and terminal chapters and is at least a subordinate theme in the chapters in between. Ensnaring and entrapping, hinted at in the preceding section, swell to basic themes in the centrally feminine Calypso chapter. For this chapter Joyce chose the house for the scene, the kidney for the organ, and the nymph for the symbol. He inaugurated the theme of his nymph's less-than-platonic relationship with her suitors, typified in this case by Blazes Boylan, and placed her in her characteristic position. Then he gave her a name ironically reminiscent of the name of the herb which Hermes gave Ulysses as an antidote to the fateful charms of Circe, and he even had his reincarnated Ulysses offer up a sacrifice of a burnt kidney to her. Although hinted at in earlier chapters, the subject of metempsychosis is here directly stated for the first time in the book, translated by Molly as "met-him-pike-hoses," with overtones appropriate to her dominant interest in life. Molly is the principal woman of the book,

not only as a human being and as Calypso the nymph at the beginning and Penelope the Earth Mother figure at the end, but also as
the embodiment of the anima, the "mover, the instigator of change,
whose fascination drives, lures, and encourages the male to all the
adventures of the soul and spirit, of action and creation in the inner
and the outward world."[17] Both women represent the most attractive
aspects of the Terrible Mother and her death mysteries; and like
Calypso, the nymph of Ogygia, the isle of the west, of death, un-
reality, and passivity, Molly, the nymph of Dublin, of Eccles Street,
of a world which both repels and attracts Bloom, holds her Ulysses
in bondage at the initial point in his adventures.

Indirection and the development of subordinate themes characterize Joyce's use of the Great Mother archetypal pattern in the next
several chapters. The bath of the Lotus-eaters chapter is related to
the mysteries of rebirth and the water theme of the Proteus chapter,
and the bath itself is one of the symbols of feminine containment.
The juxtaposition of several prior themes, united at the end of the
chapter, seems more than accidental. "He foresaw his pale body
reclined in it at full, naked, in a womb of warmth, oiled by scented
melting soap, softly laved. He saw his trunk and limbs riprippled
over and sustained, buoyed lightly upward, lemonyellow: his navel,
bud of flesh" (p. 85). The Hades chapter presents the death mysteries
witnessed in their most direct aspect. Bloom buried his Elpenor,
Paddy Dignam, his coffin and his condition suggestive of the containing and extinguishing qualities of the Feminine. The Aeolus chapter, that which was set in the newspaper office, furthered the development of the archetype only slightly through reintroduction of the
omphalos-tower theme—this time mounted by two elderly virgins—
and incidental repetition, for example, "mouth, south: tomb, womb"
(p. 137). With the Lestrygonians Joyce returns more directly to
matters archetypal as he strongly emphasizes blood sacrifice, devouring, and cannibalism, integrated with the religious Blood of the
Lamb theme. Death, too, remains in evidence with the announcement of Mina Purefoy's prolonged confinement and imminent peril
of death through childbirth. The potency of this climactic revelation
of the heart of the Terrible Mother decreases in the Scylla and
Charybdis chapter to mere implication, the feminine monster of cannibalism and the devouring whirlpool playing a role in the actualiza-
tion of the archetype that is less than nominal.

With the tenth chapter, named the Wandering Rocks, the labyrinthine motif implied in earlier chapters by Bloom's wanderings is

brought to the height of its development. The labyrinth, according to John W. Layard's *Stone Men of Malekula: Vao* (London, 1942), has archetypal characteristics. They are:

1. That it always has to do with death and rebirth relating either to a life after death or to the mysteries of initiation.
2. That it is almost always connected with a cave (or more rarely a constructed dwelling).
3. That in those cases where the ritual has been preserved, the labyrinth itself, or a drawing of it, is invariably situated at the entrance to the cave or dwelling.
4. That the presiding personage, either mythical or actual, is always a woman.
5. That the labyrinth itself is walked through, or the labyrinth design walked over, by men.[18]

Layard indicates that these characteristics of labyrinths are the same in India, Crete, the ancient Roman world, and the Christian Middle Ages. According to Neumann's interpretation of the findings of a number of scholars:

The labyrinthine way is always the first part of the night sea voyage, the descent of the male following the sun into the devouring underworld, into the deathly womb of the Terrible Mother. This labyrinthine way, which leads to the center of danger, where at the midnight hour, in the land of the dead, in the middle of the night sea voyage, the decision falls, occurs in the judgment of the dead in Egypt, in the mysteries both classical and primitive, and in the corresponding processes of psychic development in modern man. Because of its dangerous character, the labyrinth is also frequently symbolized by a net, its center as a spider. [p. 177]

Not only do these discussions of labyrinths suggest parallels with the voyaging of Odysseus and the ambulations of Bloom, but also they denote relationships between the Daedalus myth and *Ulysses*. The Daedalus myth, important because of its use by Joyce in *A Portrait of the Artist as a Young Man* and *Ulysses* to symbolize the search for freedom and flight from tyranny, and even used by Joyce to name his autobiographical hero, is closely associated with the labyrinthine ritual. According to Robert Graves:

Minos's palace at Cnossus was a complex of rooms, ante-rooms, halls, and corridors in which a country visitor might easily lose his way. Sir Arthur Evans suggests that this was the Labyrinth, so called from the *labrys*, or double-headed axe; a familiar emblem of Cretan sovereignty —shaped like a waxing and waning moon joined together back to back, and symbolizing the creative as well as the destructive power of the goddess. But the maze at Cnossus had a separate existence from

the palace; it was a true maze, . . . and seems to have been marked out
in mosaic on a pavement as a ritual dancing pattern.[19]

This was all, of course, intrinsically bound up in the myth of
Daedalus; so when Joyce borrowed from that myth he got more
than the multiple concept of flight: he got, also, the old artificer,
the Labyrinth that he constructed, and all the associations with the
Terrible Mother aspect of the feminine which the tradition of the
labyrinth entailed.

The chapters on the Sirens and the Cyclops offer little in extension
of the pattern of the feminine archetype. The sirens themselves must
have represented, both in *The Odyssey* and *Ulysses,* the dual nature
of the Great Mother, the destruction developing from attraction,
and from the negative female image. In addition, something could
probably be made from the parallels between the music of the sirens
as sung to Odysseus and the music of the tavern as heard by Bloom;
between the fact that Odysseus was strapped to the mast and carried
in a ship, and Bloom was contained in an earthbound building. The
search for archetypal symbols in the Cyclops chapter is even less
rewarding. Evidently, from the point of view of the Archetypal
Feminine, these chapters constitute a pregnant pause, a suppression
of the theme prior to its dramatic culmination.

The ultimate crescendo seems first to be announced in the Nausicaa chapter, an interruption of Homer's order, necessitated by the
rearranging to which Joyce subjected *The Odyssey* when he condensed
twenty-four books into eighteen and changed their order, interject-
ing adventures from the Lotus-eaters through the Cyclops between
Calypso and Nausicaa. If this did violence to Homer's arrangement,
it lent dramatic emphasis to Joyce's. Nausicaa, known in *Ulysses* as
Gerty MacDowell, had a real defect whereas it was only implied that
Nausicca herself had a defect, real or imagined. Why, one wonders
along with Butler, was there such emphasis on her forthcoming
marriage when no suitor was in evidence? And how could her father
provide her with a dowry if he could not even afford to give his
guest the gifts that he had promised? And it is with this defective if
virginal figure that the shift from the Terrible Mother in a variety
of forms, as presented in preceding chapters, to the transformative,
yet negative female image takes place. The midway point is witchery.
Gerty's "witchcraft" was in her harmless, time-worn, girlish wiles—
a bit of leg swinging, some exposure of her charms, the "loss" of a
talisman, and the kicking of a ball, symbolic, of course, of ancient
fertility rituals and sexual rites. From Bloom this puerile witchcraft

evoked merely an onanistic response, related to but less intense than the deeply psychological response evoked in him by the mature witchcraft of the negatively transformational Feminine in the Circe chapter.

Between the Nausicaa chapter and the Circe chapter itself, Joyce placed the Oxen of the Sun. One of the most confusing sections in his book, it takes place in the lying-in hospital where Mina Purefoy is enduring a prolonged and difficult delivery. The motif, introduced originally in the Lestrygonians chapter, is repeated with fuller development. The oxen theme represents fertility and the generative feminine earth principle, and it is darkly symbolized by the undercurrent of fear of death through childbirth. The chapter briefly reasserts earlier themes at the same time that it interrupts that of witchcraft, preparatory to the great cadenza of the Circe chapter.

The nighttown, or Circe, chapter brings together those themes which had been suggested before, and in doing this it dramatizes the very essence of the negative transformational feminine character. As Neumann indicates, this form of the Great Mother is affiliated with drunkenness, ecstasy, madness, impotence, stupor, transformation, dissolution, rejection, and deprivation. In *Ulysses*, Stephen and his friends are revealed, drunk, in Bella Cohen's whorehouse. There, Stephen comes under the protection of Bloom in a manner strangely reminiscent of *The Telegonia* rather than *The Odyssey*. The witch topic of Nausicaa continues, but the symbolism is altered. The pig, according to Neumann (p. 45) a symbol of fertility and containment, comes to be represented not by the men of Bloom, but by the massive, moustached whoremistress. Sadistically matriarchal, she dominates Bloom, evoking in conjunction with an awareness of her female superiority, his fear of discovery, his guilt for sins of desire, his masochistic need for excoriation by the many, his megalomaniacal craze for mass adulation, and his perversions of several sorts including transvestism; in short, a kind of ecstasy of normal psychological aberrations culminates hyperorgiastically with violence and the Black Mass and postorgiastically with impotence and stupor. Joyce has drawn a complete blueprint of the Circe aspects of the Feminine.

The aftermath of the storm is described in the Eumaeus and Ithaca chapters, both of which deal with a symbolic return to the womb in that each takes place in a shelter, a cavern, or a structure like that which in innumerable myths represents the earth womb (Neumann, p. 44), a place safe from the outside world. The male energies, enervated from reacting to the powerful female forces, seek to recover in some quiet backwater. And, exterior to the narrative of the events of that day containing all days, the Penelope chapter, Molly's dream, provides the summation of the feminine character of *Ulysses*. She is the Earth Mother, the basic figure of containment, protection, and nourishment, and her resounding affirmative corresponds to the initial character of the feminine theme in *Ulysses*, a character which counterbalances the negative forms developed from Calypso to Circe. She is the central or total form of the archetype, and through her embodiment of the elementary and transformative features of the other forms and their contradictions, she represents the vision of the primal Feminine around which Joyce's work revolved.

Because, like all who read *Ulysses*, we found it a strange, wondrous, and difficult work, we turned for explanation, as our guides suggested, to Homer; to help us know Homer, we turned to Butler; to confirm an hypothesis which Butler unintentionally suggested, we turned to Jung; and to rectify Jung's judgment, we turned to one who developed a theory that Jung introduced. We found that Joyce began with the initiation of the elementary Good Mother concept and that from there he developed gradually into contradictory concepts which defined the Terrible Mother. From there he continued via witchcraft into the negative transformational character, and thence back to the most essential and total containment symbol. The development was not absolutely complete. Notably lacking was one aspect of the Feminine—the positive transformational form identified with the muses, the Virgin Mary, wisdom, vision, and the inspirational mysteries. The lack of this form is most conveniently explained by Joyce's famous revolt against the church. Not that this is the only matter left unresolved. What use, for example, did Joyce make of other archetypal forms? What relationship does his work bear to certain esoteric studies? and to the other arts? The old artificer has left us in the maze he created, and we will have to search for a long time before we find our way out. But fortunately, we have had some assistance: Butler has helped identify our plight; Jung has lighted a candle; and Neumann has carried it for us for a certain distance.

Notes

1. *The Collected Works of C. G. Jung,* ed. Sir Herbert Read, trans. R. F. C. Hull (London, 1966), XV, 124. Also in *Nimbus* (1953), II, 7-20 and *Spring,* trans. W. Stanley Dell (New York, 1949).
2. *James Joyce's Ulysses* (London, 1930, 1952).
3. *The Humour of Homer and Other Essays* (London, 1913).
4. (New York, 1950), p. 124.
5. S. Foster Damon, "The Odyssey in Dublin," in Seon Givens, *James Joyce: Two Decades of Criticism* (New York, 1963), pp. 203-42.
6. Hugh Kenner, *Dublin's Joyce* (Bloomington, 1956).
7. (New York, 1954). Originally published as *Ursprungsgeschichte des Bewusstseins* (Zurich, 1949).
8. (New York, 1955).
9. *Mother,* p. 13.
10. Leon Albert, in *Joyce and the New Psychology* (Ann Arbor, University Microfilms, 1957); also, *Dissertation Abstracts* (1958), XVIII, IV, 1424-25 observed that "A note book dated 1914 contains a small collection of Joyce's dreams with analyses of each, written in Joyce's hand." The method of analysis seems similar to that set forth in *The Interpretation of Dreams.* Another notebook containing early notes and drafts used in the composition of *Ulysses* and dating from about 1914 refers to "Siegfriedmund Ueberallgemein," possibly a parody of the name of the founder of psychoanalysis. Additional "external evidence" is also explored and related to the reference in the manuscript of *Ulysses* to "the Viennese school. . . ."
11. In support of this concept one can cite Otto Rank, *The Myth of the Birth of the Hero,* and his belief that the child is trying to replace the real father by a more distinguished one, as an expression of his longing for the former lost time when his father appeared to be the most imposing and admirable man. "The queer suddenly things he popped out with attracted the elder man who was several years the other's senior or like his father." James Joyce, *Ulysses* (New York, 1934), p. 640. All subsequent references will be to this, the Random House edition.
12. Quoted by Gilbert, pp. 62 ff. Curtius's article, translated by Eugene Jolas as "Techniques and Thematic Development of James Joyce," appeared in *Transition* (June, 1929), Nos. 16-17, pp. 310-25.
13. P. 62.
14. Miles Hanley, *Word Index to James Joyce's Ulysses* (Madison, 1951).
15. The gorgon, according to Neumann, *Mother* (p. 170), "is endowed with every male attribute: the snake, the tooth, the boar's tusks, the outthrust tongue, and sometimes even with a beard."
16. In passing it is of interest to note that the word crosstrees was incorrect, that Joyce knew that it was incorrect, but that he insisted upon using it. Its evident appropriateness in subtly reminding us of the religious-archetypal motif later to be developed could explain his insistence.
17. *Mother,* p. 33.
18. P. 652 of Layard, as quoted by Neumann, *Mother,* p. 176.
19. *The Greek Myths,* I (Baltimore, 1955), Section 88.8, p. 297.

Philip Wheelwright

THE ARCHETYPAL SYMBOL

AN INCREASING INTEREST IN ARCHETYPAL SYMBOLISM, STIMULATED jointly by cultural anthropology, depth psychology, and metaphysical reflections, has enlivened much of the critical discussion of literature in recent times. My present aim is to take a fresh look at the complex but unified term, "archetypal symbol," first analyzing the purport of its two component terms, and then considering three main groups of archetypal symbols—namely, those concerned with uranian divinity, with chthonic counter-divinity, and with the perennial human idea of pilgrimage. If the much joggled word "semantics" is taken broadly and humanistically, as its etymology warrants, to cover *any ordered study of what and how something* MEANS, then it is accurate to describe the present inquiry as a semantics of the archetypal symbol.

Defining the Symbol

Some concepts, such as *meaning, being, relation, time,* are too fundamental to allow of definition. To ask what meaning means is obviously question-begging. Nevertheless, while it is impossible to define meaning from the outside by reference to a larger category, we can somewhat clarify the concept internally by distinguishing its main forms and expressions—by phenomenological examination, in short. To keep our bearings in such an examination we must acknowledge from first to last that every human experience has meaning in some way or other, whether clear or vague, articulate or dumb, intellectually respectable or offbeat. By such nonpartisan procedure we can avoid the danger of systematically omitting (as a seeming exercise of methodological virtue) unorthodox kinds of significant question.

The most general truth that can be affirmed about meaning, or a meaningful situation, is that it always involves two aspects: that which means and that which is meant, a semantic carrier and a semantic content, or (in I. A. Richards' suggested terminology) vehicle and tenor, V and T. Now V may be anything without exception; for we can inquire of anything to which our attention is turned, and implicitly we do inquire, what it means. In asking what V means we seek to give shape to its T and to the specific V-T relation. T may also be spoken of as the *referend* (from the Latin gerund, "to be referred to") or as the *meaning* of V.

The forms of the V-T relation are manifold. The relation may be distinct (for example, the word "dog" vis-à-vis the animal itself), or on the other hand V may coalesce with T and participate in it (as a friend's face will signify, and indicate the presence of, the friend himself, of whom the face is a part; and as a sacred dance may pay symbolic homage to a divine presence of which the dance is regarded as a manifestation). Or taking a different approach we may distinguish between those V-T relations that grow up naturally in a given cultural nexus (for example, the bull as a symbol-manifestation of divine potency) as against those established stipulatively by deliberate choice (for example, the Greek letter π to stand for the ratio between a circle's circumference and its diameter). Each of these two ways of distinguishing between different kinds of V-T relations develops its own set of problems for poetic interpretation and theory. The former distinction suggests questions of clarity versus vagueness and their patterns of interrelatedness in poems; the latter distinction suggests questions about the poet's acceptance of established meanings in contrast with his creative renewal of language through their remolding. Both distinctions lead by different routes to the question of the kind of *interpreter to whom* the language is clear or vague, familiar or novel. It appears that as we move toward the larger questions of poeto-cultural and religio-cultural meaning we find ourselves less and less able to say with assurance just who the fit interpreters are. Nevertheless, the concept of the able interpreter is indispensable in principle. For if we are to think, judge, and communicate, we cannot avoid supposing (however tentatively) that some ways of understanding a given matter are more adequate and nearer to the truth than other ways.

We are now in a better position to say what a symbol is—that is, to say how the word "symbol" should be used. Here as in all definitions there has to be some compromise between actual usage and prescribed usage—with an eye to practicality on the one hand, to order and clarity on the other. And we can specify three main characteristics, I think, as distinguishing the symbol from other kinds of semantic vehicle.

First, the attitude which a symbol represents and to which it appeals is contemplative rather than directive or pragmatic. A symbol refers to what supposedly *is*, not (or at least not directly) to what one is to do. It is the *logos theoretikos*, not the *logos praktikos*, which the symbol in its symbolic role expresses. Thus a red traffic light, although it indubitably "means something," is not a symbol. But if some sermonizer were to devise a remark like "The atomic bomb is God's red traffic light," then in that metaphorical usage the familiar sign would have been turned into a symbol.

Secondly, in the case of a symbol the relation between V and T is not simply determined by the natural (nonhuman) factors of (*a*) causation or (*b*) resemblance, but involves a contributory factor of human choice, whether individual or collective and whether conscious or unconscious. Thus (*a*) although black clouds may "mean" that a storm is brewing, they do not constitute a symbol; and (*b*) although a map "means," refers to, a certain geographical terrain, the map is still not a symbol.

Thirdly, a symbol has a certain stability: it endures beyond one or a few occasions. For instance, a man might make a spontaneous gesture of contempt and the onlookers might understand quite well what he meant by it: his gesture would then be meaningful, but it would not be a symbol. On the other hand the gesture of thumbing the nose, the accepted meaning of which has been commonly understood for several generations, has become a symbol of contempt.

The last characteristic, being susceptible to growth and decline, is significant for further study of the nature of the symbol. There are, it would seem, three main ways in which the V-T relation can become stabilized: by natural semantic growth and personal choice in some degree of collaboration (the way of cultural tradition and of poetic, personal utterance), by passive habituation (the way of the marketplace, of journalese, and of personal default), and by stipulation (the way of logic and theoretical science). The first and third of these procedures, which draw upon the second and give it character in different ways, eventuate in two contrasting types of symbol—the one living and organic, the other inert and formalized; the one illustrated by Mallarmé's *faune,* Rilke's angels, and Eliot's waste land, the other by the mathematical square root sign (or for that matter any arithmetical digit) and the symbols of symbolic logic. The former type may be called the *expressive* symbol, the latter the *steno-symbol;* and in larger scope we may speak correspondingly of expressive language and steno-language.

The resulting distinction is not a sharp dichotomy, but is marked by degree. The characteristics of the expressive symbol are potentials: they can be found to different degrees in one or another expressive symbol, but in the steno-symbol they tend to be entirely absent. The steno-symbol and steno-language are thus marked by a minimal degree of expressivity. In logico-scientific language the expressivity is systematically ignored as a matter of methodological policy, whereas in commonplace language it tends to be lost by default of imagination. The significance of these statements can be judged better by considering the main types of expressivity presented in the next section.

Traits of the Expressive Symbol

Since the present essay is concerned with the expressive symbol (the steno-symbol having been mentioned merely in order to make and keep the distinction clear), it is this that I shall mean henceforth when I use the simple word "symbol." In contexts where there might be some doubt I may use a capital: "Symbol." After all, this is approximately what people in general mean by the word, except for the few who have been taught to employ a technical vocabulary. But the concept needs to be clarified, and while finality in such deep and devious matters is neither possible nor desirable, I wish to point out four leading characteristics of the Symbol that are of primary impor tance. Let me repeat that these characteristics are permissive, not prescriptive; and how far each of them may be present has to be ascertained afresh in each instance.

Semantic congruity. In the case of a Symbol, as distinguished from a steno-symbol, there tends to be some degree of congruity, of appropriateness between V and T. It would make a difference to the meaning if the Symbol were altered or replaced by another Symbol. Steno-symbols, on the other hand, are always theoretically replaceable; any difficulty of replacement will be practical and contingent. The choice of "π" for its accepted role in mathematics, rather than some other steno-symbol, is stipulative. The Greek letter has no organic relation with the meaning for which it stands; its use is a matter of convenience. Any other sign could have served equally well to denote the ratio of circumference to diameter, and if a change of sign were to be agreed upon it would have no effect whatever upon the structure and validity of geometrical relations. By contrast, if Shakespeare had decided to let the Weird Sisters inhabit water like the Rhine Maidens, instead of "fog and filthie aire," the entire texture of relations composing *Macbeth*—imagistic, dramatic, and metaphysical at once—would have been profoundly changed. There can be no substitution of one Symbol for another without thereby somehow altering the meaning.

This concept of semantic congruity—that is, congruence between a Symbol and its meaning—invites some further attention. How is the congruence to be understood, if possible explained? As a working formula I suggest that V may be considered semantically congruent with T when V is related to T either by perceived similarity, by analogy from general experience, or by developed association. Let us consider briefly each of these.

Perceptual similarity gives rise to three kinds of semantic representation. *Iconic* representation (for example, a map) is based on visual similarity; *tonal* representation (for example, program music, onomatopoeia) on auditory; *mimetic* representation (for example, a sacred dance) on kinaesthetic. Similarities of smell, taste, and outward touch may usually be ignored. Now in my previous mention of maps I have already remarked that resemblance by itself, functioning semantically, does not constitute a symbolic relation. True; but nevertheless resemblance may enter into a symbolic relation as a contributing factor. Especially is this true in the case of kinaesthetic resemblance, where operative in a ritual mimetic dance. A dance which mimes the war god or the god of reproduction or the god of rain is likely to develop Symbols appropriate to that kind of ritualistic occasion.

More widely significant is analogy drawn from general experience. Symbols like "the key to the city" offer examples. The key is symbolically appropriate to what it means, because of the analogy between an actual key's unlocking of doors and the ceremonial key's bestowal, or pretended bestowal, of privileges. Analogies of this type are especially operative in those symbolic relations of very broad human acceptance, which are designated archetypal.

Developed association is a third factor that may contribute to semantical congruity: thus Christians have come to feel the appropriateness of the Cross as symbolizing resurrection, although the cross in its origin (specifically its Christian origin) was an instrument of torturing the crucified victim to death. Where the association between V and T is no more than a matter of social custom and private habituation, however, the result is likely to be a steno-symbol— as the Christian cross turns out to be for those who take it perfunctorily. What produces expressive symbolism is more likely to be some combination of these three factors of congruence.

Plurisignation. A Symbol tends to reach out semantically. As distinguished from the steno-symbol, which is governed by the principle of semantic economy, the expressive symbol is characterized by semantic plenitude. Its meanings are limited not by set rule, not by definition, but by some more organic principle. Why in the rituals of the Osage Indians of the Central Plains did the smoke from the ceremonial pipe (the *calumet,* as the French-Canadian missionaries called it) signify both war and peace?[1] Its suggestion of war doubtless came originally from the visual similarity between the smoke from the pipe and storm clouds; its suggestion of peace from the similarity of the smoke to rain-clouds, with their promise of fruitful growth of crops, hence tribal health, hence peace. The two meanings when juxtaposed look contradictory, and a steno-logical procedure would be to eliminate either the one or the other. Nevertheless, since the pipe smoking is a collective ritual, the criterion of valid interpretation is to be sought not in exercises of abstract analysis but in tribal activities and shared sentiments. In practice there is no confusion between the opposite meanings of the *calumet,* because all partakers of the ritual always know whether the purport of a particular ceremony is peace or war. There is no collective need here for applying the law of non-contradiction, nor for formulating such a law. The seeming paradox of the *calumet* takes its rise from, and finds its justification in, the complementary forms of the ritual. Again, in the ancient European ceremony of the *taurobolium* the blood of the bull symbolized on the one hand the divine power and vitality to be transferred magically to each blood-bather, and at the same time the symbolic brotherhood of all who shared the same blood.

When a poet undertakes to introduce a certain Symbol into the language of his poem, he has a reservoir of meanings from which he can draw, and he manipulates his context in such a way that the reader will think only of the meanings (assuming them to be more than one) that the poet intends. Thus Eliot's manner of contextualizing the Dove imagery in "Little Gidding" directs the reader's mind to take the Dove as symbolizing both a bombing plane and the Holy Ghost; not the Dove of Peace, however, although in other circumstances that meaning might have been suggested. In the same poem the line, "To be redeemed from fire by fire," unmistakably refers to the opposing fires of hell and purgatory, thereby symbolizing ultimate pain and loss on the one hand, spiritual cleansing on the other; it does not, however, carry another well-known symbolic reference of fire, specifically, to the Heraclitean notion of universal change.

Soft focus.   Sometimes there is doubt as to what a symbol means, even though one feels that it does mean something, that it is not meaningless. Or, what is more often and more characteristically the case, there may be a bright focussed center of meaning together with a penumbra of vagueness that is intrinsically ineradicable; which is to say, the vagueness could not be dispelled without distorting the original meaning. The meaning of a symbol in such case is problematic, or partially so, for a problem is called "problematic" when any attempted solution of it changes its nature. The symbolic meaning of Ariel and Caliban in *The Tempest,* of the poodle in *Faust,* and of the castle in Kafka's novel of that name, is in each case partly problematic. The problematic residue is largely responsible for the powerful effect, emotional and intellectual at once, which the symbol has upon us. The attention of literary critics is naturally attracted by the problematic residue; the more naïve of them may try to reduce that residue to intelligibility. But since such reduction is impossible, what they actually do is impose their own schemata of intelligibility upon the symbolic situation, thereby diminishing rather than strengthening their grasp of it.

The relation of plurisignation to soft focus is of some theoretical interest. Schematically we might take our bearings from those two complementary laws of logic, the law of non-contradiction and the law of excluded middle—interpreting plurisignation as transcending the domain of the one, soft focus of the other. William Empson's justly influential book, *Seven Types of Ambiguity*, causes some confusion, I think, by failing to distinguish between these two basic relations, subsuming them both under the common name of "ambiguity."[2] In accuracy, however, V is ambiguous when it means simply either T_1 or T_2 without further specifications; it is plurisignative when it means both T_1 and T_2 together. And of course it is possible for both characteristics to be present in the same symbolic situation. Both proceed in poetry out of a certain psychological magnanimity: plurisignation from a disposition to symbolize luxuriously, ambiguity (soft focus) from a lordly indifference to excessive details.

Contextual variability.   In the stipulative procedure of logico-scientific method it is required that a symbol, whether it be a word or something else (for example, the square root sign in algebra, red lights on highways), should be employed with identically the same meaning throughout a given science, a given type of situation, or a given argument. By contrast consider a Shakespearean symbol. The symbolic role of stormy weather is not quite the same in *King Lear,* in *Macbeth,* and in *The Tempest.* Its meaning is limited and developed differently in each dramatic context. Yet there is a strong affinity of meaning (not a logical identity, however) in all Shakespearean uses of tempest imagery and tempest incident; for at least we never doubt that all those tempests point in an opposite direction from the meanings and moods evoked by such Shakespearean symbols as music, jewels, and feasting.

On Archetypes

Some symbols have more universality and durability than others. This statement, coupling the ideas of universality and durability, has significance only as applied to expressive symbols, not to steno-symbols. Wherever steno-symbols are in question their degree of universality presents no depth-problem; for it is a matter of plain logical demonstration that *animal* is a more universal concept than *dog*, and *dog* than *terrier*. Here "more universal" means simply having a wider denotation, a more extensive applicability. Questions of humanistic universality, on the other hand, can be raised only regarding Symbols. And such Symbols as are found to be universal or nearly so, in their broadly human manifestations, are called archetypes.

Methods of discovery in the field of archetypes must be approximate and tentative rather than exact or final, but even so there are certain Symbols that are indubitably archetypal. The sky father, the earth mother, the serpent, the eye of the sun, the ear of grain, the vine, the sprouting tree, ritualistic bathing, the road or path and the pilgrimage along it, kingly power as both blessing and threat, the soaring bird, the circle or sphere, and so on—these Symbols are not the products of a single culture as the Christian cross is, but are to be found exercising their powers in cultures widely separated in time and in historical trends of influence.

The full breadth of this meta-anthropological phenomenon has been known only recently, since the establishment a century ago of anthropology as a field of scientific inquiry. As the prevalence and importance of archetypes became known the question of their cause or causes began to be raised; but while that type of question is natural to the scientific disposition, the persistent pursuit of it can be misleading and distractive from the main issue. Accurate description and comparison, graced by sympathetic receptivity, should take precedence over theoretical etiology in the study of archetypes; we can make headway with the former by a phenomenological study of the evidences drawn diversely from literature, anthropology, and ancient art, but the latter is bound to contain an element of unverifiable speculation.

The late Dr. C. G. Jung's desire to couple the study of ancient evidences with the findings of clinical psychoanalysis in the study of archetypes seems to me of ambiguous value for a sound understanding of the ancient archetypes themselves.[3] We may grant without cavil Jung's discovery of a few (and they are only a few!) striking analogies between ancient man's preconceptual life and certain images and configurations "which drift into consciousness in our dreams and in abnormal states of mind." As an adventure in theorizing it may even be allowable to postulate that there is not only analogy but somehow a hypopsychical "continuity" between the ancient anthropological and the modern clinical. As a corollary of this assumption it was perhaps natural to devise the non-empirical concept of a "collective unconscious," as a theoretical explanation of so vast a world-organism of seeming correspondences. But when Jung unguardedly let this idea of hypopsychical continuity provoke the question of how transmission from generation to generation was possible, and answered with his theory that archetypes are *inherited* "like the morphological elements in the human body," he therein flouted empirical method in a way that unfortunately discredited his approach and even his legitimate discoveries in the eyes of many psychologists. Inasmuch as the word "archetype" has become so widely associated with Jung's name and method I think it wise to specify that the present study of archetypes is altogether independent of Jung's special theories. The ancient evidences on which I draw are open to all, and they are drawn mainly from ancient literary sources, amplified and sometimes interpreted by philology, archeology, and anthropology; for after all it is through the medium of syntactical language that the nature of ancient archetypes is most clearly shown.

Three groups of archetypes will here be examined: those having to do with sky and sun, fatherhood and kingship, as related symbolic expressions of divinity; those which express what in one way or another is complementary, sometimes antithetical, to the power and majesty of sky-divinity; and those pertaining to the basically human experiences of aspiration and alienation. No survey of archetypal symbols can be final; but it may be that the present threefold classification offers a patterned standpoint from which, by extension, most of the greater archetypes and archetypal relations can be envisioned and judged.

Father Sky and King Sun

The sky, as Professor Eliade has remarked, tends by its very nature to suggest transcendence.[4] Doubtless three characteristics present themselves, however inarticulately, to the primitive imagination as it looks upwards in awe and wonder. There are the sky's beneficent gifts of warmth and brightness alternating with life-giving rain; there is the menacing threat sometimes announced by the lightning flash and thunder clap and carried out in the destructive violence of storms; and there are the suggested ideas both of unlimited upward reach and of semi-sphericality of form. These three aspects of the sky tend to stir respectively, in a vaguely transcendent and proto-religious way, early man's gratitude, his terror, and his contemplative wonder.

In mythopoeic perspective the sky is more comprehensive than the sun, since the sky furnishes both warmth and rain while the sun is limited to the former. Although both sunshine and rain are needful to life, it was more suggestive metaphorically to think of rain as the sperm dropped from the sky into the womb of earth. Thus Aeschylus writes: "The pure sky [Uranos] desires to penetrate the earth, and the earth is filled with love so that she longs for blissful union with the sky. The rain falling from the beautiful sky impregnates the earth, so that she gives birth to plants and grain for beasts and men."[5] After the explicit sexuality of this Aeschylean account one is prepared to interpret Euripides' more restrained use of the same metaphor: "Parched earth loves the rain; and high heaven, rain filled, loves to fall earthward."

The spontaneous metaphor of impregnation must have given early currency to the idea of Father Sky; and the strong sense of filial piety in ancient societies made it easy and natural to fit out the cosmic picture. The sun, on the other hand, by reason of its unique position among the sky's luminaries, suggests regal power and distinction, and hence was more likely in mankind's early outlook to suggest kingship. It should be added, however, that in primitive communities the ideas of king and father were more closely related than in subsequent historical times, and that in the symbolism and mythology that have come down to us there is frequent intermingling of the two.

As Friedrich Max Müller demonstrated a century ago, there is etymological evidence that among the Indo-European language groups, before their early dispersal, the ideas of fatherhood, upward brightness, and giver of nutritive rain were evidently combined into the same god-figure.[6] The plainest clue lies in the word "Jupiter." The syllable "*Ju-*" (preserved in Latin in the oblique cases as "*Jov-*") is from the same root as the Greek "*Zeus*" and the Sanskrit "*Dyaus*"; the common meaning of all three variants is brightness, as applied to the sky. Since there are traces in older Greek of the form "*Zeu-pêter*" (Father Zeus) and in Sanskrit of the form "*Dyau-pitar*" (Father

Dyaus), employed in the vocative case in prayer, it appears likely that before the proto-Latin, proto-Hellenic, and proto-Aryan language groups split apart there was a common tendency to address the upward bright sky-god as "Father." Granted that a broad view of world religions does offer some instances in which the name of father was applied to the sun, but these are comparatively few and may quite possibly have resulted from a kind of primitive metonymy.

Did sun worship come later, on the whole, than sky worship? The question is controversial and a definite answer would be hazardous; nevertheless, it does appear that among the more developed religions of the world there have been some notable cases of sun worship and virtually none of sky worship. Dante, who developed his symbolism within and as expressing Christian doctrine, could declare: "There is no visible thing in all the world more worthy to serve as symbol of God than the Sun; which illuminates with visible life itself first and then all the celestial and mundane bodies."[7] Moreover, even after the anthropological view of the sky had been dropped the sun could still serve as a compelling religious metaphor because of its two main attributes of heat and brightness, symbolizing respectively creativity and wisdom (Plato) or divine love and divine wisdom (Swedenborg).[8]

Two great documents of sun worship have come down to us from ancient times. Both are by dedicated emperors: a prayer to the Sun by the Pharaoh Amenhotep IV, better known as Ikhnaton, who ascended the throne of Egypt in the fourteenth century B.C., and a devotional discourse by the Emperor Julian (called by his Christian enemies "the Apostate") who ascended the Roman throne in the fourth century A.D. Despite the seventeen centuries that separate the two philosopher-kings and the vast differences between the cultural environments in which they lived and thought, there are significant similarities of content and imagery between their doctrines.

On the death of Amenhotep III of Egypt his son, a lifelong cripple and newly come of age, succeeded to the throne as Amenhotep IV. Doubtless the physical affliction contributed to his contemplative disposition and his metaphysical and religious interests. To become Pharaoh meant attaining to the status of godhood. Apotheosis of the Pharaoh was a central tenet of Egyptian religious faith—specifically the elevation of him to the role of the sun god Rê (or Ra). But the usual manner of conceiving such elevation was more akin to what is expressed in perhaps the most famous of early Egyptian religious hymns:

Flying aloft like a bird
He settles down like a beetle
On the seat in the ship of the sun god.
Now he rows your ship across the sky, O glowing one.

The sky is darkened, the stars rain down,
The bones of the earth-god tremble
When this one steps forth as a god
Devouring his fathers and mothers,
With his sacred serpents on his forehead.

The long chant from which these lines are taken was uttered by the Pharaoh's surviving subjects, assembled to mourn his death and to exult in his divine translation. In this ambivalent ceremony the Pharaoh is raised as high as imagination can conceive: at the poem's climax he is represented as swallowing the heart and lungs of the sky gods themselves so that "their wisdom and their strength have passed into his belly."

When the crippled and introspective Amenhotep IV inherited the Egyptian throne (in 1367 B.C., some have estimated) there was no immediate change in the royal pattern of behavior. The new Pharaoh took to wife that exquisite lady Nefertiti, whose head, enshrined in the Dahlem Museum of West Berlin, shows her unique beauty miraculously preserved over thirty-three centuries, undiminished by changing styles. For seven years they continued in the imperial palace at Thebes following the traditions of their ancestors. But in the eighth year of his reign the Pharaoh proclaimed that the sun god was thenceforth to be worshipped under the name of Aton, and he removed his palace and court, together with the Queen and the three young princesses, to a new city, established midway between Thebes and the sea, to which he gave the name Akhetaton, "the horizon of Aton." His own name he changed to Ikhnaton.[9]

Several hymns or prayers (it is hard to know which to call them) of Sun worship have been preserved from the ensuing brief but brilliant period of solar monotheism in Egypt. Their authors appear to have been the Pharaoh himself, the Queen Nefertiti, and those royal architects of palace and city, the twin brothers Suti and Hor. Whether the Pharaoh or his architects composed the striking Sun hymn from which the following lines are taken is a matter of dispute, but in any case the sentiments and images authentically express that striking religion of solar monotheism, which came to its end in Egypt with Ikhnaton's death.

O living Aton, creator of life,
Beautiful is your dawning.
Coming forth as Rê you take all captive with your beams.
You bind them with your love.
Your footprints are the day.

If in the god's older, traditional manifestation as Rê he is the conqueror, in his newly declared universal character as Aton he breathes life and activity into all forms, both of growing things and of human activity and intercourse. There is coalescence between Rê and Aton, to be sure, nor was it natural to Egyptian religious thinking to stipulate clear distinctions. Yet the new tone of Aton worship is distinctive:

As Aton you rise in the eastern sky
Driving away darkness and brightening the earth.
Then the cattle browse upon their pasturage,
The birds flutter out of the marshes,
Their wings uplifted in adoration,
While the sheep dance nimbly.
The barques begin to sail up and down stream,
And on the highways men's traffic becomes active.
Your rays strike the green sea and the fishes leap up.

Moreover the sun's power and warmth are generative, stirring the germs of new life in male and female:

Creator of the seed in man and in woman
You gave life to the child in the womb of the mother,
Nursing him there that he may not weep,
Giving him breath that he may be alive.
And when he comes forth on the day of his birth
You open his mouth with speech.

The generative power of the sun was an essential part of Egyptian religious belief, symbolized particularly by the figure of the scarab. In zoological fact the scarab was the dung-beetle, marked by a curious set of birth preparation activities. The female of this species would lay her eggs in animal dung, then shaping the nitrogenous stuff into a spherical pellet she would roll it along the ground to a place chosen by her instinct as suitable for hatching and breeding. The Egyptians, unable to see the eggs but observing the newly born beetles, supposed the pellet to possess inherent generative powers.

Furthermore, as they watched the little brown sphere being rolled along they were struck by its resemblance to the sun rolling across the sky. Might it not be that an invisible beetle was pushing the sun? Thus both in its motion and in its generative power the dung-pellet became associated with the sun; and correspondingly the gold scarab, the beetle-shaped emblem of the Sun, came to symbolize especially the Sun's own attributes of new birth and immortality. Accordingly, in the special Egyptian ceremony of mummification the physical heart would be cut out and replaced by a gold scarab as symbol and assurance of the departed soul's immortality. The Sun, whether as Rê or as Aton, thus becomes the majestic higher power which bestows and symbolizes not only the bright significance of day but also the generative potency of birth into the world and of rebirth into immortality.

Another characteristic of the Sun symbolism as developed by Ikhnaton around the divine figure of Aton, is a new emphasis on universality. The mythology surrounding the traditional figure of Rê, besides being unusually fragmentary, and scarcely lending itself to any kind of coherent account or conception of the god, had to do mainly with the daily journey of Rê high above the land of Egypt, supplemented by his night journey underneath the earth, through the twelve compartments of the underworld from the western gate of sunset to the eastern gate of dawn. By contrast Ikhnaton's worship of Aton shows a wider and loftier imaginative reach:

> How manifold are your works!
> They are hidden from plain view,
> O sole God, whose power is unique.
> You have made a Nile in the nether world,
> Which you bring forth [annually] as needed,
> To preserve the life of your [Egyptian] people.
> But for those who live elsewhere
> And for their shambling cattle
> You have placed a Nile in the sky.
> To every man you have given his own possessions and
>   his allotted span of days,
> Whether he lives in Egypt or in distant Syria or Kush,
> And however strange his features, his skin, and his
>   ways of speech.

Between the two great sun-worshipping emperors, Ikhnaton of Egypt and Julian of Rome, there is an interval of about seventeen centuries. Julian is less of a poet than Ikhnaton and more of a metaphysician, although his name will not be found in histories of philosophy. As for the shortcomings of his published philosophy let it be remembered that he was handicapped both by the isolation of the throne (for how can an emperor get strong honest criticism?) and by the brevity of his life. Had it not been for that fatal javelin at the battle of Maranga in the second year of his reign when he was but thirty-two, who can guess what his studious dedication might have accomplished? As matters stand, however, we must deal as we can with his literary remains, particularly with the discourses entitled *On King Helios* and *On the Mother of the Gods*. My present attention is confined to the former of these.[10]

The best clue to Julian's symbolism of the Sun, to the what and why of it, lies in his statement of the main characteristics of the physical sun which make it the worthiest symbol for the ultimate Supreme *(On King Helios* 135 C). This brief but weighty statement deserves more consideration than it has hitherto received—not only as an indication of the Emperor's philosophy but also as an oblique contribution to the functioning of a major archetypal symbol.

1. The physical sun *"enables us to see objects of a visible kind."* Thanks to the sun (all lesser lights being derived from it) our eyesight is enabled to distinguish one physical thing from another. Analogously what we may describe as the light of the mind enables us to distinguish among intelligibles, preeminently discriminating true from false and good from evil.

Intellectual distinctions, however, are not self-justified. Unmotivated analysis is a dead end. Any real distinction between this and that, as Plato had taught, involves a discrimination of the specific good of each; which means that it involves a knowledge of the Good as manifesting itself differently in the things compared. To judge something objectively is not to appraise its external characters and utilities, but to apprehend the specific way in which Good manifests itself in that thing and in that kind of thing. The best scorpion *qua* scorpion is not the least injurious to humankind. In Plato's metaphor, we know the sun's existence from observing the qualities and degrees of brightness it produces on the various landscape. So Julian, by a quasi-Platonic dialectic only half-developed, sees the realm of intelligibles, which is to say of intelligible distinctions, as midway between the physical world, which symbolically points to it, and the supreme Good, to which it symbolically points.

2. The physical sun has *"creative and generative power, as shown by the changes he has wrought in the universe."* As the Egyptian em-

blem of the scarab had already indicated, the sun by the spermatic virtue of its warm rays penetrates the earth and produces life. But in order to grasp the symbolism of this biological process correctly we must interpret it in the teleological manner to which the ancients, both Egyptians and Greeks, were disposed. The sun acts telically, they held, as a *causa finalis*; the sunbeams are its emissaries, carrying gifts of warmth and spermatic power; sprouting seed and growing plant are not operated on in the modern materialistic sense, but are *attracted* toward the light. The Good works analogously, never coercing but attracting men's wills and wavering dispositions towards itself; and therein again the sun stands as a fitting symbol of it.

3. *The physical sun "joins all diverse motions into one whole, making a harmony* [symphonia] *of them. For he stands midmost, and the reason why he is established* [symbolically] *as king in the realm of the intelligibles is the fact that he holds a middle position among the planets."*

Is it surprising that a Roman emperor should know and accept the heliocentric theory less than a century after Aristarchus of Samos had propounded it? Perhaps not when we stop to reflect. In the first place Julian would probably have heard of the theory during his early years of study at Nicomedia and at Athens, and as a dedicated Mithraist he would have grasped eagerly at a scientific view so congenial to his own religious faith. In the second place we are largely ignorant of the background of Aristarchus' theory. Historians of science usually depict him as an out-of-season Copernicus, too advanced for the scientific climate of his time. But whereas Copernicus' principal declared motive was to find a conceptual means for simplifying the computation of planetary movements, Aristarchus meant the heliocentric pattern not merely as a pragmatic device but as a true statement of how the universe is really arranged. The idea of the sun's central position had already been propounded by some Mithraists, as by some later Pythagoreans, not on any scientific ground but because centrality symbolized primacy, so that the center was deemed the rightful position for the sun to hold.

At any rate, what the sun symbolizes, according to Julian, "holds the royal place in the realm of intelligibles," connoting both highest honor and supreme power. Julian's restatement of the Platonic analogy has peculiar interest for the present inquiry because of its combined use of three archetypal symbols—light, kingship, and centrality. The first two are essentially uranian as we have seen, but the archetype of the Center goes altogether beyond the dualism of sky and earth. It is a geometrical image employed symbolically, and in ancient thought it tends often to be embodied in the more concrete image of the Wheel. For the revolving wheel has a special property that made it a highly suggestive symbol in Greek and Buddhist thought alike: the fact that when a wheel revolves uniformly its central point is motionless, and vice versa. Clearly the idea has implications at once metaphysical and moral: metaphysically it points to the stasis of Being in relation to the dynamics of Becoming; morally it suggests a pattern for serene living by finding the "still point" at the center of one's selfhood. Thereby the Center of the Wheel, connotatively connected with the brightness and majesty of the Sun, becomes one of the great archetypes for the understanding and ordering of human life.

God's Symbolic Counterparts

One does not need to demonstrate that reality as lived and known is imbued with polarity, but the forms of polarity are widely varied according to the standpoint adopted. Imagistically the light of the sun is contrasted with the nether darkness (Erebus, Hades, Sheol); mythologically the Sky Father is related conjugally to the Earth Mother; dramatically some sky-born hero fights against and conquers the enemy dragon; conceptually the oneness and perfection symbolized by the solar disk is dialectically contrasted with the manyness and temporality of the shifting world of things and events; psychologically the contemplative quietude of Being is qualified by the sensuous, emotional, and impulsive unevenness of Becoming. Briefly let us look at three main archetypal symbols which in one way or another represent antithesis or complementation to the initial idea of pure upward divinity: specifically, Woman, the Serpent, and the Evil One.

Woman. There are four main general forms which the archetypal Feminine tends to assume, with a confusing variety of blendings and transformations. She is (1) the Mother, the *Magna Mater*, somehow identified with Earth, from whose womb all life germinates and comes to birth; (2) the Virgin, the Feminine Ideal, for whose sake the hero, and the heroic in every man, bestirs himself to confront dangers and attain the goal; (3) the Siren, the temptress, the symbol of sensual allurement which distracts man from his essential task; and (4) the Harpy, which is to say femininity in its repellent and frightening aspect, whether as witch, vampire, erinys, lamia, medusa, or whatever other configuration of female horror.

But such distinctions, though perhaps helpful in giving us our bearings, can mislead by their seeming clarity. That woman is essentially mysterious, eluding rational analysis and explanation, has been a popular article of faith in most periods of cultural history. The Egyptians symbolized this mystery by the Veil of Isis; and the inscription in her shrine at Sais reads:

> I am all that has been, and that is, and that shall be, and no mortal has ever raised my veil. The fruit which I have brought forth is the sun.

That is to say, the feminine kind of reality precedes and gives birth to the clarity and predictability and more overt kind of power represented by the sun. Yin gives birth to Yang. Herself, however, is eternally veiled.

The combinations among the four aspects of the Woman archetype are many and various. Only one of them, dramatically the most striking, can be considered here. The *Magna Mater*, as Erich Neumann has demonstrated with a wealth of examples,[11] is inherently ambivalent, combining the aspects which correspond to our (1) and (4). Although the Great Mother on the one hand is the beneficent source of life and nourishment, she also represents all that is menacing in life, men's unconscious terror of the unknown. For the earth which nourishes is also the black hole into which man must eventually disappear. "Disease, hunger, hardship, war above all, are her helpers," Neumann writes, "and among all peoples the goddess of war and the hunt express man's experience of life as a female exacting blood." The most conspicuous mythic instance of the Dreadful Female (as Neumann calls her in this aspect) is the Hindu goddess Kali, "the bone-wreathed lady of the place of skulls," as Heinrich Zimmer calls her. In the many statues and paintings of Kali in all parts of India she is most commonly depicted as tearing human flesh and devouring it, often with children as her victims. Yet there is another side to her nature, for she is worshipped in India as "Mother

Kali" and we learn from the biographies of Mahatma Ghandi that she was for him a principal object of worship and veneration. Probably Zimmer and other interpreters are right in seeing Kali as symbolizing, in large part at least, the destructive and devouring action of Time.[12] On that interpretation the worship of Kali by thoughtful Hindus symbolizes what is perhaps man's ultimate and only successful choice: "the courage to be," a stalwart acceptance of the total risk of blessings and banes that time imposes.

The Serpent. It would be far too large a task here to survey all the species of animals that have played important symbolic roles. Lion, eagle, snake, bull, cock, peacock, owl, fish, fox, cat, horse, and many others have had some importance as symbols in the myth, folklore, and literature of the world. Frequently they have been supplemented by fabulous beasts—dragon, chimera, sphinx, phoenix, centaur, unicorn, griffin, hippogriff, and so on. But in their symbolic role the difference between real and fabulous animals is blurred by the fact that even real animals tend in a mythopoeic setting to develop fabulous qualities.

Of all symbolic animals none has such a related variety of meanings as the snake, or, as it is usually called in its archetypal role, the Serpent. On the one hand it is widely regarded as a fertility spirit, while at the same time it carries overtones of mystery and potential hostility to man. Its traditional relation to fertility seems to be based in part on its closeness to the ground and its emergence from holes and caves, and partly on its annual shedding of its skin, tending to make it a symbol of both physical and spiritual rebirth. Perhaps less consciously than these are the suggestions latent in its beady eyes and almost mesmerizing gaze, its elusive wriggle, its phallic shape, and the general air of non-human otherness it exudes. Such implications of fertility, sexuality, and biological regeneration explain why there was a snake coiled around the staff of Aesculapius, the legendary founder and patron god of medicine in ancient Greece; while their natural sublimation into the idea of spiritual rebirth accounts for the various representations of a snake coiled about the Tree of Life.

A quite different set of meanings arises from the *ouroboros*—the Gnostic word for a snake in circular shape with its tail in its mouth. Many representations of this figure bear the letters *Alpha* and *Omega*, signifying absolute first and last, hence immortality when it is placed on a mortuary *stêlê*, and more generally divine wisdom. In

India the same ouroboric figure represents the Wheel of Life, or the life-force which manifests itself alike in birth, death, and rebirth; such symbolism, too, carrying overtones of a divine wisdom and cosmic order that transcends human vicissitudes. The notion of the serpent as crafty, expressed in the Garden of Eden legend and in many another folklore, is perhaps a popular debasement of an older idea of supernatural and quasi-divine wisdom.

Personified evil. The idea of absolute moral antithesis and its symbolization by God in Heaven versus Devil in Hell can arise only within monotheism. Where there is a plurality of gods the antagonisms among them are political rather than ethical, and generally more shifting. A mythos of one inflexible righteousness is needed if there is to be a single cosmic Adversary.

Evil has in general two meanings: the evils that one suffers and the evils that one does. One of the primary philosophical insights about the human condition, affirmed by the greatest teachers in the East and the West alike, is that what one does, rather than what one suffers, should be our principal (some say our only) concern. The vicissitudes of fortune and the kind of external evils it can bring do not concern us here, but rather those symbols pertaining to the existential enigma of evil choice.

Where internal evil is concerned its symbolization has two phases. An evildoer may recognize that he has failed to "see" the right course or that he has failed to "listen to" the voice of duty or of wisdom; hence arise the symbols of blindness to the Light and of deafness or indifference to the Word. The Light and the Word represent the two indispensable factors in moral goodness: the need to discern the good and the need to hearken to That which speaks with a higher authority than impulse, desire, or custom. But since unalloyed acknowledgement of one's own failings is humanly difficult, there is an almost universal desire for mythic symbols by which one can seem to explain, excuse, and shift the blame. Homer wryly illustrates this need, or perhaps parodies it, in Agamemnon's petulant speech to the Argive assembly:

> It is not I that am the cause; rather it is Zeus, and Destiny, and Epinys who walks in darkness,—it is they who put blind fury into my chest on that day in the assembly when I robbed Achilles of his rightful spoil. [*Iliad* XIX, 86–9.]

Whereas Agamemnon is a polytheist, man's moral predicament becomes more fully dramatic when the various sources of evil and temptation are thought of as arrayed under a single enemy banner. Ahriman in Zoroastrian and Satan in Christian theology are the two outstanding examples of such monokakology.

According to early Zoroastrianism as it can be pieced together from the prayers, ponderings, and affirmations in the *Zend-Avesta*, a great cleft runs through the whole of reality dividing it into two great warring camps: the realm of Ahura Mazda ("Lord Light") and that of Angra Mainyu ("Enemy Spirit"), characterized on the one side by truth and justice, symbolized as Light and personified as the angel Asha, and on the other side by falsehood, symbolized as Darkness and personified as the *daeva* (demon) Druj. In the course of time Ahura Mazda and Angra Mainyu became more succinctly known as Ormazd and Ahriman respectively. Ahriman is the primordial source and proponent of evil, the eternally irreconcilable enemy of Ormazd and of good. Even while Ormazd was creating the world Ahriman busied himself devising faults and obstacles to plant in it. When Ormazd created Gâyômart and Goshûrvan, the primeval man and the primeval ox, Ahriman slew them both, thus thwarting Ormazd's original plan for perfect human and animal life on earth. Finally, when Ormazd created the present race of mankind, endowing the seed of the progenitor so that each individual would have both freedom of choice and a sense of responsibility to his Creator, Ahriman thenceforth devoted himself to enticing the human soul and inciting it to rebel against Ormazd, denying the Light and what it represents. Thus the moral battle is a real one, of cosmic proportions, fought and re-fought in the soul of every individual.[13]

Compared with early Zoroastrianism the moral dualism of the Judaeo-Christian Old Testament is more shaky and problematical. Satan is not here an independent source of evil in the full sense that Ahriman is. In the earlier-written books of the Old Testament the Hebrew word *"sātān"* evidently means nothing more than either an opponent or an accuser (or both) in a quite general sense. Even where Satan has become personified, as in the Book of Job, he is plainly going about his persecution of Job with the Lord's permission and connivance. The older connotations of the Hebrew word still invest his personality, and he seems to be something like God's *agent provocateur*, tempting a human soul to evil and then accusing it before God's high tribunal.

The present Christian notion that Satan (subsequently named also by the Greek word for accuser, *"diabolos,"* translated "the Devil") is the author of all evil, who brought death into the world, appears to stem from *The Wisdom of Solomon,* ii: 24, although that book is excluded from the Protestant canon. The identification of Satan with the serpent who seduced Eve appears to have developed rather late in Old Testament apocryphal literature.[14] By the time of the New Testament it is evident that Satan, now more variously named and described, is accepted as a fully substantial entity, the source and power of evil, "the lurking adversary" (*antikeimenos,* 1 Timothy 5: 14) "seeking whom he may devour" (1 Peter 5: 8). In the episode of Jesus' temptation in the desert (Matthew 4) there is evidently no ground whatever for questioning the real and independent existence of Satan, who is here called "the Devil." Nor is there the slightest indication that he here acts with God's connivance or permission as he did in the Book of Job. And yet, while the New Testament Satan appears repeatedly as an independent power of evil, acting on his own initiative to corrupt God's created world wherever he can, the balance of power does not remain poised, for subsequent theology (doubtless drawing on Revelation 20: 2–3) developed the reassuring doctrine that God was sure to be the ultimate victor and that there was no question of Satan's being finally overthrown. God, in short, *seems* to be playing the game for stakes, but he has things arranged so that he is certain to be the eventual winner.

Thus the contest between God and Satan is melodrama rather than tragedy. Two things determine it as such. In melodrama there is a fast line between virtue and sin, between hero and villain; while secondly there is assurance, perhaps half-suppressed for the pleasure of rediscovering it, that the good will triumph in the end. Zoroastrian and Christian ethics share the first of these characteristics. The second of them is absent from the earlier and sturdier phases of Zoroastrian thought, where the cosmic warfare is taken as genuine, but later it comes more and more to be accepted; for if it were not, the worshipper would be faced with the unpleasant corollary that even though he chooses the right side, the side of truth and justice, he might quite possibly find his cause and himself hopelessly overthrown. Few men can face so formidable a prospect steadily, and consequently the two doctrines of sharp ethical dualism and eschatological rectification tend to be accepted or rejected jointly. Christianity accepts them both, and therefore maintains the symbol of the Last Judgment as an essential part of its total mythos.

Image of the Pilgrim

Man is the questing animal. He is the animal who can formulate and pursue ideals that are different in kind from the goals of animal instinct, even though the relations between the ideal and the instinctual are intricate and confused. To regard man in his transzoic capacity (never pure but nonetheless real) is to regard him existentially; and in existential perspective the purport of symbolic archetypes takes on a riper significance.

A stern fact about man's existential goal is that it is never completely attainable or perfectly formulable. It is not like a prize to be won. For when the prize has been secured, or the particular project accomplished, it no longer has the character of a goal. Thus from the start it was an empirical, not an existential goal. The object of man's existential quest is always receding, attainable from time to time in fragmentary particulars but never totally. Satisfaction from grasped success is small and temporary compared with the never-ending itch for something more. Out of this changing and persistent desire for transcendence of particularity arise certain typical relations between the psyche and its world. When these relations are conceptualized they provide terms and questions for metaphysical inquiry; when they are projected into images and narratives they produce certain archetypal symbols and myths.

There are, it seems, three main existential moods, each marked by its characteristic symbols. In human life they are intermixed, but since they enter the mixture in different proportions we can usually distinguish them in tenor and bearing. For brevity they might be called the moods of Innocence, of Alienation, and of Aspiration. Subjectively everyone knows something of all three, but since they not only intermingle but also sometimes wear one another's features, subjective approaches to them are prone to self-deception. At all events, self-deceived or no, we can recognize certain characteristic symbols that mark the presence, real or imaginary, of each: respectively, for example, the Garden, the Desert, and the Path.

The mood of Innocence is the most elusive and self-deceiving of the three. Our real innocence both individually and racially has been lost (if, indeed, it ever existed), and the ideas of innocence that we formulate bear the stamp either of fairytale fantasy or of ethical rationalization. But whatever the degree of self-deception they tend always to wear the double countenance of nostalgia and of hope. In terms of the Judaeo-Christian-Mohammedan mythos we look backward to the Garden of Eden and forward to the garden-like splendor of Paradise. Innocence resides thus at both beginning and end of the archetypal cycle: there is pristine innocence, then loss or corruption of it, then redemptive reaffirmation, pointing to a heavenly goal that somehow renews and fulfills whatever was essential in the original innocence lost. Be it noted, however, that the symbols of innocence can validly appear to us only as overtones and evanescently—as "bright shoots of everlastingness" (Vaughan), as "a green thought in a green shade" (Marvell), as vague interminglings of memory and desire, the remembered and hoped for "moment in the rose garden" (Eliot). When the nostalgia and the hope are too consciously dwelt upon they inveigle us into self-deception; then, as in "Burnt Norton," a cloud passes and the pool is empty.

Symbols of the phase of Alienation, though various, bear a family likeness. The Desert or Wasteland may be taken as central; connected with it are such component and subsidiary images as sand (connoting spiritual barrenness), murky darkness (Dante's *l'aere bruna*), cacophony (producing deafness to, or distraction from, the Logos), bodily wounds (particularly those affecting the sexual centers), chaos, the abyss, and directionless wandering. The idea of Hell is the idea of hopeless immersion in the kind of being that these symbols represent.

By contrast there is the image-symbol of the Path, and of the Pilgrim who travels it. The Pilgrim differs essentially from the Wanderer, in that the one has assurance of direction, the other not. Precisely this assurance of direction is the valid core of meaning in the theological virtue of Hope, when it has been purged of "hope of the wrong things" including supernatural fantasies. Other symbols of this third existential phase, besides the Path and the Pilgrim, are the Stair or Ladder, the Bird or Winged Soul, Cleansing whether by water or by fire or in other contexts by blood, Unveiling, Change of Heart (*metanoia*), and, in some areas of belief, Purgatory.

As an illustration of the Pilgrim archetype let us consider a passage that has rarely received the attention it merits—Parmenides' symbolic description of his journey from nether darkness upward into the light of philosophical truth. The description is placed as prologue to his didactic poem *On Nature,* the main body of which is devoted to the only doctrine of metaphysics that can be perfectly expressed in a single word: "Is."

> The steeds that draw my chariot were conducting me to the farthermost reach of my desire, bringing me at length on to the resounding road of the Goddess, along which he who knows is borne through all cities. Along this road I was carried—yes, the wise horses drew me in my chariot as maidens held the reins. The axle, urged round and round by the whirling wheels on either side, glowed in the sockets and gave forth a singing hum. The handmaidens of the sun, who had left the realms of night and had thrown back their veils from their faces, were driving the chariot speedily toward the light.
>
> We came to the gates of day and night, which are fitted between a lintel above and a stone threshold below. Although the gates are of aetherial substance they have the strength of mighty doors when closed, and Justice the rectifier secures them with bolts that both punish and reward. But the maidens cajoled her with gentle words and soon managed to persuade her to pull back the bolts from the gates. When the gates were flung back on their hinges, which were nailed to bronze posts on either side, a wide expanse was revealed through the open doorway: it showed a broad avenue, along which the maidens steered my horses and chariot. The Goddess greeted me kindly, and taking my hand in hers she spoke these words:
>
> "Welcome, my son, you who come to our abode with immortal charioteers at the reins! It is no evil fate that has set you on this road, but Right and Justice [*Themis* and *Dikē*] have brought you here, far away from the beaten paths of men. It is needful that you learn of all matters—both the unshaken heart of well-rounded truth and the opinions of mortals which lack true belief. For it is needful that by passing everything under review you should learn this also—how to judge of mere seeming."[15]

As a reader will partly see and further suspect, the passage teems with symbolic meanings and suggestions. The principal symbols of it are those which serve to define the journey by giving it the character of Pilgrimage. There are the usual metaphors of Upwardness and Light, the symbolic purport of which is well known. More specifically there are several solar references. The maidens who drive the chariot are described as "handmaidens of Helios." Since the chariot reaches "the resounding road" ("the renowned road"?) before it reaches the gates of day and night (that is, the portals of dawn), it seems to follow that the first part of the chariot's course has been a night journey. Now Parmenides, like the other philosophers of his day, was virtually certain to have had some knowledge of Egyptian thought and myth; and his description here strongly suggests the Egyptian mythos of the night journey of Rê the sun god through the under-world realms of the dead, on the way to arriving at the eastern gate whence every morning he comes forth in divine splendor. Adjunc-tively there is the image of the whirling axle producing both a fiery glow and a singing hum—representing the combined solar symbols of light, circular form, and that cosmic music which Pythagoras had named the Music of the Spheres.

Furthermore, the passage emphasizes in a special way the primary philosophy of *Gnosis*, which is the principle that essential ritual, ceremony rightly enacted, brings a validly higher awareness. The Dionysian dance, when authentic, produces Apollonian vision. An implicit postulate of the Purgatorial mythos is that the Pilgrim wins new and genuine insight through his pilgrimage. In the case of Parmenides' journey the demigoddesses who were guiding the chariot had already left the realms of night and thrown back the veils from their faces, even before reaching the crucial gates. The gates are bolted and unbolted by Justice herself, and when a worthy aspirant is allowed to pass through he attains thereby a new *gnosis,* for in the words of the story he perceives a broad avenue in a wide expanse and he comes at last into the presence of the Goddess. Although the God-dess is neither named nor explicitly characterized it is evident that she is the Goddess of Truth, who proceeds to impart her high wis-dom to the aspiring philosopher by telling him:

> Gaze steadfastly at things which, though far away, are yet present to the mind. . . . Do not let custom, born of everyday experience, tempt your eyes to be aimless, your ear and tongue to be echoes. Let Reason [*Logos*] be your judge when you consider this much disputed question [of what truly Is]. The heart when left to itself misses the road.[16]

That is to say, let divine Logos impart the criterion of worthy choice, in thought and action alike. Most men, Heraclitus had re-marked contemptuously, think and act by what they take to be their own private intelligence, with the result that they are like sleepers, each inhabiting a dream world of his own. The Logos, he pro-claimed, is eternally valid, but it reserves its fiery wisdom for the Dry Soul—which is to say, for the soul self-purified from the moral sluggishness of emotional attachment. Wakefulness is the essential condition; which means, in terms of the auditory metaphor, a con-stant alertness, a self-sustaining readiness to Listen.

Beyond Symbolism

A study of archetypal symbols tends to raise the hauntingly futile question, "Symbols of what?" The question is futile because it seems to express a hope of getting beyond symbols altogether and grasping cleanly their non-symbolic purport. Such escape from semantics is roughly possible where empirical meanings are involved —meanings either digital, where one can point, or practical, where one can exemplify in action. Where meanings are expressive, on the other hand, and particularly where they have archetypal status, there is no exit from semantics. To elucidate a Symbol is to replace it with a set of words, which are symbolic operators of another kind. To explain the sun as symbolizing God, or "Alpha and Omega" as a symbol of Being, or the Pilgrim as standing for human aspiration, is to invoke the special symbolic languages of theology, metaphysics, and psychology respectively. Do we move any closer to the heart of reality when we discourse in terms of Aristotle's *to on* or Heidegger's *das Sein* than when we employ the language of Symbols? "Every concept is framed in its own irony," Santayana has remarked; and perhaps we are in a better way to acknowledge our semantic limitations when we employ images than when we resort to the more solemn claims of verbal exposition.

The ancient Hindus, perceiving this semantic dilemma, and realizing that even the word *"Brahman"* is historically conditioned and not at all identical with the ultimate What which it intends, proposed an ingenious solution. Since any word by which to signify ultimate Being is itself a verbal sound, let us discover (they reasoned) what phonetic sound partakes most nearly of Being's own nature. Open your mouth wide (they prescribed) and emit the sound that most naturally flows from it, *"ah."* Close slowly, emitting through rounded lips the unforced sound *"oo"* (that is, that of the Latin long *"u"*), and then with closed lips the sound *"mm."* Three Sanskrit letters represent these sounds, and their composite result is the emergent word *"Aum."* Subsequently *"Aum"* became simplified into *"Om,"* the verbal form that is now most familiar, employed particularly to introduce Hindu prayers and Upanishadic discourses. Thus the word *"Om"* (*"Aum"*) stands as a perpetual reminder and test of the limited possibility of breaking through semantic and symbolic conventions. But the semantic irony of which Santayana speaks is not dispelled even here, although altered perhaps into a subtler and quainter form.

What the *"Om"* tradition illustrates is the double-headed truth that while symbolism in one sense or another is inescapable for any thinking and intending creature, yet some symbolic devices are closer to the reality which they represent than others. The gap between vehicle and tenor cannot be removed, but it can often be narrowed. Context collaborates. To speak of love on a right occasion, to a right person, in a right tone, and so on, comes somewhat closer to the existential fact than an impersonal discourse could do. The difference is highly germane to the poet's task. For the first of his aims, giving body and poetic significance to the rest, is to explore fresh possibilities of creating closer verbal, imaginistic, and intentive rapport. Poetic discipline is not a manipulation of concepts, but an ordering developed out of just this kind of flexibility and nearness. Upon such a merger of light and warmth the Symbol, as distinguished from the steno-symbol, is reared; and the great archetypal Symbols, even when their glow has been dimmed by time and sophistication, are still lasting memorials to shared magnanimities of meaning out of the human past.

Notes

1. Dablon's *Relation* (i.e., *Narrative*, 1674). Relevant passages, French and English, in Francis B. Steck, O.F.M., *Marquette Legends* (Pageant Press, 1959), pp. 76-77.
2. William Empson, *Seven Types of Ambiguity* (London and New York, 1930). Specifically, the line of verse by which he illustrates his third type (p. 130) contains three good examples of plurisignation, whereas on pp. 28, 236-37, etc. he is dealing with ambiguity.
3. *The Collected Works of C. G. Jung* (Bollingen Series: Pantheon Books), Vol. IX, Part I, "Archetypes of the Collective Unconscious"; cf. Vol. VIII, "The Structure and Dynamics of the Psyche." More pertinent to the literary archetype: Northrop Frye, *Anatomy of Criticism* (Princeton University Press, 1957), esp. pp. 100-12, 131-60; cf. "The Archetypes of Literature" in his *Fables of Identity* (Harbinger paperback).

4. Mircea Eliade, *Patterns in Comparative Religion* (Sheed and Ward, 1958; Meridian Books, 1963), chap. II, "The Sky and Sky Gods."

5. From a lost play by Aeschylus, *The Danaids:* Fragment 25 in the Loeb Classical Library edition of Aeschylus, Vol. II. The Euripides quotation which follows is from a lost play, title unknown; quoted by Aristotle, *Nicomachean Ethics* 1155b 4. The translations of both are taken from *The Presocratics* (Odyssey Press, 1966).

6. F. Max Müller, *Introduction to the Science of Religion* (London, 1873), p. 172; cf. 393. Cf. *Chips from a German Workshop*, Vol. I (London, 1868), pp. 358-60, 367.

7. "*Lo quale di sensibile luce sè prima e poi tutte le corpora celesti e le elementi allumina.*" Dante, *Convivio*, eds. Busnelli and Vandelli III (2d ed.; Florence, 1954), xiii, 7. Dante carries out the analogy by adding: "*Così Dio prima sè con luce intelletuale allumina, e poi le [creature] celestiali e l'altre intelligibili.*" I have translated "elementi" as "mundane bodies," because the reference is to the primary physical substances—earth, water, air, and fire.

8. Plato, *Republic*, Book VI, 506 E-509 E. Swedenborg, *Angelic Vision concerning the Divine Love and Divine Wisdom* (Eng. ed. of 1868). The title of Sec. 99 bears on the point: "That spiritual heat and spiritual light, in proceeding from the Lord as a Sun, make one, as His Divine Love and His Divine Wisdom make one." Cf. *Heaven and Hell*, Secs. 132-38. Cf. *The Apocalypse Revealed*, Sec. 53.

9. Among the English versions of Ikhnaton's *Hymn to the Sun* are notably those given by: James Henry Breasted, *Development of Religion in Ancient Egypt* (New York, 1912); same, *The Dawn of Conscience* (New York, 1933); same, "Ikhnaton, the Religious Revolutionary" in *Cambridge Ancient History*, Vol. II, chap. VI; T. Eric Peet, *A Comparative Study of the Literature of Egypt, Palestine, and Mesopotamia* (London, 1931); Josephine Mayer and Tom Prideaux, *Never to Die / The Egyptians in their Own Words* (New York: Viking Press, 1938), pp. 162-65. For a fuller text of the older hymn, on the apotheosis of the deceased Pharaoh, see Adolf Erman, *The Literature of the Ancient Egyptians* (London, 1927); also Mayer and Prideaux, *op. cit.*, pp. 42-46.

10. *The Works of the Emperor Julian*, Vol. I of the Loeb Classical Library edition, pp. 352-435, "Hymn to King Helios."

11. Erich Neumann, *The Origins and History of Consciousness* (Pantheon, Bollingen Series, 1954): esp. Part II, pp. 266-312, on the development out of the original ouroboric condition. Cf. Neumann, *The Great Mother* (same, 1955).

12. Heinrich Zimmer, *Myths and Symbols in Indian Art and Civilization* (Pantheon, Bollingen Series, 1946), pp. 211-15.

13. *Zend-Avesta*, Yasna 31. 11; 32. 3-5. Cf. A. V. W. Jackson, *Zoroaster* (1898); Robert G. Zaehner, *The Dawn and Twilight of Zoroastrianism* (Putnam, 1961); art. "Zoroastrianism" by K. F. G. in *Encyclopaedia Biblica* (London, 1903).

14. *Encyclopaedia Biblica:* art. "Satan" by T. B. G. According to this source the identification of a fully personified Satan with the Serpent in the Garden of Eden story makes its first known appearance in the Slavonic *Book of Enoch*, where incidentally Satan the Serpent carries his seduction to the point of becoming Eve's paramour. There is no mention of all this in the Western *Book of Enoch* as edited by R. H. Charles.

15. The translation of Parmenides is taken from *The Presocratics* (Odyssey Press, 1966), pp. 95-96, corresponding to Fragment 1 in Diels-Kranz. Cf. C. M. Bowra, *Problems of Greek Poetry* (Oxford University Press, 1953), chap. III, "The Poem of Parmenides."

16. *Ibid.:* Frags. 2 and 3 in the Odyssey Press collection, corresponding to Frags. 7 and 4 in Diels-Kranz.

George Mauner

MANET, BAUDELAIRE, AND THE RECURRENT THEME

MOST MODERN STUDIES OF ÉDOUARD MANET'S PAINTING INCLUDE SOME reference to the mysterious quality of his group subjects. Indeed, the lack of psychological communication between his figures is the most haunting feature of his art. His dispassionate handling of figures, as people, is in strong contradiction to his sensual technique of recording their appearance and their environment. In others words, it is in the *métier* of painting that Manet reveals his human warmth, while in the role of narrator he remains cool and distant. Modern criticism has recognized in this duality Manet's importance for the development of abstract art. As a "pure painter" he has early contributed to the growth of our taste for color and texture at the expense of our interest in subject matter. While there can be no doubt that his painting, as surface, new and personal as it was, did have far-reaching effects, his figures, in their very coolness, in their compositional relationships, in their penetrating, expressionless gazes, are impossible to dismiss as the result of indifference to their life-roles, and to a willful distinction between art and life.

Certainly, many a viewer of *The Luncheon on the Grass, The Old Musician, Olympia, The Balcony* and a host of other paintings, mostly dating from the 1860's, has felt the expression of timelessness behind the vibrancy of the light, the fashionable costumes, and the many other references to the time-bound phenomenon of modern life. That Manet, while remaining strongly responsive to the sensual stimuli of daily life, appreciated the unchanging values of human nature and saw his characters as examples of principles, would help explain his attachment to the "Salon" and his refusal consciously to serve as a revolutionary by openly joining the Impressionists. He was won over to the art of Monet only when he discovered in the great painter of nature a philosopher, and was able to describe him as *"le Raphael de l'eau."*[1] Manet knew, of course, that the realism of some "Salon" artists was empty, while the classicism of others was devoid of any contact with life. His intention was to express accurately his own visual sensitivity in the elaboration of important ideas, as the great masters of the past had done. His method was to relegate the world of ideas and that of perception to different areas of his art, yet to make one a function of the other.

These general observations also recall Manet's friend, Charles Baudelaire. It was Baudelaire who cried out for the painter of modern life, while holding in contempt the popular view of progress. He expressed the principal aim of the modern painter thus: *"Il s'agit pour lui, de dégager de la mode ce qu'elle peut contenir de poétique dans l'histoire, de tirer l'éternel du transitoire."*[2] In his diaries he wrote that the artist must find the infinite in the finite, the same idea but in reference to space rather than time. In his article Baudelaire named Constantin Guys as the painter who fulfills his requirements. To claim that the poet thereby failed to recognize Manet's genius is to overlook the fact that the piece was probably written in 1859–60, when Manet had not yet painted anything of importance.

It is unfortunate that the Manet-Baudelaire friendship is so poorly documented. A few of the accounts we do have indicate that the two men were very close. A journalist, after Baudelaire's death, noted: *"Dans ces derniers temps, son meilleur ami était M. Manet; le fait est que ces deux natures devaient se comprendre."*[3] Another account tells us that it was Mme. Manet who comforted the dying poet with her renderings of Wagner at the piano.[4] Yet Baudelaire the art critic mentioned Manet in print only once, in 1862,[5] although he did take the trouble to write a letter defending Manet's originality to the critic Thoré-Bürger in 1864.[6] If we make the assumption, however, that the *œuvres* of the poet and the painter share a major theme (a theme long identified with Baudelaire and not yet discovered for Manet), then the few documents linking the two men invite new interpretations. Baudelaire's demand that the artist seek the infinite in the finite can, as a generality, be said to find fulfillment in the duality of immanence and timelessness in Manet's art. This philosophy of art necessarily takes more specific forms in Baudelaire's poetry and prose, and it is in an examination of his themes that we shall seek the key to a better understanding of Manet's intentions.

The central problem of Baudelaire's troubled life was the coming
to grips with the opposing forces of good and evil. Even the title of
his collection of poems, *Les Fleurs du Mal,* proclaims this theme. He
saw the problem as a cosmic condition to which all men are subject,
and to which the artist is particularly sensitive since the "higher"
and "lower" spheres project their own kinds of beauty, and beauty is
the artist's main concern. The two principles are part of an ancient
unity and are therefore deceptively interchangeable. The artist is
aware of their similarity and is also conscious of his struggle as he
moves between them.[7] While this idea recurs in a multitude of ways
in Baudelaire's writings, it finds clearest expression in his diaries:
*"Il y a dans tout homme, à toute heure, deux postulations simul-
tanées, l'une vers Dieu, l'autre vers Satan. L'invocation à Dieu, ou
spiritualité, est un désir de monter en grade; celle de Satan, ou
animalité, est une joie de descendre . . . Les joies qui derivent de ces
deux amours sont adaptées à la nature de ces deux amours."*[8]

When Baudelaire was attracted to another artist, it was when he
sensed in him an awareness of the same dual attraction. Thus, he
wrote of Wagner: *"Tannhäuser représente la lutte des deux prin-
cipes qui ont choisi le coeur humain pour principal champ de
bataille, c'est-à-dire de la chair avec l'esprit, de l'enfer avec le ciel, de
Satan avec Dieu."*[9] It was largely for the same reason that Baudelaire
was attracted to Poe and to Hoffmann. No doubt, he considered the
similarity of his own temperament to that of earlier artists as evidence of the timeless nature of really significant discoveries. It was,
in fact, in his letter to Thoré-Bürger that he likened Manet's similarity to Velasquez to his own spiritual kinship with Poe, attributing
such phenomena to "mysterious coincidence," rather than to vulgar
plagiarism.

We know, nevertheless, that Manet was in the habit of borrowing
motifs from the old masters. The fact was known in Manet's lifetime, and the discovery of his pictorial sources has progressed apace
in our own century. Our current view of Manet as a pure painter
has prevented our making any sense of his borrowings, save for their
probable formal interest to him, or even simply to prove his indifference to subject, seeking only to rework a given motif in his own
manner. Not many years ago it was commonly thought that Manet
was dependent on these sources due to a lack of imagination and
ability to devise his own compositions. It has even been discovered
that for some works several sources were used, although no pattern,
no system or guiding principle in the selection of these sources has

Fig. 1. Manet. *The Luncheon on the Grass.* 1863. 84 x 106″. Louvre, Paris.

(Photo: Giraudon).

Fig. 2. Giorgione. *Concert champêtre.* c. 1509. 45½ x 57½". Louvre, Paris.
(Photo: Alinari).

Fig. 3. Marcantonio Raimondi, after Raphael. *The Judgment of Paris*. c. 1520. Engraving.

Fig. 4. Raphael. *The Miraculous Draught of Fishes*, tapestry cartoon (detail). 1515. Victoria and Albert Museum, London.

Fig. 5. Manet. *Dead Christ with Angels*. 1864. 70⅝ x 59″. Metropolitan Museum of Art, New York (gift of Mrs. H. O. Havemeyer).

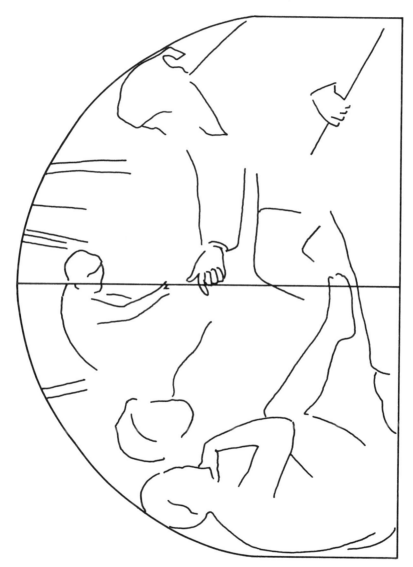

Fig. 6. *Luncheon on the Grass*, schema.

Fig. 7. Raphael. *The School of Athens* (engraving after). 1510–11. Fresco. Camera della Segnatura, Vatican Palace, Rome.

Fig. 8. Manet. *The Old Musician* (detail). 1862. 73¾ x 97¾″. National Gallery of Art, Washington. (Chester Dale Coll.)

yet been proposed. Manet's overall talent as a painter, including his skill in composition, is far too apparent from a number of works for us to accept the theory of his dependence on the designs of others. Furthermore, the works for which the compositions have been borrowed are so stiff and unnatural, so "incorrect" by academic standards, that it is easy to believe that his borrowing was a matter of choice, not need. Let us propose the hypothesis that when Manet entered into what has often been referred to as a "dialogue with the old masters" on the basis of compositional similarity, the subject of that dialogue was a common theme of interest. We can test this theory by examining a number of his paintings from the 1860's, the period of his friendship with Baudelaire, and their sources. Space limitations will restrict us here to the examination of one major work, *The Luncheon on the Grass (Fig. 1)*, with only some indispensable references to a few others.

This famous painting was the first by Manet to create a scandal and has furnished us with a conveniently dramatic moment for the birth of modern art. Like many of his paintings from the 1860's, it is now prized as an early example of the artist's superb, lyrical handling of paint. Its subject, however, while no longer shocking, still lacks an adequate interpretation and remains the enigma it has always been. Because of the fame of this work we have rather more information about it than about a good many equally compelling pictures by the artist.

Manet spoke to Antonin Proust of his admiration for Giorgione's *Concert Champêtre (Fig. 2)* in the Louvre, although he had made the reservation that it was too dark and stated that he wished to redo it in the transparency of natural light.[10] The remark obviously stresses Manet's interest in realism and further documents his position as forerunner of the Impressionists. But we should ask as well why he was particularly attracted to Giorgione's masterpiece. The Venetian's sensual style must have appealed to him, but this alone does not explain his desire to reinterpret this particular subject. Proust is silent on the matter, and it is entirely possible that Manet had said no more about it to him. But if Manet's pictures are enigmatic, we can certainly say as much of those of Giorgione, particularly of the *Concert Champêtre*. Only recently has an acceptable explanation of its theme been proposed. Patricia Egan has demonstrated that it is an allegory of two kinds of poetry which she describes as "higher" and "lower."[11] If it is unlikely that Manet knew this (although he may have been familiar with Giorgione's sources, the Tarot cards, through Baudelaire), it is, nevertheless, highly probable that he recognized the fused duality of the work. The women are clearly allegorical and the two men, while together, are opposites in dress and manner. Our present knowledge of Manet's ability to store images in his memory also justifies the supposition that he recognized the affinities between the woman at the well and the embodiment of sacred love in Titian's famous allegory of a "higher" and "lower," of sacred and profane love. Giorgione's soft rendering and his use of musical instruments imbue the naturalistic subject with a poetic other-worldliness which Manet achieves by his own means. But we need not belabor the similarities between Giorgione's and Manet's pictures. At any rate, Manet found the *Concert* too dark, and his own *Luncheon* reflects such a strong immanence as to discourage any suspicion of allegory within it. The grouping and presentation of the figures is, nevertheless, contrived and ambivalent.

It was known in Manet's lifetime (and Gustave Pauli rediscovered it in 1908) that the group of three seated figures is based on the trio of river gods in Marcantonio Raimondi's engraving after Raphael's *Judgment of Paris (Fig. 3)*. Although this fact is widely known and almost always reprinted in studies of the *Luncheon,* we really have not yet discovered any convincing reason for Manet to have decided to build his painting on this composition. Of course, we might observe that, as in Manet's group, the river gods, while sitting together, do not look at one another. The central figure looks heavenward toward a celestial chariot, and Manet has altered the direction of the glance of his equivalent figure so that it nearly, but not quite, meets that of his conversational partner. The approximation of sociability is part of an elaborate and precise composition that suggests genre, while transcending it. This formal, anti-psychological quality, however, is not an adequate explanation for the borrowing, nor is it as obvious as the one which Nils Sandblad deduced from a thematic comparison. The original title of Manet's painting was *Le Bain,* and Raphael's trio is composed, after all, of two river gods and a water nymph.[12] In neither case do the bathers bathe, but the aquatic theme in conjunction with a tight, classical composition was evidently what Manet sought in his source. Furthermore, Manet's two sources are themselves thematically related, and this relationship may have seemed particularly strong to the painter. We have pointed out the duality implicit in Giorgione's masterpiece as well as its relationship to Titian's *Sacred and Profane Love.* The Raphael source, of which the river gods are a detail, is the *Judgment of Paris,* also a subject dealing with a choice of love. We now have more substantial grounds for considering the *Luncheon on the Grass* as an allegory of a similar kind, namely, as a presentation of a dual principle and its implication of choice or resolution.

Let us not forget that it was Giorgione's painting that Manet proposed to reinterpret and that that painting includes two feminine figures. Thus, Manet has inserted the distant wading figure in the convenient space within the closed form supplied by the group of river gods. A convincing pictorial source for this figure has never been proposed, and if we leave the hope of discovery to a chance encounter among the countless images of the history of art, it may well continue to elude us. If, on the other hand, we assume that Manet followed a principle then our search is not nearly so hopeless. We have seen that it was the theme of Giorgione, in a setting of modern life, that attracted Manet. He apparently set about finding his arrangement in the classical composition of a related theme by Raphael. If the design of the foreground group is Raphael's, let us make the assumption that the wading figure is also borrowed from Raphael, and even that it derives from an aquatic subject. These suppositions substantially limit the amount of material to be investigated and quickly provide the image we seek. It is more than likely that Manet's bather derives from the figure of St. John in Raphael's tapestry cartoon, *The Miraculous Draught of Fishes* (Fig. 4).[13] St. John stands ankle-deep in a rowboat and reaches down for the full net. Manet's bather, separated from her boat which is over at the right, is ankle-deep in the water and plunges her hand into it.[13a] Since attention to subject matter has led to this discovery we must now extend this interest to the next level of investigation and inquire why, specifically, an image of St. John was chosen.

The subject of the fisherman had interested Manet before he undertook the *Luncheon on the Grass*. There is a painting entitled *Fishing* in the New York Metropolitan Museum in which Manet has represented himself and his bride, Suzanne Leenhoff, in seventeenth century costumes. This gesture was perhaps meant as an homage to Rubens since two of the Flemish master's compositions served as sources for this work. The young couple, however, is placed at the extreme right side of the painting, while its center is occupied by a fisherman in his boat. This position, in an obviously personal painting, is evidence of the importance of the symbol of the fisherman to Manet. In a watercolor done at approximately the same time, the fisherman in his boat is again the central motif, and, in this instance, is very close in design to the wading figure in the *Luncheon* and its Raphael source. It is in the fusion of the act of fishing with the person of St. John, given in the figure from the tapestry cartoon, that Manet reveals the spiritual symbolism which he attaches to the activity. For further evidence of Manet's interest in St. John we must now turn our attention to another of the artist's major paintings.

In a corner of the *Christ with Angels (Fig. 5)* Manet has painted a serpent crushed by a rock. On this rock he has written, "Evang. S. Jean XX, 5-12." Here, in Manet's own hand, is the clear reference to the St. John Gospel as the textual source of his religious painting. If we read the cited passage of the Gospel we find that Manet's image bears an imperfect relationship to the text. The story of the angels at the tomb of Christ is told by all four evangelists. It is true that Matthew and Mark speak of only one angel, but Luke, as well as John, speaks of two. Manet's image, if interpreted literally, is as close to the description of Luke as it is to that of John. In one important particular it differs from all the Gospels, for the Evangelists speak of the resurrected Christ who is no longer in the tomb. John alone adds the information that the angels were placed one at the head and the other at the foot of where Christ had lain. Manet has, the literal description notwithstanding, made Christ his central image and has placed one angel on either side of him. It is not possible to belittle or to ignore this discrepancy, as Mrs. Hanson has recently reminded us,[14] since Manet invites the comparison by citing his source.

The Christ is rendered very naturalistically as a cadaver, and we can appreciate Zola's defense of the figure as a bit of superb realistic painting. Yet Christ sits up and reveals the stigmata willfully, and the expression of death on his face mingles with an other-worldliness which mitigates it. Our feeling that this figure is both dead and alive accords, of course, with the story of the Resurrection, and it gains visual support from the opposed character of the two angels. The one at the left covers his face in an obvious gesture of grief, while the other looks forward, transfixed, as if possessed by a superior knowledge. In a subsequent etching which Manet made after this painting, the expression on the face of this angel is intensified and is framed by a shock of hair which stands away from the head as if electrically charged. Furthermore, we note that Christ is received by this angel and that the direction of wings and key compositional lines all move toward the right. Finally, the angel at the left has wings of a rather dull color, while those of the other angel are a brilliant blue.

On the ground, at the left, is a row of snails, symbols of the earth. Baudelaire used this image in a poem entitled *Le mort joyeux,* which greets death as a comfort:

> *Dans une terre grasse et pleine d'escargots*
> *Je veux creuser moi-même une fosse profonde.*[15]

On the ground, at the right, is the rock which bears the inscription citing St. John and which crushes a snake, old image of the spiritual triumph of Christ over the powers of darkness. Thus, we have a painting of which the left side speaks of Christ the man and of his physical death, while the right proclaims his spiritual rebirth and its significance. One angel mourns the man and expresses the sufferings of the flesh, while the other welcomes the God. This is Manet's translation of the line in St. John which places the angels at the head and foot of the tomb. He has seen in these words the "higher" and "lower" of spiritual and physical life. This description of the angels is given in verse 12, the one that closes Manet's inscribed reference.

The Gospel of St. John has always been considered the most mystic of the four versions of the life of Christ. It is St. John who stresses the meaning of the "Logos" become flesh and the role and lesson of love in the Passion. It is pertinent to our discussion to observe that only St. John speaks of the lance wound in Christ's side. We know that Baudelaire had written to Manet suggesting that he place the wound on the other side of Christ before submitting the painting to the "Salon," in order to avoid ridicule. John does not say, however, on which side the wound was inflicted, and Manet, since he cites John, obviously knew this. However, John does write that Jesus was the only one of the three martyrs to receive the wound, rather than to have legs broken like the others, in fulfillment of the Old Testament prophesy of the Messiah. From this wound, writes the Evangelist, flowed blood and water, symbols of the Eucharist and the Baptism. It does not seem, therefore, to be a coincidence that Manet placed the wound on Christ's left side (the right side of the painting), with the angel of the Resurrection and the symbol of the triumph of spiritual love, for of all the stigmata only the lance wound is described specifically as a symbol of His divinity.

Manet sent the *Christ with Angels* to the "Salon" of 1864 together with *An Incident in the Bull Ring,* of which he later detached the *Dead Toreador.* His friendship with Baudelaire in this year appears to have been particularly close, for the poet wrote not only to Manet regarding Christ's wound but also to the critic Thoré-Bürger defending the originality of the toreador figure. It is a striking fact that both pictures have death as their theme, one sacred the other secular. We have seen that the *Christ with Angels,* the religious subject, contains sacred and secular portions within it. The same is true of the *Dead Toreador,* but it is contained in a different, still more secret way. This figure derives from two sources, the *Dead Orlando,* thought by Manet to have been painted by Velasquez, and Gérôme's *Dead Caesar,* which had been exhibited at the "Salon" of 1859. Both figures are exemplary prototypes, one of the Christian, the other of the pagan soldier. A normal amount of skepticism would dictate that these facts be considered coincidences were it not that the pattern is so often repeated in Manet's *œuvre.* The duality of the toreador is to be found in its sources.[15a]

We have seen that the two women in the *Luncheon on the Grass* derive from two compositions by Raphael. We are now disposed to recognize at once that one is drawn from a pagan, the other from a Christian theme. To Baudelaire such juxtapositions were perfectly in order and even necessary. In his diaries he had made the following observation: *"Mysticité du paganisme. Le mysticisme, trait d'union entre le paganisme et le christianisme. Le paganisme et le christianisme se prouvent reciproquement."*[16] The example of Christian and pagan principles, opposing each other yet part of one another, is one of the forms in which the poet expressed his belief in the cosmic polarity of equivalent "higher" and "lower" forces. I have tried to show by the analysis of Manet's painting that he shared Baudelaire's great interest in the problem. The most surprising evidence for this aspect of the friendship of the poet and the painter, however, is provided by Baudelaire in a short story. As part of his series of vignettes, *Le spleen de Paris,* Baudelaire published a tale entitled *La Corde,* which he dedicated to Édouard Manet.

The story tells of an event in Manet's life, although the painter is mentioned by name only in the dedication. It is the incident repeated by Manet's biographers concerning the ragamuffin whom Manet had befriended and engaged as assistant and model. Upon returning to his studio one day, Manet found that the boy had hanged himself, and the artist consequently abandoned that studio. Evidently Baudelaire was attracted by the horror of the event and wrote it up, he explains, as it was told him by a painter friend. Even if we allow for the poet's freedom to alter facts, it is surprising that the story has never been read more critically in an effort better to understand the bonds of the Baudelaire-Manet friendship.

The painter in the story describes the boy's expression as both *"ardente"* and *"espiègle."* He found him to be both *"charmant"* and given to *"des crises singulière de tristesse précoce."* In the two descriptive sentences Baudelaire reiterates the double nature of the child. In another passage the poet has his painter recall the roles in which he had the boy pose: *"Je l'ai transformé tantôt en petit bohémien, tantôt en ange, tantôt en Amour mythologique. Je lui ai fait porter le violon du vagabond, la Couronne d'Épines et les Clous de la Passion, et la Torche d'Eros."*[17] The casual tone of the passage with the repeated use of the word "tantôt" gives the impression of a random listing of traditional characters and obscures the fact that these have been carefully chosen. The two sentences are parallel in that each contains three characters and in that the second set is a repetition, in the same order, of the first. The difference is that while the first set deals with figures the second describes their attributes. Thus, we have: *"petit bohémien—"violon du vagabond"; "ange"— "Couronne d'Épines et les Clous de la Passion"; "Amour mythologique"—"Torche d'Eros."* The first pair is the beggar-philosopher, a character often depicted by Manet; the second is the symbol of Christian love; and the third is that of pagan love. We cannot doubt that these themes were premeditated.

In *The Luncheon on the Grass* we have the foreground nude borrowed from Raphael's pagan nymph who attends Paris' choice among beauties, and the distant figure borrowed from the same master's St. John, the embodiment of Christian love. As a final touch, Manet associates each woman with an animal symbol. A bird, freed from terrestrial restraints, hovers over the wading figure, while a "lowly" frog, an animal associated with an attraction to material things, sits beside the shed clothing of the nude.[17a] Manet has also given us the philosopher in the man at the right. He is not, here, the vagabond he had been in the slightly earlier *Old Musician,* but has been transformed into the boulevardier and dandy and plays the same central, coordinating role. We have mentioned the "near-miss" of the glances of the two men in the painting which makes the superficial genre aspect of the painting suspect. The same double impression of the trivial and the symbolic is conveyed by the hand gesture of this reclining figure. It is casual yet compelling, for it coordinates the psychologically and spatially separated figures.

If we suppress the space that lies between the foreground trio and the more distant bather (and this distance is difficult to measure in any case), we more readily see that all the figures fall within an arch on the surface of the canvas. This arch is defined by the contour lines of the figures, and just encloses the heads, as shown in *Figure 6*. If we draw a vertical line through the center of the arch, we discover that it runs through the middle of the gesturing hand. We find, too, that the bathing figure is at the center and top of that arch. It is no longer difficult to see that the thumb of this central hand points toward the bather and, when the picture is seen as surface, almost touches her hand. The index finger points forward and left toward the seated nude.

The wading figure, while retaining the pose and the proximity to the water of Raphael's St. John, has, nevertheless, been separated from her boat. This object is found at the right side of the background and, again if we suppress depth, serves as a kind of aureole around the head of the gesturing figure. The position of the oars even echos that of the man's right hand and cane. He has become the mortal fisherman who seeks his way between the two poles of his nature. Perhaps Manet has made technical use of a poetic image by Théophile Gautier to whom Baudelaire had dedicated the *Fleurs du Mal* and who, in turn, had praised Manet's *Guitar Player* at the "Salon" of 1861:

> *La vie est un plancher qui couvre*
> *L'abîme de l'éternité;*
> *Une trappe soudain s'entr'ouvre*
> *Sous le pécheur épouvanté;*
> *Le pied lui manque, il tombe, il glisse,*
> *Que va-t-il trouver? le ciel bleu*
> *ou l'enfer rouge? le supplice*
> *ou la palme? Satan ou Dieu?*[18]

In these lines we find not only the image of the mortal caught between the forces of good and evil, but also the description of life as a surface behind which lies eternity. Manet has made symbolic use of the inter-penetration of his two-dimensional and three-dimensional designs. It is in the surface arch that the distant figure, bathed in light and framed by trees, is brought into the immediacy of modern life.

Manet's device of dissembling the meaning of a significant gesture while placing it in a crucial area of his composition is not unique to *The Luncheon on the Grass*. It exists, too, in the slightly earlier *Old Musician* (*Fig. 8*). Here, the beggar-philosopher seemingly holds his violin bow (one of the attributes described by Baudelaire in *La Corde*) casually at rest. In this work, too, the figures are psychologically isolated from one another while an unorthodox composition brings them all into surface contact. Here, again, strange gazes greet the viewer, and here, once again, the bow changes character before our eyes and is transformed from a traditional attribute into a pointer directed toward the fraternally linked boys at the left. This pair of figures, one light, the other dark, are fused into a unity of opposing forces.

Obviously, Manet's indebtedness to Raphael was great, but his dependence on the Renaissance master was self-imposed. Manet welcomed the discovery of his own ideas in the art of the past as inevitable. Baudelaire claimed that all ideas and forms created by men are immortal,[19] and it was in the art of the past that Manet sought the forms which he reinvigorated with the artistic gifts which were uniquely his own. He appears to have completely identified form with meaning in his borrowing of images, and the iconography of his paintings is frequently to be discovered in the iconography of his sources. The images which Raphael's art gave to *The Luncheon on the Grass* do not, of course, represent Manet's overall theme but are assembled form-idea fragments. Raphael did, however, paint the subject of "higher" and "lower" forces on a monumental scale in the frescos of the Camera della Segnatura. Each of the four great hemicycles, while representations of Theology, Philosophy, Poetry, and Jurisprudence, has this metaphysical problem as its central theme. Its presence in the four great branches of knowledge only serves to magnify its cosmic character. Under the arch of the *School of Athens (Fig.* 7) Raphael has represented the fusion of the superior and inferior realms in the persons of Plato and Aristotle, who point upward and outward respectively. Within the rectangular format of *The Luncheon on the Grass* Manet has constructed a similar arch at the center of which is the single hand pointing both upward and outward toward sacred and profane love.

Manet's stylistic modernism, his stress on surface and contrast, cannot be considered apart from his thematic interests. He did, indeed, use his medium in a new way, but he did so in an effort to convey ideas of a complexity and importance which could not be transmitted with equal subtlety by either the narrative or allegorical approaches of his contemporaries. The true tradition to Manet was the series of "mysterious coincidences" which led artists of the past to rediscover the same forms in the expression of a few significant ideas. He gives evidence of a belief in the almost magical meaning of forms created by the masters, and of a rare faith in the power of painting, by its very silence, to intensify ideas. Baudelaire held an equally strong conviction concerning the unchanging nature of the inner theme of all great art, and he expressed it in one of the best known poems of the *Fleurs du mal, "les Phares."* After evoking the art of Rubens, Leonardo, Rembrandt, Michelangelo, Puget, Watteau, Goya, and Delacroix, he writes that in this series we have *"un echo redit par mille labyrinthes . . . un cri répété par mille sentinelles"* and concludes,

> *Car c'est vraiment, Seigneur, le meilleur témoignage*
> *Que nous puissions donner de notre dignité*
> *Que cet ardent sanglot qui roule d'âge en âge*
> *Et vient mourir au bord de votre éternité!*[20]

Notes

1. Antonin Proust, *Edouard Manet, souvenirs* (Paris, 1913), p. 84.
2. "Le peintre de la vie moderne," in: Y. G. Le Dantec and C. Pichois (eds.), *Œuvres complètes,* (rev. ed.; Paris, 1961), p. 1163. Published originally in *Le Figaro,* Nov. 26 and 29, Dec. 3, 1863.
3. W. Bandy and C. Pichois (eds.), *Baudelaire devant ses contemporains* (Monaco, 1957), p. 310. The article, by Victor Noir, contains many errors of fact. This citation, however, is interesting for the rare information, given in the tone of common knowledge, concerning the similar natures of the two men.
4. *Ibid.,* p. 224. The information is contained in a letter from Jules Troubat to Eugene Crépet. In the chronology of Baudelaire's life given in the *Œuvres complètes* Mme. Paul Meurice is named as the pianist who comforted Baudelaire with her performances of Wagner.
5. "Peintres et aquafortistes," *Le Boulevard* (Sept. 14, 1862). See *Œuvres complètes,* pp. 1145-51.
6. The letter is cited in: E. Moreau-Nelaton, *Manet raconté par lui-même* (Paris, 1926), vol. I, pp. 58-59. We do not pretend to present all the known data linking Baudelaire and Manet. Profs. Francis and Lois Hyslop are currently preparing an article which will review this documentation.
7. For an extensive study of Baudelaire's occultism and its literary sources, see: Paul Arnold, *Das Geheimnis Baudelaires* (Berlin, 1958).
8. "Mon coeur mis à nu," *Œuvres complètes,* p. 1277.
9. "Richard Wagner et Tannhäuser à Paris," *Œuvres complètes,* p. 1223. Originally published in *La Revue Européenne* (April 1, 1861).

10. A. Proust, *op. cit.*, p. 43.

11. P. Egan, "Poesia and the Fête Champêtre," *Art Bulletin*, XLI (Dec., 1959), pp. 303-13.

12. N. G. Sandblad, *Manet, Three Studies in Artistic Conception* (Lund, 1954), p. 91.

13. Manet may well have known the design of the cartoon from the engraving by Nicholas Dorigny which includes the appropriate quotation from the St. Luke Gospel.

13a. It is an interesting coincidence that Sir Kenneth Clark has compared Raphael's *Miraculous Draught of Fishes* with Manet's art, although purely on the basis of style. In his *Looking at Pictures* (London, 1960, p. 70) he writes: "the pink and grey cranes in the foreground of the *Miraculous Draught* are as visually exciting as a *Gitane* by Manet."

14. Anne C. Hanson, "Notes on Manet Literature," *Art Bulletin*, XLVIII (Sept.-Dec., 1966), p. 436.

15. *Œuvres complètes*, p. 67. Snails traditionally symbolize the Resurrection. Such a reference would not be inconsistent with the argument.

15a. These findings tend to support Theodore Reff's suggestion that Manet, in submitting the *Olympia* together with the *Christ Crowned with Thorns* to the Salon of 1865, may have consciously been emulating Titian's example, as reported by Northcote, of presenting Charles V with a "religious and a worldly" subject. These were also a *Christ Scourged and Crowned with Thorns* and "a Venus . . ." (T. Reff, "The Meaning of Manet's *Olympia*," *Gaz. des Beaux-Arts*, vol. 63, Feb. 1964, pp. 115-6.)

16. "Mon coeur mis à nu," *Œuvres complètes*, p. 1273.

17. *Œuvres complètes*, p. 278. Published originally in *Le Figaro*, (Feb. 7, 1864).

17a. Furguson, in his *Signs and Symbols in Christian Art* (London, 1961, p. 19) says specifically that the frog "is interpreted as a symbol of those who snatch at life's fleeting pleasures; hence it represents worldly things in general."

18. "Les affres de la mort," *Poesies complètes* (Paris, 1855), p. 343. This poem is in the collection, *Espagna*, which also includes evocations of the painters Ribeira, Valdes Leal and Zurbaran. It is highly probable that the hispanophile Manet was familiar with these pieces.

19. "Mon coeur mis à nu," *Œuvres complètes*, p. 1298.

20. *Œuvres complètes*, pp. 12-14.